Dissertation Research and Writin
Built Environment Studer

Dissertation Research and Writing for Built Environment Students is a step-by-step guide to get students through their final year research project. Trusted and developed over three previous editions, the new fourth edition shows you how to select a dissertation topic, write a proposal, conduct a literature review, select the research approach, gather the data, analyse and present the information and ultimately produce a well-written dissertation.

The book simplifies dissertation research and writing into a process involving a sequence of learnable activities and divides the process into three parts.

Part One covers the necessary groundwork, including: identifying the problem, writing a proposal and reviewing the literature.

Part Two covers the research design and includes: approaches and techniques for data collection and constructing and sampling a questionnaire.

Part Three covers: measurement of data, analysis of data with SPSS, structuring and writing the whole dissertation, and supervision and assessment.

This new edition is packed with updated examples and research samples, making this the ideal resource for students involved in research in built environment subjects such as construction management, construction project management, facilities management, real estate, building surveying, quantity surveying and civil engineering.

Dr Shamil G. Naoum is currently a Senior Lecturer in Construction Project Management at the University of West London and a Visiting Fellow at London South Bank University. He has over 25 years' experience teaching and researching in construction management and related built environment topics.

Dissertation Research and Writing for Built Environment Students

Fourth Edition

Dr Shamil G. Naoum

LONDON AND NEW YORK

Fourth edition published 2019
by Routledge
2 Park Square, Milton Park, Abingdon, Oxon, OX14 4RN

and by Routledge
52 Vanderbilt Avenue, New York, NY 10017

Routledge is an imprint of the Taylor & Francis Group, an informa business

First edition published by Butterworth-Heineman 1998
Third edition published by Routledge 2013

British Library Cataloguing-in-Publication Data
A catalogue record for this book is available from the British Library

Library of Congress Cataloging-in-Publication Data
Names: Naoum, S. G. (Shamil G.), author.
Title: Dissertation research and writing for built environment students /
S. G. Naoum.
Description: Fourth edition. | Abingdon, Oxon ; New York, NY : Routledge,
2019. | Includes bibliographical references and index.
Identifiers: LCCN 2018060703| ISBN 9780815384625 (hardback) |
ISBN 9780815384632 (pbk.) | ISBN 9781351203913 (ebook)
Subjects: LCSH: Building—Research. | Dissertations,
Academic—Authorship. | Academic writing.
Classification: LCC TH213.5 .N36 2019 | DDC 624.072—dc23
LC record available at https://lccn.loc.gov/2018060703

ISBN: 978-0-8153-8462-5 (hbk)
ISBN: 978-0-8153-8463-2 (pbk)
ISBN: 978-1-351-20391-3 (ebk)

Typeset in Goudy
by Deanta Global Publishing Services, Chennai, India

Visit the eResources: www.routledge.com/9780815384632

To my mother, Rose

Contents

Part II   Research design and methodology

Figures

Tables

Boxes

Preface

This book has grown out of my involvement in supervising BSc and MSc dissertations as well as my accumulated experience of teaching research methods to postgraduate students at London South Bank University. Over the years, I became convinced that construction students needed something akin to research methods lectures, in addition to tutoring, that could provide them with guidance on basic research techniques and how to write a dissertation. There have been an enormous number of textbooks which presented research design and methodologies but few, if any, are related to built environment studies.

This book approaches dissertation research and writing as a process, involving a sequence of learnable activities. Each activity prepares the student for the next step and some steps are best taken before others. I have divided the process of dissertation research into three parts, which are best carried out in the order presented.

Part I is 'preparing the ground'. It involves:

1 identifying the problem (including narrowing and clarifying the problem);
2 writing a proposal (including the aim, objectives, hypothesis and/or key research questions);
3 reviewing the literature (including critical appraisal of literature).

Part II is 'research design'. It involves:

4 approaches to data collection (deciding whether to use a survey or a case study);
5 techniques for data collection (deciding whether to use the post or go for interviews);
6 constructing and sampling the questionnaire.

Part III is 'analysis of the results' and producing the dissertation. It involves:

7 measurement of data;
8 analysis of data (including interpretation and discussion of results);
9 structuring and writing the whole dissertation;
10 dissertation supervision and assessment.

This book is aimed specifically at BSc and MSc students who are embarking on research as part of their degree. It will provide students with a clear explanatory text which is supported by numerous examples illustrating good practice. Students of built environment subjects such as construction management, facility management, building surveying, quantity surveying, town planning, estate management and civil engineering will find this book of use. It will also be of use to anyone else involved in research work.

About the fourth edition

It has been very pleasing to receive the many complimentary and positive comments from reviewers and users of the first and second editions. These comments have been most appreciated and provided the encouragement for, and formed the basis of, the fourth edition.

The fourth edition covers wider built environment disciplines but retains the same underlying theme, aims and approaches. It also carries forward the same basic framework with the same sequencing and ordering of the chapters.

There is, however, a general review and update of material and references. Moreover, the rationalisation of the text recognises the need for new sections such as the following:

Chapter 2

- Examples of dissertation topics.
- Examples of writing a working title.
- A further example of a typical methodology road map.

Chapter 3

- List of refereed journals related to courses related to built environment.
- Links to databases in built environment.
- Example of summary note-taking of literature review.
- Using the 'Zotero' software tool to organise the literature.
- Example of developing a contextual framework of the literature.
- A new example of writing a literature chapter.

Chapter 4

- Steps for building up a theoretical framework with examples.

Chapter 5

- The SurveyMonkey tool.

Chapter 6

- Update to examples of factual questions related to built environment.
- Update to examples of attitudinal questions related to built environment.

Chapter 9

- New example of writing the rationale section of the introduction chapter.
- New example of writing the research goals.
- New example of writing the methodology chapter.
- New example of writing the dissertation structure.
- New example of writing a literature chapter.
- Example of presenting the 'theoretical' framework.
- Example of writing the rationale section of the research design and methodology chapter.
- Example of writing the research sample.
- A general guide to referencing.

Chapter 10

- Example of a marking grid for dissertation.
- Examples of supervisors' feedback.

Acknowledgements

I would like to give special credit to other contributors in the field of built environment. In particular, I wish to record my acknowledgements to the work of the following writers:

Borden, I. and Rüedi, K. (2003) *The Dissertation: An Architecture Student's Handbook.* Architectural Press, Elsevier, Oxford.

Farrell, P., Sherratt, F., Richardson, A. (2017) *Writing Built Environment Dissertations and Projects – Practical Guidance and Examples.* 2nd edn. Wiley Blackwell, Chichester.

Laycock, E., Howarth, T. and Watson, P. (2016) *The Journey to Dissertation Success for Construction, Property and Architecture Students.* Routledge, Abingdon and New York.

I am also grateful to the following students for their permission to extract information from their dissertations: Miss H. Cooper, Mr S. Green, Mr B. Hemmings, Mr M. Howard, Mrs Z. Mulholland, Mr F. Rassam and Mr T. Whitworth.

I also wish to thank Longman Group Ltd, London, for permission to adapt appendices from their book *Statistical Tables for Biological, Agricultural, and Medical Research*, sixth edition (1974); to Pitman Publishing, for permission to adapt a table from their book *Management and Organisational Behaviour*, fourth edition (1996); and to Unwin Hyman Publications, for permission to adapt a table from their book *Quantity and Quality in Social Research* (1988). Last but not least my thanks go to my colleague D. Fong for his permission to use his SPSS lecture notes, which are exhibited in Appendix 5.

References to sources of information and material are given as accurately as possible throughout this book. Apologies are expressed if any acknowledgement has inadvertently not been recorded.

Finally, I wish to express my gratitude to the staff of Routledge who masterfully crafted the production of this book.

Dr Shamil G. Naoum
School of Computing and Engineering
University of West London

Part I

Preparing the ground and reviewing the literature

1   *Introduction*

This book serves as a guide and learning support document in the preparation of a dissertation for honours undergraduate students and for students undertaking dissertations on taught master's degrees. The book focuses specifically on built environment subjects with a special emphasis on construction-related degree programmes. It covers issues such as the selection of a dissertation topic, writing a proposal, conducting a literature review, selecting the research approach, devising research instruments, collecting information, analysing and presenting information and producing a well-researched and written dissertation.

The meaning of research

To set the scene for this book, I begin by defining the meaning of 'research'. The *Concise Oxford Dictionary* defines research as 'careful search or inquiry; endeavour to discover new or collate old facts etc. by scientific study of a subject; course of critical investigation' (Soanes and Stevenson, 2004). From this, we can conclude that the word 'research' may be used interchangeably with 'inquiry', 'study' or 'investigation'. And yet something more is implied: the inquiry, study or investigation must be conducted in a careful, scientific and/or critical manner. Others have added 'methodical' and 'systematic' to this list of adjectives. It does not really matter which combination of words is chosen (systematic inquiry or critical investigation) so long as both words are kept clearly in mind.

In addition to a specific method of inquiry, a research project has to have an aim or objective. In general terms, the aim of all research is to expand knowledge and develop a product or a message. But we do not simply want a list of facts. A good piece of research will focus on certain aspects of a topic. It will seek to answer specific questions, solve a particular problem or test a hypothesis. The issue(s) to be addressed must be clearly stated at the outset in the objective(s) of the research proposal.

Rationale for conducting a dissertation

The rationale for including a dissertation as a major component of the BSc and MSc courses is that it provides for the development of intellectual skills of a kind that is not fully facilitated on the other components or modules of the teaching course. The dissertation requirement accords with the educational philosophy of the BSc and MSc courses in that it requires students to take responsibility for their own learning, specifying and defining the task and defining the learning outcomes. Therefore, the dissertation provides the opportunity for you to undertake an independent piece of research, investigating in depth a subject in which you have a particular interest and which is of your own selection. Normally, you will submit a dissertation of between 12,000 and 15,000 words and sometimes 20,000 depending on the requirement of your university.

There are two main phases. First, you propose a subject area and, during the course of the lecture sessions, develop a dissertation proposal, which is submitted for approval. Second, after approval, you are assigned to work under the supervision of a selected member of the academic staff and submit a dissertation according to the submission dates specified by your university.

Aim of conducting a dissertation

To undertake an independent piece of research of a demanding nature on a subject related to a particular discipline and then write an academic report. It has a beginning (proposal and literature), a middle (research design and methodology) and an end (analysis of findings and conclusions). The purpose is to deliver a 'product' or a 'message' that has an impact on other researchers and the industry as a whole, such as devising a new methodology, reaching a solution to a particular problem, developing a theoretical model, designing a particular system, delivering a guideline and the like.

Objectives of the dissertation

1   To enable students to investigate, in depth, a subject in which they have a particular interest and is, usually, of their own selection.
2   To provide students with an opportunity to stretch their intellectual and technical skills.
3   To encourage students to develop new forms of analysis, conclusions and policies which may make an original contribution to the knowledge in the field of study concerned.
4   To encourage both clarity and depth of thought in that the project involves analysis of a problem and the development of a logical sequence of ideas.
5   To provide students with an opportunity to learn how to acquire detailed information on a particular issue. It will involve students in the use of bibliographies, libraries and library reference systems. It will involve their using primary sources of data such as a census and the collection of new data through interviews, surveys and archival research.
6   To identify and critically analyse issues with reference to relevant arguments and evidence.
7   To identify and critically analyse issues with reference to pertinent arguments and evidence and formulate 'contextual' and 'theoretical' frameworks.
8   To assemble information and data from a variety of sources and discern and establish connections.

9 To evaluate current procedures and approaches, investigate routine and unfamiliar problems and apply professional judgment in order to devise solutions and/or recommend appropriate actions.

Transferable skills of conducting a dissertation

On completion of your dissertation, you should be able to:

1 Effectively communicate complex ideas, information and data by written and sometimes oral and visual means in a form appropriate to the intended reader and/or audience, with appropriate acknowledgement and referencing of sources.
2 Apply statistical and numerical skills at an advanced level.
3 Use information and communications technology (ICT) to locate and access opinions, information and data from a wide range of sources and communicate information to others.
4 Exercise initiative and personal responsibility in employment and possess the independent learning ability required for continuing professional development.

Purpose of the book

This book fulfils a need within the construction industry by providing students with a useful guide to undertake a piece of research. The construction industry is now developing a community with a new attitude to research. Although a number of texts are available on research design and methodology, there is little applied in construction. This book is specifically designed to assist:

1 Honours undergraduate students and MSc (taught Masters) students in built environment conducting a dissertation or final year research in construction such as construction management, construction project management, quantity surveying, building surveying, architecture and facility management. However, as the book follows the interrelated process of conducting research, it can also be useful to undergraduate and postgraduate students of related construction disciplines such as civil engineering, town planning and estate management. It covers issues such as the selection of a dissertation topic, writing a proposal, conducting a literature review, selecting the research approach, devising research instruments, collecting information, analysing and presenting information and producing a well-researched and written dissertation.
2 Students in the social sciences and people concerned with social surveys.
3 This book also provides a useful 'foundation' guide to students who are about to start an MPhil/PhD programme. However, it is not designed to provide a manual for PhD students, nor does it provide the type of analysis that a doctorate deserves.

Plan of the book

As mentioned earlier, this book will follow the interrelated stages of conducting a piece of dissertation research. Figure 1.1 illustrates the research process stages with their corresponding chapters. This book is therefore composed of ten chapters.

Chapter 1: Introduction

This chapter provides a general introduction to dissertation research and outlines the main aims and objectives of the book.

Chapter 2: Selecting a topic and writing the dissertation proposal

The choice of a dissertation topic usually comes from your interest in and value of a particular subject, which are usually interrelated. The interest and value will eventually be developed into a series of questions, which you will be keen to find answers to. Selecting a topic is discussed in the first part of the chapter. After selecting the subject of your dissertation, you need to formulate a proposal that should contain a rationale, research goals (aim, objectives, hypothesis or key questions), outline methodology and a programme of work. The extent and degree of details for the dissertation proposal are given in the second part of this chapter.

Chapter 3: Reviewing the literature

This activity will most likely be carried out throughout the whole research process but more extensively at the earlier stages of the research. It basically involves reading and critically appraising what other people have written about your subject area. The chapter also gives details on how to conduct a systematic literature search and design a 'contextual' framework for the literature.

Chapter 4: Approaches to data collection

After deciding on the topic that you wish to study and having conducted an extensive literature search, you will be in a position to design your research. Designing the research involves the following activities:

1   Deciding on the type of data that has to be collected (quantitative or qualitative data). This chapter provides further description of these terms.
2   Confirm the method of data collection (i.e. should you conduct a survey or a case study?). The chapter describes each of these methods in great detail.
3   Designing the 'theoretical' framework for your research (if applicable).
4   Deciding on the techniques for data collection (i.e. should you gather the data by interviews, by telephone or by postal questionnaire?).
5   Designing your sample. The research design should tell you how your sample needs to be drawn, to whom you should target your questionnaire and how many to issue.

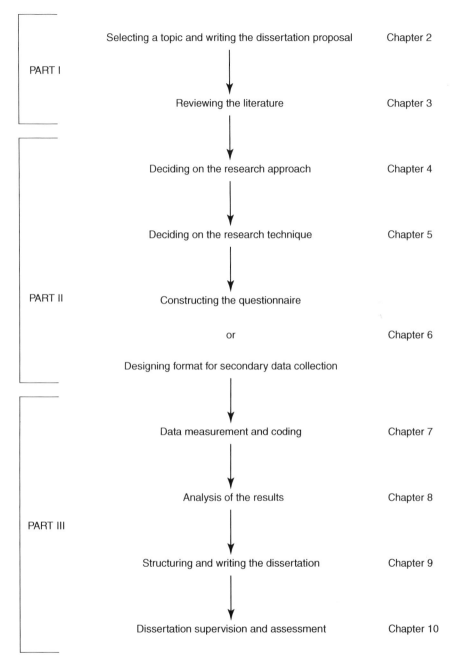

PART I

Selecting a topic and writing the dissertation proposal — Chapter 2

Reviewing the literature — Chapter 3

PART II

Deciding on the research approach — Chapter 4

Deciding on the research technique — Chapter 5

Constructing the questionnaire

or — Chapter 6

Designing format for secondary data collection

PART III

Data measurement and coding — Chapter 7

Analysis of the results — Chapter 8

Structuring and writing the dissertation — Chapter 9

Dissertation supervision and assessment — Chapter 10

Figure 1.1 *Research process diagram.*

Chapter 5: Techniques for data collection

After deciding on your research approach, you will be involved in collecting the data for your research study. If you are collecting 'primary' data (data collected at first hand), you need to undertake certain activities such as inviting your sample to complete the questionnaire, preparing the data summary sheet or taking whatever action is required for your fieldwork. If you are collecting 'secondary' data (data gathered from some other sources), you need to contact those organisations that store the data (if not stored in the library), such as the state and its agencies, statistical offices such as Her Majesty's Stationery Office (HMSO) and the Health and Safety Executive (HSE). Chapter 5 explains the main features of the postal survey and the interview technique, together with showing the advantages and limitations of both techniques.

Chapter 6: Questionnaire construction

This chapter describes and illustrates methods of questionnaire construction: the content of questions, types of questions, question format and the sequence of questions.

Note to students

After constructing your questionnaire, it is strongly recommended to conduct a trial run on the questionnaire before circulating it to the whole sample. This trial is called a 'pilot study'. The pilot study involves testing the wording of the questions, establishing the length of the questionnaire, avoiding ambiguous questions and suggestions for analysing the data, as well as testing the technique selected for collecting the data. In large research projects such as an MPhil or PhD, the researcher should even try to analyse the results of the pilot study to ensure the reliability of data collected. Chapter 6 gives further details on the pilot study.

Chapter 7: Measurements and probability

This chapter prepares the ground for analysis of your results. It is concerned with the nature of measurement in research. It includes the explanation of the four levels of measurement: nominal, ordinal, interval and ratio. The main point to recognise about measurement is that each level of measurement requires a certain type of analysis that is more appropriate than others. This chapter will also explain the meaning of the term 'probability' and its relevance to the analysis of your results.

Chapter 8: Analysis of the results

Once you have collected all the completed questionnaires and/or gathered the archival data, you will be ready for the next stage: the analysis of the data and determining the direction of the study. This stage involves processing the data, putting answers to categories and generally finding out the pattern of the responses. Some results require statistical analysis, as in the case of a large sample survey, and some results involve finding out the trend of the responses, as in the case of in-depth interviews. Chapter 8 gives details on how to analyse the results both manually and with the use of the SPSS (Statistical Package for the Social Sciences) software.

Chapter 9: Structuring and writing the dissertation

After you have completed the literature review and analysed the data, you will be ready to write up the whole dissertation. Writing your dissertation involves reporting and critically appraising the literature review, the analysis of the data and the discussion and interpretation of your findings. Bear in mind that the writing-up stage can overlap with any of the above activities and may start as early as the literature review stage. Chapter 9 provides details on structuring and writing a typical dissertation project.

Chapter 10: Dissertation supervision and assessment

Once you have decided on the topic of your study and your proposal gets approved, your department should then appoint a personal supervisor for you. It is therefore important to know the role of your supervisor and what can be expected from him/her.

This chapter will discuss the basics of what you should expect from your supervisor. It first explains what the role of the supervisor is and what it is not. Second, it illustrates how you may plan your dissertation and finally how you would expect to be assessed in the end.

Reference

Soanes, C. and Stevenson, A. (2004) *Concise Oxford English Dictionary*. Oxford University Press, Oxford.

2 Selecting a topic and writing the dissertation proposal

The first step of the research process involves selecting a research topic and writing your dissertation proposal. This means that you need to do a great deal of reading and clear thinking to identify the gap in knowledge, the problem and your area of interest. This chapter deals with choosing a topic for research and gives guidance on writing your dissertation proposal. The contents of Chapter 2 are illustrated in Figure 2.1.

Choosing the topic

When embarking upon research as part of an undergraduate or a postgraduate study programme, it is important that you pay particular attention to the choice of subject or topic of the research. The choice of topic usually comes from your interest in and value of a particular subject. This interest and value will eventually be developed into a series of questions that you are keen to find answers to. If you are finding difficulty in choosing a researchable topic, you can consider the following:

1   Consulting the library catalogue and inquiring about theses and dissertations, articles in academic journals, reports, books and the like.
2   Using web searches to find areas of interest.
3   Talking about problems and possible topics with your colleagues and/or with your lecturers who are experts in the field.
4   Arranging an informal interview with professionals in the industry and discussing what you should emphasise and what are the possible practical outcomes.

There are a number of criteria that need to be considered when deciding on your research topic. These are summarised below:

1   *A dissertation topic should be realistic.* You need to identify a problem (supported by published materials), investigate the causes and possible solution. You might wish to investigate a problem on-site, for example, the causes of variation orders and their effect on the project outcome, or the problem of material management on-site. Alternatively, the research subject might cover an office procedure or the appraisal of a particular system.

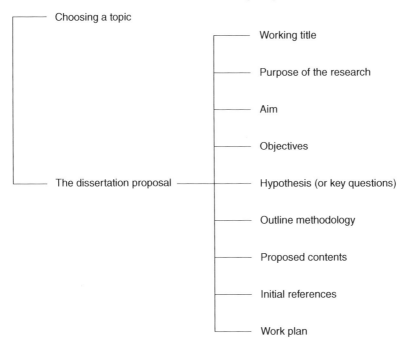

Figure 2.1   *Contents of Chapter 2.*

Here you will be investigating what should be done and what is actually done.

2   *Your topic should be specific and narrow.* For example, if you are conducting a detailed case study, do not investigate all the factors that may influence site productivity as a topic, but rather limit yourself to the influence of financial incentives on productivity. You might be tempted to study job satisfaction in the building industry, but this again is too broad. A better way is to narrow it down and investigate job satisfaction of operatives who are working for small-size firms. Narrowing down the topic can be diagrammed as in Figure 2.2. Bouma and Atkinson (1995, p. 30) comment:

> [T]he first thing to do if we are to narrow and clarify a problem question is to 'unpack' it. Most of the starting-points contain many issues and suggest many different avenues of research. The questions we begin with are usually quite complex. They may sound simple, but they are probably far from it. If we are to narrow and focus the issues for research, we have to list the issues involved in the question. We are then in a position to choose from that list, a question that will focus our attention on a narrowed problem.

3   *Your topic should show individuality – that is your personal contribution to the study.* What is new about your investigation? This can take the form of case studies, a series of interviews, postal questionnaires or analysing archival data.

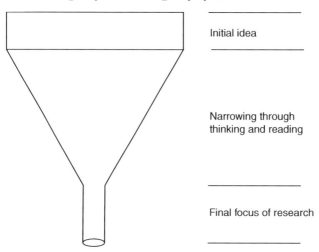

Figure 2.2   *A diagram showing the narrowing down of the research topic.*

For example, if you are conducting an architecture dissertation, you should rely on research that is:

- Original, in that it is undertaken by you.
- Acknowledges other people's ideas and work as appropriate.

In this context, 'originality' means examining material that is rarely or has never been studied before or providing new interpretations of well-known material. According to Borden and Rüedi (2006), the process by which you do this should entail:

- The study of some specific architectural objects, e.g. persons, ideas, buildings or drawings.
- The application of some interpretive or analytical framework, particularly one which:
- Explores a particular theme or asks a specific question about architecture.
- The writing or other exploration of these ideas in a way that conveys your investigation to yourself and to others.

The result is then a dissertation which:

- Provides new information and/or interpretations about architecture.
- Allows you to learn more about architecture yourself.
- Makes a contribution to architectural knowledge in general. (Chapters 4 and 5 discuss these approaches in detail.)

☞ **For more information go to http://www.ut-ie.com/s/sample_diss.html**

4 *Accessibility of information.* Your topic should be in an area for which you can have access to the data necessary for the successful completion of the dissertation.

5 *Personal ability.* The subject and extent of the research should be within your intellectual and physical resource ability.

6 *Personal interest.* Last but not least, you should be interested in the subject of research. It is of no use if you do not like or enjoy the research subject.

Tips for choosing topics in architecture

Apart from criteria 1–6 that you need to consider when deciding on your research topic, the following tips might help you think about your own subject:

Your portfolio work – The portfolio you have produced in the design studio over the years is in many ways a record of yourself, your architectural thoughts and how they have developed. Therefore, pick a subject related to your architectural design interests, but do not make it a slave to studio projects. Writing directly solely about your design work is not normally acceptable. Borden and Rüedi (2006, p. 5) state:

> One particular question that you may want to bear in mind is the connection between your design work and your dissertation subject. The essential thing to bear in mind here is that the word-based work should not be a commentary on the design-based work, and nor should the design-based work be simply the supporting visual evidence for the word-based work. Rather works and designs should be used as equivalent and inter-related ways of exploring the same subject matter.

Other work – If you have already written about, for example, contemporary architecture, perhaps it would be a good time to explore something older, such as Victorian Gothic architecture, or perhaps something outside of the immediate architectural profession, such as the way architecture has been represented in theatre design (and vice versa) (Borden and Rüedi, 2006).

☞ **For more information about selecting a dissertation subject in architecture, go to Borden and Rüedi (2006, pp. 5–6).**

Examples of dissertation topics in architecture

Next is a list of previous research related to various disciplines which may broaden your thoughts to the type of subjects that you might be interested in researching. These topics have been extracted from various UK universities' websites and the British Library. Others are from the ARCOM database (some of which have already been published as journal papers).

☞ **For more published topics, go to http://www.arcom.ac.uk/abstracts-search. php or simply type ARCOM abstracts into Google Search.**

Note to students

- The following topics have been selected randomly and are not based on grades, date, themes or other criteria. They are merely to demonstrate examples. Your university should also store a list of dissertations in the library that have already been completed in your course.
- Some of the following topics are multidisciplinary and can apply to other courses.
- Some titles require fine-tuning and it can be a good exercise for you to put them right (see how to write a working title in the following proposal section).

Examples of dissertation topics in architecture

- Virtual generative BIM workspace for maximising conceptual design innovation: a paradigm of future opportunities.
- Optimal process integration architectures in off-site construction: theorising the use of multi-skilled resources.
- Building information modelling (BIM): now and beyond.
- The potential for gender equality in architecture: an Anglo-Spanish comparison;
- Distributed ontology architecture for knowledge management in highway construction.
- Characteristics and evolution of innovative collaboration networks in architecture, engineering and construction: study of national prize-winning projects in China.
- Matching supply networks to a modular product architecture in the house-building industry.
- Knowledge management in the architecture, engineering and construction industry.
- Marketing importance and marketing performance measurement of architecture firms in Singapore: an exploratory study.
- Is radical innovation in architecture crucial to sustainability? Lessons from three Scottish contemporary buildings.
- Evolutionary, not revolutionary – logics of early design energy modelling adoption in UK architecture practice.
- Product architecture model for multistory modular buildings.
- Critical appraisal of design management in architecture.
- Needs and technology adoption: observation from BIM experience.
- Architectural and cultural responses to global environmental concerns in the 21st century: an investigation.
- Architecture and graphic design: case studies on the use of image and text in the built environment.
- Materiality and spirituality: the architecture of Peter Zumthor, George Pace, Peter Celsing and Sigurd Lewerentz.
- Phenomenology in architecture.

- Seaside regeneration and the role of architecture as a regeneration tool.
- The final churches?: an examination of the work of four post-war European church architects: Rudolf Schwarz, George P.
- The influences of Chinese and Portuguese cultures in Macau architecture.
- The use of natural light in architecture through case studies.

☞ **For more information on selecting a dissertation subject in architecture, go to http://www.dissertationcooperative.com/dissertation-topics-in-architecture/ (The best dissertation topics in architecture: 20 questions to look into).**

Examples of dissertation topics in property, town planning and estate management

- Community involvement in planning: the debate and the reality.
- Contaminated land redevelopment: a viable development option for the small-scale developer.
- Delivering affordable homes in London: a critical evaluation of town planning policy in inner London boroughs.
- Financing the provision of infrastructure in major urban growth areas in the UK: the challenges facing the designated growth area of the Thames Gateway.
- Making the case for strategic rail infrastructure provision as precedent to urban regeneration: why the government should be spending on the railways to support their Sustainable Communities.
- The impact and effect of flooding and flood risk on property development in England and its implication for the UK.
- The investment performance of private rented residential property: a historical comparison with the equity returns.
- The role of place marketing within the strategies of urban regeneration companies.
- An appraisal of Local Authority employment: planning in selected inner cities of the United Kingdom.
- The changing cultural identity in the urban fabric of the contemporary Islamic city: the case of Cairo.
- Architecture as Building the sustainable city: compact or dispersed? a catalyst for urban regeneration.
- The skyscraper and urban design.

Examples of dissertation topics in construction management, construction project management, quantity surveying and building surveying

- A conceptual model into the formation and preservation of trust in client/ contractor partnering agreements.
- An investigation into whether there is a difference in the motivational and demotivational factors affecting directly employed and subcontract staff in the rail renewal industry.
- Critical success factors in NHS PFI projects.

- Diversification and the QS firm: a review of strategies and implications.
- Managing risks associated with modular construction in the UK budget hotel sector.
- Off-site manufacture and modular construction: the future of house building?
- Partnering procurement and the benefits for the UK construction industry from the quantity surveyor's perspective.
- The influence of integrated project teams on health and safety performance in the UK construction industry.
- The quantity surveyors' contribution to sustainable construction.
- What drives and constrains the use of standardisation in the construction of school buildings in the UK?
- Hierarchy of criteria used to select or reject hybrid concrete construction as a structural frame in the UK.
- Integration and Collaboration: is it an asset or a burden to existing duties between consultants and contractors?
- Post-occupancy evaluation: how can project managers effectively collect project feedback and feed it forward to manage future design?
- Sustainable construction in the recession.
- The inter-relationships of trust in partnering and disputes resolution.
- The selection of building procurement systems: a guide on how to choose the most appropriate procurement method for a building based on client's requirements.
- Transferring the success of the lean theory: quantifying the relationship between leanness and productivity in the UK construction industry.
- Use of team building on improving project performance.

The dissertation proposal

After deciding on a topic for research, your dissertation proposal should contain the following:

1 Working title or the approved title
2 Purpose (rationale for the study)
3 Research goals
   i Aim
   ii Objectives
   iii Key questions
   iv Hypothesis (if applicable)
4 Initial literature review
5 Outline methodology
6 Proposed contents
7 Initial references
8 Work plan

The extent and degree of detail for your proposal should ideally take the following into account.

Working title

A working title is a short line that gives your research a 'direction', and the title might change slightly at the final stages of research. The title should give your research an identity/name that reflects the focal point and area of the research. It should therefore be clear and to the point. There are a number of questions to bear in mind when selecting a final title. These are:

1   Does the title identify precisely what is being studied?
2   Is the title clear and concise and at the same time sufficiently descriptive to allow for rapid categorisation?
3   Has the title been stripped of superfluous words and redundancy? Phrases such as 'A contribution to …' or 'Towards a theory of …' are nothing more than padding.
4   Are the key nouns correctly chosen and in the proper order?

Appendix 1 gives examples of working titles but below are tips to construct one (this idea is adapted from the following website:

☞ **http://dissertation.laerd.com/what-the-reader-learns-from-a-dissertation-title.php**

Example 1

Barriers to sustainability in construction: a qualitative study among medium-size contractors operating in Greater London.

Example 2

Problems with partnering in the public sector: lessons from 20 completed case studies in the UK.

   The two main parts of these two titles are the area of interest (and focus) of the research, which are grouped together, and the methodological components that the researchers want to draw attention to. Looking at these titles again, the author <u>underlined</u> the area of interest (and focus) and *italicised* the methodological components.

The structure of the two titles

Example 1

<u>Barriers to sustainability in construction</u>: *a qualitative study among medium-size contractors operating in Greater London.*

<u>Barriers **[focus]** to sustainability</u> **[area of interest]**: *a qualitative study **[qualitative research design]** among medium-size contractors **[population]** operating in Greater London **[situated nature of the study]**.*

Example 2

Problems with partnering in the public sector: lessons *from 20 completed case studies in the UK.*

Problems **[focus]** with partnering **[area of interest]** in the public sector **[population, situated nature of the study]**: lessons **[proposed outcome]** *from 20 completed case studies* **[sample methodology]**.

The second example is similar in structure to the first example, but with one important addition in the second title in that it highlights the *proposed outcome* of the research.

Exercise for students: Go back to the examples of dissertation topics in various disciplines above and try to rephrase them following the principles of writing a working title discussed in this section.

Purpose of the research (or rationale for the study)

The second part of your proposal is the rationale which should be a discussion of approximately 500–1000 words that sets out (with supporting empirical facts that are fully referenced) the problem and the reason for the proposed study, highlighting the issues to be investigated (see example in Chapter 9).

The research goals

The third part of your proposal contains four sections, namely, the aim, the objectives, key questions, hypotheses or assumptions.

Aim

Ideally, a *one*-sentence aim should be provided, highlighting your ultimate goal. Appendix 1 provides examples of aims but here are some more specimens:

Example 1: To *provide professional guidelines* to engineers who are required to undertake the role of the project manager.
Example 2: To *develop a conceptual model* for analysing productivity barriers of subcontracting.
Example 3: To *develop a theoretical model* for identifying the different factors that may influence the behaviour and effectiveness of project managers.
Example 4: To *construct a comparative table* showing the difference in performance between various types of procurement methods.
Example 5: To *design a management system* for improving the safety performance to small-size contractors.

Example 6:	To *develop a chart* that demonstrates the strength of the relationship between implementing lean construction initiatives and productivity level on site.
Example 7:	To *develop a mathematical formula* to predict the productivity level of various construction techniques.
Example 8:	To *construct a scoring matrix* showing the level of performance between management and traditional form of contracts.

Note to students

Notice that the aforementioned aims are phrased as if the researcher is seeking to deliver some kind of a 'product' that would benefit the industry and other future researchers, such as to provide professional guidelines, to develop a conceptual framework, to construct a comparative table, to design a management system, to develop a chart, to develop a mathematical formula or to construct a scoring matrix.

In the conclusion chapter, you need to deliver the product that you have aimed for at the start of your research. Appendix 7 shows an example of an achieved aim.

Objectives

Ideally, between three and five single-sentence objectives should be developed. Objectives are the breakdown of your aim (sub-aims), which focuses on finding out or establishing certain issues while achieving your aim (see Appendix 1 for examples). The objectives will then pose a number of questions that will form your research questionnaire later in the research process. As shown, try to phrase each objective in the form of:

To investigate …
To analyse …
To assess …
To examine …
To compare …
To test …
To critically appraise …
To find out …
To evaluate …, etc.

Key questions

A number of 'key questions' need to be formulated in your proposal that would state the position for the argument or investigation. Appendix 1 provides various types of key questions.

The research initial hypothesis

If your research is designed to test or validate a hypothesis or a theoretical framework, or to explain a phenomenon, then a one-sentence main hypothesis needs to be established that should clearly and specifically state the position for the argument or investigation. This main hypothesis can be broken down into a number of sub-hypotheses (see Proposal 2 in Appendix 1).

A hypothesis is a tentative proposition that is a subject of verification through your investigation. Your conclusion will either support or reject your proposed hypothesis, or support part and reject others. Hypotheses can often be formulated as 'if … then' statements, or as a hunch that you have about the existence of a relationship between issues or variables. Your hypothesis should also be sharp and specific. Appendix 1 provides various types of hypotheses.

Initial literature review

This is the fourth part of your proposal which is an expansion of your rationale section and you should write an initial literature review of approximately 1000 words on your topic. (See examples of writing-up styles in Chapters 3 and 9.)

Outline methodology and research road map

In this fifth part of the proposal, you should highlight your proposed methodology for obtaining the information necessary for the study. Research methods can take many forms (see Chapter 4). At the proposal stage, however, all you need to provide is an outline methodology, for example, on which academic journals you will concentrate your reading. If you intend to interview personnel, who will they be and approximately how many of them will you interview? and so on (see Box 9.4, Chapter 9, page 152 and Appendix 1 for examples).

It is strongly recommended to include a road map for your research methodology (see a typical example of a research road map in Figure 2.3 on page 21 and also Figure 2.4 on page 22).

Proposed structure of the dissertation

This is the sixth part of your proposal. Naturally, you would not be expected to provide the precise structure of your dissertation at this stage, but an initial indication is necessary. So in this part, you need to provide the proposed titles of your chapters, which will be subject to verification and can be tweaked at the end. This table shows an example (see also Box 9.5 on page 154):

Chapter 1:	Introduction and background to the problem
Chapter 2:	Previous project management models
Chapter 3:	Apparent advantage and disadvantages of project management
Chapter 4:	Research design and methodology
Chapter 5:	Analysis of the interviews, results and discussion
Chapter 6:	Conclusions and recommendations

☞ See Appendix 1 for more examples.

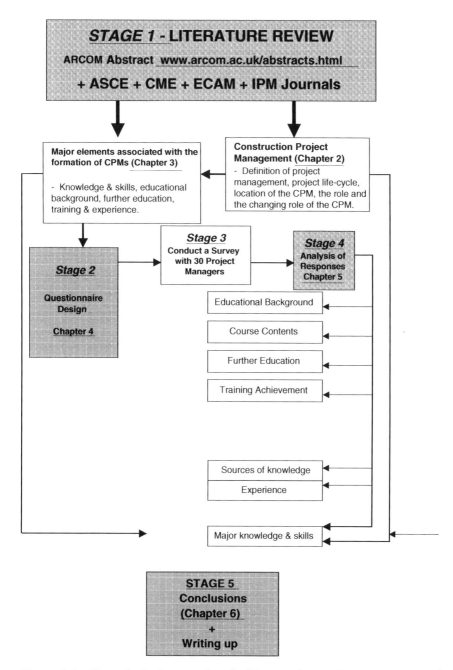

Figure 2.3 *Example 1 of a typical methodology road map. Source: Naoum and Al-Dhyaf (2006).*

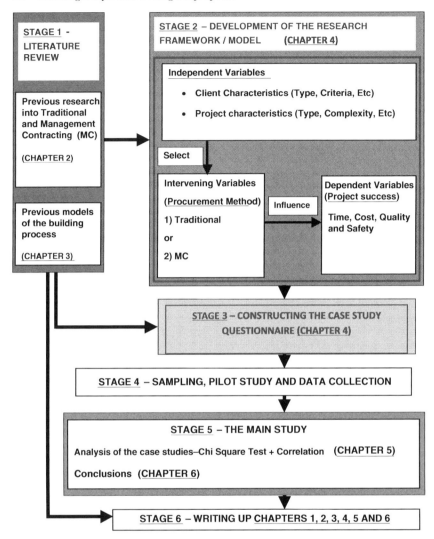

Figure 2.4   *Example 2 of a typical methodology road map. Source: Naoum (2013).*

Initial references

Section seven of your proposal should provide details of the core sources of references, particularly those that have been consulted in order to provide the basis of evidence and information necessary to enable the dissertation proposal to be developed. Each reference should provide author, year, title, publisher, edition and publication data (see Appendix 1 for examples).

Work plan

This is the last part of your proposal and it should be a simple work plan or time-table. A bar chart of activities over the weeks of study is often helpful, indicating what you intend to do and when (see Figure 10.1, page 207).

Summary

Selecting your dissertation topic is an important task. Therefore, you should allow a reasonable amount of time in which to develop your proposal. The first step is to identify areas that have potential and seem interesting to you. Consult your library and read articles, books, dissertations, etc. that are related to your area of interest. Discuss your ideas with your colleagues and/or lecturers. The second step is to write your initial proposal following the instructions given in this chapter (see Appendix 1 for examples). The three most important parts of your proposal are the purpose of study, objectives and methodology. Finally, discuss your initial proposal with your appointed supervisor and make amendments, if required. Start your investigation as soon as you can and stick with your work plan.

References

Borden, I. and Rüedi, K. (2006) *The Dissertation: An Architecture Student's Handbook*. 2nd edn. Architectural Press, Elsevier, Oxford.

Bouma, G. and Atkinson, G. (1995) *A Handbook of Social Science Research: A Comprehensive and Practical Guide for Students*. Oxford University Press, Oxford.

Naoum, S.G. (2013) *Dissertation Research and Writing for Construction Students*. Routledge, London.

Naoum, S.G. and Al-Dhyaf, S. (2006) 'Formation of Construction Project Manager'. CIB W65 conference on building and construction, 10–14 October, Rome, Italy.

3 Reviewing the literature

The literature review is an essential stage in conducting a research project and amounts, on average, to between 20 and 25 per cent of a dissertation's content, although certain dissertation subjects may require a literature review amounting to up to 50 per cent of the content. The literature review involves reading and appraising what other people have written about your subject area. It can be both descriptive and analytical. It is descriptive in that it describes the work of previous writers and it is analytical in that it critically analyses the contribution of others with a view to identifying similarities and contradictions made by previous writers.

There are seven main activities involved in undertaking a literature review:

1 Knowing the sources of information.
2 Understanding how the library works.
3 Knowing the search engines related to your discipline.
4 Collecting existing knowledge on the subject and systematically organising the literature.
5 Reading and note-taking.
6 Designing the contextual framework for the literature.
7 Appraising and writing up the literature review.

This chapter focuses on discussing the seven activities highlighted above. The contents of Chapter 3 are illustrated in Figure 3.1.

Rationale for undertaking a literature review

In order to be able to make an original contribution to knowledge in your research area, the literature review should demonstrate that you have a comprehensive grasp of existing knowledge. The literature review serves two purposes. First, it seeks a systematic reading of previously published and unpublished information relating to your area of investigation. The gathered information will develop issues and themes and should drive you to the next important stage, namely research design. Second, the literature review will help you to improve your research study by looking into previous research design or questionnaires, which will give you some insights into how you can design your own study more effectively. The authors of past dissertations, theses and published journal articles gave their research work

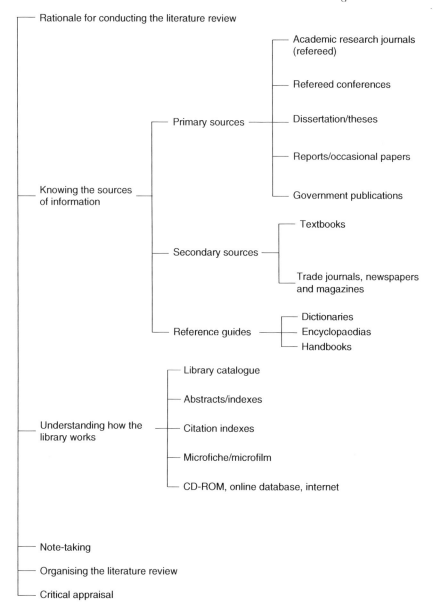

Rationale for conducting the literature review

Knowing the sources of information

- Primary sources
  - Academic research journals (refereed)
  - Refereed conferences
  - Dissertation/theses
  - Reports/occasional papers
  - Government publications
- Secondary sources
  - Textbooks
  - Trade journals, newspapers and magazines
- Reference guides
  - Dictionaries
  - Encyclopaedias
  - Handbooks

Understanding how the library works

- Library catalogue
- Abstracts/indexes
- Citation indexes
- Microfiche/microfilm
- CD-ROM, online database, internet

Note-taking

Organising the literature review

Critical appraisal

Figure 3.1 *Contents of Chapter 3.*

a great deal of thought, and you can frequently benefit from their thinking when conducting your literature search. In other words, a literature review attempts to integrate what others have done and said, criticise previous scholarly works, build bridges between related topic areas and/or identify the central issues in a field. The following sections describe the activities involved in undertaking the literature review.

Knowing the sources of information

Starting the literature review process involves the identification of appropriate literature. Generally speaking, there are three types of literature sources available for you to look at. These are primary sources, secondary sources and reference guides.

Primary literature sources

Primary literature is the most accurate source of information as it publishes original research. The following publications fall within these primary sources.

Academic research journals (refereed)

Refereed journals related to construction publish original research work and technical papers, which usually report innovative developments in the built environment field such as architecture, town planning, urban planning, civil engineering, construction and estate management. By publishing papers from both industry and academia, refereed journals provide an excellent source for discussing recent developments in your field.

Here is a list of refereed journals related to construction (architecture, construction, project management, quantity surveying, building surveying, commercial management and facility management):

- *Journal of Construction Engineering and Management (ASCE).*
- *Journal of Professional Issues in Engineering (ASCE).*
- *Journal of Management of Engineering (ASCE).*
- *Construction Management and Economics.*
- *Construction Economics and Building.*
- *Engineering, Construction and Architectural Management.*
- *International Journal of Project Management.*
- *Journal of Performance of Constructed Facilities.*
- *Journal of Management Procurement and Law.*
- *International Construction Law Review.*
- *International Journal of Law in the Built Environment.*
- *International Journal of Architectural Computing.*
- *Journal of Architectural Engineering.*
- *International Journal of Construction Education and Research.*
- *Facilities.*
- *Construction Repairs.*
- *Architectural Engineering and Design Management.*
- *Journal of Cost Analysis and Management.*
- *Economic Journal.*
- *International Journal for Construction Marketing.*
- *Journal of Construction in Developing Countries.*
- *International Journal of Construction Management.*

- *International Journal for Managing Projects in Business.*
- *International Journal of Productivity and Performance Management.*
- *Journal of Architecture.*
- *Journal of Architectural Conservation.*
- *Journal of Production Planning & Control, The Management of Operations.*
- *Constructing Technology.*
- *International Journal of Construction Education and Research.*
- *Journal of Engineering, Design and Technology.*
- *Smart and Sustainable Built Environment.*
- *Building Research & Information.*
- *Australasian Journal of Construction Economics and Building.*

☞ **Also see list of journals in the field of construction management in Farrell et al. (2017, p. 47).**

Refereed journals related to property, estate, urban and town planning:

- *International Journal of Urban and Regional Research.*
- *Built Environment Project and Asset Management.*
- *Journal of Urban Planning and Development.*
- *Urban Studies.*
- *Urban Design* journal.
- *International Journal of Strategic Property Management.*
- *Journal of Property Research.*
- *Journal of Property Valuation and Investment.*
- *Property Management.*
- *Journal of Real Estate Literature.*
- *Journal of Corporate Real Estate.*

Other refereed journals (mixed disciplines):

- *Building and Environment.*
- *Building Research and Information.*
- *Construction Innovation: Information, Process, Management.*
- *Architectural Engineering and Design Management.*
- *International Journal of Environmental Research and Public Health.*
- *Journal of Engineering, Design and Technology.*
- *Journal of Asian Architecture and Building Engineering.*
- *International Journal of Disaster Resilience in the Built Environment.*
- *Journal of Housing and the Built Environment.*
- *Journal of Property Investment and Finance.*
- *International Journal of Sustainable Engineering.*
- *Journal of Finance Management of Property and Construction.*
- *Journal of Environmental Engineering.*
- *Intelligent Buildings International.*
- *Journal of Information Technology in Construction.*

- *Structural Safety.*
- *Building Research and Information.*
- *Construction and Building Materials.*
- *Journal of Composites for Construction.*
- *International Journal of Civil, Structural, Construction and Arch. Eng.*
- *Journal of Structural and Construction Engineering.*
- *Energy and Buildings.*
- *Resources, Conservation and Recycling.*

Refereed journals related to civil engineering:

- *Journal of Computing in Civil Engineering (ASCE).*
- *International Journal of Impact Engineering.*
- *Structures.*
- *Journal of Structural Engineering.*
- *Cement and Concrete Research.*
- *Structural Concrete.*
- *Composite Structures.*
- *Journal of Constructional Steel Research.*
- *Journal of Structural Engineering.*
- *Computers and Structures.*
- *Soils and Foundations.*
- *Automation in Construction.*
- *Journal of Materials in Civil Engineering.*
- *Journal of Bridge Engineering.*
- *Research in Engineering Design.*
- *Journal of Environmental Engineering and Science.*
- *Construction and Building Materials.*

☞ **Also see list of journals in the field of civil engineering in Farrell et al. (2017, p. 46).**
☞ **Also visit http://www.icevirtuallibrary.com/ for more lists of journals.**

Refereed conferences

The term 'conference' also applies to symposiums and congresses. In many fields, conference proceedings can be a main source of information and the main aim of these conferences is similar to that of academic journals (i.e. discussing current developments in your field of study). Papers published in proceedings contain a collection of themes such as mega projects, developing countries projects, productivity, design, procurement, economics, law, technology, sociology, psychology, organisation, management and many more. The majority of international conference papers are based on 'primary' research and are accepted for publication after they have been refereed by at least two members of the paper review committee. Therefore, the quality of some conference papers can be as good as refereed journal articles. The British Library Lending Division (BLLD) publishes an 'Index' of conference proceedings.

Here is a list of some international conference proceedings related to the built environment:

- Organisation and Management of Construction Symposium (known as CIB W65).
- Procurement Systems Symposium (CIB W92).
- Building Economics and Construction Management (CIB W90).
- Economic Management of Innovation.
- Congress on Computing in Civil Engineering (organised by the ASCE).
- The Design and Environment Conference.
- International Conference on Computers in Urban Planning and Management.
- Association of Researchers in Construction Management (ARCOM).
- Information Technology in Civil and Structural Engineering Design.
- International Congress on Construction.
- Automation and Robotics in Construction.
- International Cost Engineering Council Symposium.
- Financial Management of Property and Construction.

Here is a list of some international conference proceedings related to civil engineering:

- International Conference on Civil Engineering and Materials Science.
- Internal Conference on Concrete Engineering and Technology.
- International Conference on Sustainable Civil Engineering Structures and Construction Materials.
- International Conference on Sustainable Civil Engineering and Environment.

Dissertations/theses

It is most important for undergraduate, postgraduate and higher degree students to look at other people's dissertations or theses, where appropriate. Dissertations and theses serve two purposes. First, they enable you to have an idea about the content of the work, the standard expected, the methodology adopted and the structure and style of writing up. Second, you can benefit from the list of references and bibliography that are attached at the back of the work.

Most libraries have an on-site dissertation and thesis collection as well as a borrowing service through inter-library loans. Students registered for higher degrees can obtain a list of theses from the British Library Lending Division (BLLD). Another option for finding out about other theses is to contact academic institutions and request a list of accepted dissertations or theses. The contact is usually made through the departmental secretary or the academic thesis supervisor. Once you have identified what you want, your library should do the rest by borrowing the material through the inter-library loan service. A dissertation or a thesis may take four to six weeks to arrive and overseas PhD theses may take longer.

Reports/occasional papers

Technical reports and occasional papers can be of great use to you because they are comprehensive and often publish up-to-date information. Moreover, occasional papers and reports of certain research groups are sufficiently prestigious for the researchers concerned to favour them as a method of disseminating their results (Sharp et al., 1993).

Here is a list of institutions that disseminate such reports and occasional papers relating to the built environment:

- Chartered Institute of Building (CIOB).
- Royal Institute of Chartered Surveyors (RICS).
- Royal Institute of British Architects (RIBA).
- Building Research Establishment (BRE).
- Construction Industry Research and Information Association (CIRIA).

Here is a list of institutions that disseminate such reports and occasional papers relating to civil engineering:

- Institution of Civil Engineering (ICE).
- Institution of Structural Engineers (IStructE).
- Institution of Highways and Transportation (CIHT).
- Chartered Institute of Water and Environmental Management (CIWEM).

Here is a list of institutions that disseminate such reports and occasional papers relating to property, estate, urban and town planning:

- Royal Town Planning Institute (RTPI).
- Institute of Real Estate Management (IREM).

Government publications

Government publications are one of the largest and most important sources of information, especially for those students analysing secondary data. Government documents may be classified as (a) government administration records and (b) research records for specialists, including a considerable number of statistics and data of value to science and business.

Finding your way around government publications can sometimes be complicated and confusing. This is because of the sheer volume of information published under the category of government documents and because they are often placed outside the normal subject index system. For instance, most people ask for government documents by their popular name and not by their official name (the Latham Report instead of Constructing the Team, or the Egan Report instead of Rethinking Construction, or the Tavistock Report instead of Communication in the Construction Industry, and so on). Therefore, the best way to get around this problem is to ask for the monthly list or catalogue of yearly government publications of the UK, USA or elsewhere. For example, in the UK you should be asking for the monthly lists of materials published by Her Majesty's Stationery Office (HMSO) or the catalogue of British Official Publications not published by HMSO (Sharp et al., 1993).

Secondary literature sources

Secondary literature sources are those that cite from primary sources such as textbooks and newspaper articles.

Textbooks (hard copy)

Most research is initially based on information from books which the researcher has either come across at the proposal stage or found in a dissertation/thesis bibliography. Textbooks are much easier to trace and obtain than other references. However, one significant difference between books and journals is that research work published in a journal is more recent. It takes less time to have a paper published in a journal than it takes to publish a book. A second difference is that journals contain a range of articles, whereas books often deal with a particular issue. In the initial reading phase involving books, more can be gained from reading edited collections as they are likely to contain a wide range of perspectives on a particular subject.

E-books

A growing number of key textbooks are available online on the database of your university library.

Note to students

See the best route into the database via the Electronic Resources link of your university.

Trade journals, newspapers and magazines

These are mass media sources of information which often summarise research or provide views on a particular subject. It is very useful to refer to these sources at the start of your dissertation. Students often become interested in a particular topic as a result of reading an article in a newspaper, magazine or trade journal.

Here are some mass media sources that are related to the built environment:

- *Contract Journals.*
- *Building Magazine.*
- *Architects Journal.*
- *Construction News.*

Here are two mass media sources that are related to civil engineering:

- *New Civil Engineers* magazine.
- *Construction and Civil Engineers* magazine.

Here are two mass media sources that are related to property, estate, urban and town planning:

- *The Planner.*
- *Planning and Urban Design.*

However, caution should be taken in reporting the findings of mass media sources. Such sources are usually non-refereed and may easily distort or exaggerate scientific claims. Remember that most refereed journals' editorial boards practise peer review for the purpose of ensuring high-quality reporting.

Reference guides

Reference guides are very useful sources of information for short and quick answers to basic questions. The function of the reference guides is to introduce the basic information about a particular subject area. Sources that fall within these guides are dictionaries, glossaries, encyclopaedias and handbooks.

Dictionaries and glossaries

These provide definitions of terms and can be useful in helping you clarify your thoughts. Some of the preferred dictionaries are:

- *The Concise Oxford Dictionary.*
- *Webster's Third New International Dictionary of English Language.*
- *The Random House Dictionary of English Language.*

Other specialised dictionaries are *Kister's Dictionary Buying Guide*, the *Penguin Dictionary of Sociology* and *Dictionary of Social Behaviour and Social Research Method*.

Encyclopaedias

These give a concise description of the main aspects of a topic. The most up-to-date and authoritative English encyclopaedia is the *New Encyclopaedia Britannica*. Because encyclopaedias can go out of date fairly quickly, most scientific disciplines encourage and support a variety of specialised handbooks.

Handbooks

The function of handbooks is similar to that of encyclopaedias, except that they are more current. Handbooks, however, have limitations in that they are written by and for other scholars with similar interests and vocabularies (Smith, 1991, p. 46). These usually assume that the user understands the methods and logic of particular disciplines, and they may not have subject indexes.

Understanding how the library works

Having identified the sources of information, the next step that you need to take is to know how to find the material. It is absolutely vital that you understand the library and how to use its sources most effectively. Bell (2014) lists three important points that you need to bear in mind while conducting literature research:

1   Find the most relevant published materials quickly.
2   Avoid getting 'bogged down'.
3   Get into the habit of recording information derived from your reading so that it can be easily found and understood weeks, months or years later.

Therefore, you may have to spend a few days getting to know the services offered by your library, what materials it holds and where, as well as the coding or shelving system it uses (usually the Dewey decimal system). Each library should contain the following:

- Library catalogue.
- Abstracts/indexes.
- Citation indexes.

Library catalogue

This lists all the material which the library has in stock including books, journal titles, videos, and so on. Around the late 1980s, most academic libraries had replaced card catalogues with computer-based catalogues. However, they both register the same details. Typical computer-screen information displays record the location of the book, the title of the book, author's name, number of pages, year of publication and library code number. Magazines, journals and newspapers are catalogued in the same way as the books but include detailed information about which issues/volumes the library holds. Issues/volumes of journals that are not held in the library have to have a special reference to inform the user of the closest library which holds that particular journal volume.

Indexes and abstracts

Indexes and abstracts can help you to trace articles in journals. They both give the title, author and issue/volume details, but abstracts also include a short summary, often fewer than 200 words, of the article. An abstract gives you information about the problem and the survey findings. Indexes and abstracts provide not only a short-cut means of access to information since they curtail endless random searching through periodical titles on the shelves, but also a large number of references which would not be found by such a haphazard method (Haywood and Wragg, 1982). Most abstracting services classify articles in accordance with the subject they cover. The natural way to start your search on a particular subject is, first, to look at the journal abstract/index. Second, study the abstract and find out whether the article is likely to be worth reading or is merely duplicating material already studied. Third, if it is worth reading, you then start searching the volume you need in order to locate the pages of the article in that volume.

Example from ARCOM

It is strongly recommended to visit the following link from the ARCOM website (Association of Researchers in Construction Management):

☞ Visit http://www.arcom.ac.uk/abstracts-search.php

This website address states the following:

> One of our most important publications is the CM Abstracts and Indexes. This contains the full titles, authors, abstracts and keywords of articles from several leading Construction Management journals, from recent ARCOM Conference Proceedings, and from PhD theses.

Enter one or more words into any of the boxes below. You may enter a phrase (several words) to search for an exact match. Use + to separate two or more search terms.

Paper title: [   ]

Author: [   ]

Keyword: [   ]

Searches keywords and abstract text

☞ Find out more at: http://www.arcom.ac.uk/abstracts-search.php or simply type ARCOM abstract in Google Search.

Citation index

Citation indexing reports alphabetical lists by authors of papers cited in published articles. This source of indexing provides standard bibliographic information on individual articles written in a particular time period. Their permuted subject index classifies each of these articles by significant words used in each article's title, and the citation index lists by author or by referenced articles.

Citation indexing is important because it graphically depicts scientific networks by quantifying who cites whom (Smith, 1991). Almost all scientific articles or reports published at any time and cited during a particular year will have an accompanying bibliographic list of authors, books, articles, reports and the like which cite the article or author. The researcher may then create a snowball sample of citations in a particular area by looking up each new list of citations. For example, if you know that Professor X is an expert on leadership, you could look up his/her name in the Social Science Citation Index to start tracing a collegial network of experts.

☞ Find out more about 'sources of written information' in Thomas, G. (2017, pp. 60–61).

Knowing the search engines related to the built environment

All libraries subscribe to a number of online databases providing a wide range of different types of information. These can be accessed via the electronic resources or e-resources link on your university library webpage. Below are the databases which are most relevant to the built environment:

- **British Standards Online (BSOL)** – a comprehensive online database of internationally recognised standards.
- **Building Cost Information Service (BCIS)** – gives access to independent data. It is a tool to help quantity surveyors and cost estimators to provide advice and prepare cost plans for clients.
- **Construction Information Service** – provides information, regulations, legislation, standards and guidance material (including BRE publications). Includes many e-books.
- **DCP** (Development Control Practice) **Online** – a comprehensive reference on planning: best practice, legislation, with expert analysis of how this is applied.
- **Digimap** – mapping service delivering maps and data from the Ordnance Survey. Also includes a number of other data collections, including historical, geological, Lidar and spatial data.
- **Estates Gazette Interactive (EGi)** – UK news, research and information service for the commercial property market.
- **ICONDA** – Contains summaries (and some full text) of journal articles on building, construction etc.
- **ISURV** – online database of information and best practice guidance for surveyors including interpretative legal guidance on all aspects of built environment projects.
- **Lexis Library** – law reports and full text articles, includes *Butterworths Property Law Service Bulletin.*
- **Occupational Health and Safety Information Services (OHSIS)** – provides health & safety documentation and other resources including approved codes of practice, case law and selection of guides and presentations.

- **RICS Red Book online** – RICS Red Book, Surveyors' Construction Handbook, Guidance Notes, Information Papers and Practice Statements plus case law database.
- **Westlaw** – includes legal journals, statutes, a case locator service and law report – includes *The Encyclopedia of Planning Law and Practice* and Woodfall's *Landlord and Tenant.*

There are also many other multidisciplinary databases which will give you access to many publications relevant to built environment:

- **ABI/Inform Global** – full text articles mainly relating to business but also including property, construction and planning journals.
- **EBSCO** – covers a range of subjects in both full text and abstract form, with content from journals and other sources.
- **Emerald** – database of business and management information journals including the latest research, ideas and case studies in many subjects including construction.
- **ProQuest** – this database covers a wide variety of topics and is a suitable research tool for most subject areas including built environment.
- **Science Direct** – full text articles on scientific, technical and environmental issues.
- **Web of Science** – The world's leading source of high-quality, multidisciplinary scientific information and scholarly research data.

Collecting existing knowledge on the subject, systematically organising and summarising the literature

It is absolutely essential to start, from day one of your research, to maintain a literature file to store the material that you collect. If it is a four-month dissertation, one large file will probably be enough to store all the information you gather. However, whether it is a dissertation, a thesis or a research project, the principle of structuring the literature file is the same:

1 Subdivide your file into a number of topical areas. For example, suppose you are investigating the use of procurement methods for construction projects. In this case, subdivide your manila file into a number of sections. You may create a section on definition and types of procurement methods, another section on previous research that investigated the factors that determine the selection of the appropriate procurement methods for the project, another on previous decision-making charts and so on.
2 In each of these sections, you will include all the literature review that falls under the relevant topic area together with your summary note-taking literature review (see Table 3.1). Such file(s) will later help you to:
   a Suggest hunches and possible research design to test these hunches.
   b Intellectually argue the acceptance or refutation of various authors' arguments.

c Define key concepts and derive into logical relationships between these key concepts.

d Write your literature review chapters. After all, your literature chapters will contain the same topic areas as in your file(s).

3 Create an index sheet at the front of the file. This sheet will provide you with a list of all the articles, book chapters and so on that are included in the file. Each piece of literature needs to have a separate code, which will be the same code as in the index sheet. The purpose of this exercise is to provide you with a clear view of what you have covered and where.

Using software tools to organise the literature

There are free software tools available such as 'Zotero' or 'Endnote' to organise all necessary literatures for your research work which can allow you to manage and evaluate a large amount of listed references. For example, Zotero is a free, easy-to-use, open-source tool to help you collect, organise, cite and share your research sources. The Zotero Connector automatically senses content as you browse the web and allows you to save it to Zotero with a single click.

☞ To find out more about 'how to use Zotero step by step', visit https://libguides.uwlax.edu/c.php?g=274023&p=1829224 or simply type 'Zotero' into Google Search.

☞ To find out more about 'using software to help with references', see section 3.11 in Farrell et al. (2017, pp. 60–62).

Reading and note-taking

After collecting and organising the relevant material to your studies, you should then start making notes of what you have read. 'Making notes should *not* be simply a shorthand *copy* of the original text. They should be an attempt to pick out the 'bone' of the text – or more specifically those points in the text which are relevant to your studies' (Northedge, 1997).

☞ Find out more about 'how to make notes' in the Good Study Guide by the Open University Team led by Andrew Northedge (1997, pp. 40–51).

☞ Find out more about 'how to make diagrammatic notes' in the Essential Study Skills – The complete guide to success at university by Tom Burns and Sandra Sinfield (2006, pp. 79, 81, 127, 138).

Designing the contextual framework of the literature

While collecting the relevant literature material, you should be in a position to design the 'contextual' framework of the literature. This framework provides a visual picture of previous research that has been conducted in your area of investigation. It also shows links between the issues/topic/subjects/chapters that you wish to include in your literature review and dissertation. This will help you

Table 3.1 *Example of a summary note-taking of literature review. Note to students: This table can be inserted either in the introduction chapter or at the beginning of the relevant literature chapter or in the Appendix*

*Year *Publisher *Volume no. *Issue no. (for articles)	Author/s	Title of article, book, report, etc.	Purpose – This could be the aim of the research, the purpose or the main question.	Research methodology	Main findings or conclusions (can be extracted from the ABSTRACT)
2016 (IJMPB) Vol. 3 Issue 5	Naoum, S.G. and Egbu, C.	Modern selection criteria for procurement methods in construction. A state-of-the-art literature review and a survey.	The aim is to develop an up-to-date multi-attribute procurement decision-making chart for selecting the appropriate method for the project.	Literature and a survey of 57 construction professionals.	Modern initiatives such as sustainability, lifecycle costing, standardisation are being integrated with procurement. The selection depends on the nature of the issues or problem at hand. Decision-making is not a punctual act. It is often a complex process. Effective decision-making also demands quality and timely information, and a careful consideration of alternatives. A multi-attribute decision-making chart is presented.
2014 JMIE (ASCE) Vol. 31 Issue 3	Ruparathna, R. and Hewage, K.	Review of contemporary construction procurement practices.	Reviews traditional and emerging procurement methods, revising strengths and weaknesses of procurement methods.	Literature review.	Modern initiatives such as sustainability, lifecycle costing, standardisation can be integrated with procurement.

| 2014
J. Construction Innovation
Vol. 15
Issue 1 | Van Duren et al. | Perceptions of success in performance-based procurement: Differences between clients and contractors. | The purpose of this study is to analyse, from the perspective of agency theory, differences between client and contractor in their perceptions of changes in uncertainty and in inclination to opportunistic behaviour while using a performance-based procurement procedure. | Through a survey, the perceived effects of the Performance Information Procurement System (PiPS) safeguards for both clients and contractors were investigated. | Both clients and contractors believe that applying PiPS introduces safeguards that reduce transaction uncertainty. The perceived changes in the discouragement to use opportunistic behaviour when using PiPS differ between client and contractor. Clients do not know and contractors are sceptical as to whether applying PiPS discourages opportunistic behaviour. This difference in perceptions can be explained by the often-traditional background of the two parties' project teams and the existence of information asymmetry. |
| 2013
J. Construction Innovation.
Vol. 13
Issue 4 | Sebastian et al. | Performance-based procurement for low-disturbance bridge construction projects. | This paper aims to introduce a method of performance-based procurement, based on the Most Economically Advantageous Tender (MEAT), for low-disturbance bridge construction projects in urban environment. | Review of KPI for projects vs procurement method with further case study of two projects. | The research findings demonstrate the possible inclusion of the KPIs of low-disturbance construction into the MEAT criteria. The MEAT principles can then be used in combination with either a traditional or an integrated procurement strategy. |

(continued)

Table 3.1 (Continued)

*Year *Publisher *Volume no. *Issue no. (for articles)	Author/s	Title of article, book, report, etc.	Purpose – This could be the aim of the research, the purpose or the main question.	Research methodology	Main findings or conclusions (can be extracted from the ABSTRACT)
2013 ECAM Vol. 20 Issue 6	Weisheng, L., Liu, A. and Hongdi, W.	Procurement innovation for public construction projects: A study of agent-construction system and public-private partnership in China.	The purpose of this paper is to attempt to shed light on procurement innovation by examining two state-of-the-art procurement systems in China – an Agent-Construction System (ACS or in Chinese *Dai Jian Zhi*) and Public-Private Partnership (PPP), with special consideration given to the (PESTEL).	The paper does so by using content analyses, semi-structured interviews and a 'PESTEL-Procurement Innovation' framework.	It is found that PPP has not been as popular as expected, while the ACS, which is little known to the international construction management community, is widespread in China. The study of ACS and PPP further reveals that congruence between a procurement system and its external PESTEL conditions is essential for procurement innovation.
2012 CEM (ASCE) Vol. 138 Issue 3	Love et al.	Participatory action research approach to public sector procurement selection.	Appropriate procurement selection reduces costs by 5%. Lots of procurement methods but not always suitable for public sector needs.	A robust procurement selection process is developed and examined using a participatory action research. Focus groups, comprised of key stakeholders involved with delivering an educational project, examined the approach's applicability and use in determining a suitable method.	Application of the approach presented in this paper, by the public sector agency responsible for delivering its social infrastructure projects, provides a clear indication of demonstrable impact. The procurement approach that is produced enables decision makers to constantly reevaluate outcomes in the form of recommendations that are grounded in practice, reflection and detailed evaluation.

Year / Journal	Authors	Title	Purpose	Method	Findings
2011 IJPM	Eriksson, P. and Westerberg, M.	Effects of cooperative procurement procedures on construction project performance: A conceptual framework.	To develop a testable holistic procurement framework that examines how a broad range of procurement related factors affects project performance criteria.	Based on a comprehensive literature review.	Cooperative procurement procedures (joint specification, selected tendering, soft parameters in bid evaluation, joint subcontractor selection, incentive-based payment, collaborative tools and contractor self-control) generally have a positive influence on project performance (cost, time, quality, environmental impact, work environment and innovation).
2008 IJMPB Vol. 2 Issue 3	Adekunle, S., Dickenson, M., Khalfan, M., McDermott, P., Rowlinson, S.	**Construction project procurement routes: An in-depth critique.**	The purpose of this paper is to examine different categories of building project procurement routes based on organisational, contractual, financial and technical issues.	The paper is based on review of literature and conditions of contracts. The UK construction industry serves as a general frame of reference. The Royal Institution of Chartered Surveyors survey of *Contracts in Use* from 1985 to 2004 is used to probe the value of contracts along different methods and different conditions of contracts in the UK.	Traditional routes remain the main type of procurement route for the construction project industry sector, within which different management and incentivisation systems are applied for greater efficiency. The conditions of contracts in the UK support this assertion by aligning different procurement routes to different conditions of contracts and additionally specifying different forms of agreements, special provisions and incentivisation in order to increase performance, reduce risks and improve compensation methods.

organise your ideas for the ease of structuring and writing your literature chapters. The contextual framework will also help you design your questionnaire later. In short, it puts the sections of your literature review and chapters into 'context' like the one that is shown in Figure 3.2. In this example, the researcher identified eight main subjects from the literature review that would determine the selection of the most suitable procurement method for a project.

Note to students

The contextual framework of the literature should *tie* with the summary note-taking table shown in Table 3.1, as well as with the reference list of your dissertation.

If your research involves testing a theory, then the contextual framework of the literature should help you develop your 'theoretical framework' that shows a

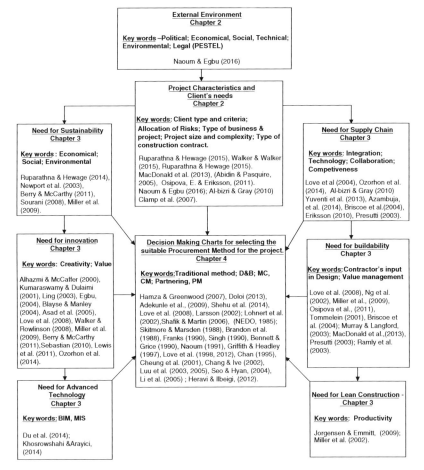

Figure 3.2   *Example of designing the contextual framework of the literature. Note to students: The example in Figure 3.2 can be inserted either in the introduction, at the beginning of the relevant literature chapter or in the Appendix.*

more 'focused and testable' relationship with a set of hypotheses. The theoretical framework provides an analytical approach to the cause-and-effect relationship among the specific variables/factors. It outlines the independent, moderating and dependent variables of your theoretical investigation (i.e. the research paradigm). (See Chapter 4 – Steps for building up your theoretical framework.)

In summary, below is the sequence of developing these two frameworks (i.e. the contextual framework of literature and the theoretical framework) and where they fit within the overall research process:

Step 1. Initial reading leads to selecting your topic and establishing the research goals.

Step 2. Afterwards, you write your proposal with aim, objectives, assumptions or hunches.

Step 3. More reading leads to the development of the contextual framework of the literature. Sometimes, this framework can be developed at a very early stage of your research and can even be inserted in your proposal. (This, of course, depends on how much reading you have done at the proposal stage.)

Step 4. After designing the contextual framework of the literature, you can then start thinking of designing your questionnaire.

Step 5. If your research is analytical in nature and requires you to test a theory, then you would need to design the theoretical framework before designing your questionnaire. Your research hunches/assumptions (stated in your proposal and at the early stages of your research) become 'firmer, sharper and more focused' leading to the development of your 'theoretical' framework for you to investigate and test. In other words, these hunches/assumptions will be converted to 'concrete' research hypotheses.

Step 6. You will then design your research strategy for data collection, i.e. survey, interviews, case studies, etc. (See Chapters 4 and 5.)

Step 7. Collect the data.

Step 8. Analyse your data and discuss it.

Step 9. Reach your dissertation conclusions.

Writing up and critical appraisal of your literature review

During or after you have compiled the sources of information, taken notes and drawn your literature framework, you will be ready to write your literature chapters and critically appraise the information. A literature review should be descriptive, analytical and critical in nature. It critically examines the contribution of other people's work with the view to identifying the following:

1   Similarities in the statements made by previous writers.
2   Common issue(s) raised by previous writers.
3   Differences or contradiction of statements made by previous writers.

☞ **See 'Judgment or opinion' in Farrell et al. (2017, p. 43).**

4   Criticisms made by previous writers.

The following example in Box 3.1 might serve as a model to show the style of writing a literature review and provide a critical appraisal section at the end. (Also see Chapter 9, Box 9.6, page 157, for another example as well as examples in Biggam, 2014 and Wallace, 2016.) The example in Box 3.1 is an extract from the author's learning material as well as an extract from his journal paper (Naoum and Egbu, 2016). The title of the paper is 'Modern selection criteria for procurement methods in construction: A state-of-the-art literature review and a survey'. Published by the *International Journal of Managing Projects in Business*, Issue 3/4, April 2016. You may not be fully familiar with the field of study, but the review puts you in the picture as to what is expected from you.

Box 3.1 Example of writing a literature chapter – Extract from the author's learning material and an extract from a published paper by Naoum, S.G. and Egbu, C. (2016)

CHAPTER 3 – Literature review into modern concepts associated with selecting suitable procurement methods for construction projects

EXAMPLE

3.1 Scope of Chapter

Note to students

Start the scope of each chapter by summarising what was reviewed in the previous chapter. For example, you may state:

In Chapter 2 of this dissertation, an overview of the types of procurement methods in construction was provided. It outlined and discussed the four standard sets of procurement methods, namely: (a) the fragmented method such as the traditional contracts; (b) fully integrated such as the design and build; (c) partially integrated such as management contracting; and (d) the partnership philosophy.

This chapter addresses modern criteria and concepts that are associated with the selection of various procurement routes. Chapter 3 is divided into six main sections, these are:

1 Procurement methods and sustainability.
2 Procurement methods and supply chain management (SCM).
3 Procurement methods and innovation.
4 Procurement methods and buildability.
5 Outline of decision-making charts and their limitation.
6 Critical appraisal of chapter.

Next is a critical review of those six sections:

3.2 Procurement methods and sustainability

The topic of sustainable construction and development has been widely discussed by Lutzkendorf and Lorenz (2005), Lapinski (2006), Waddell (2008), BERR (2009). The most widely accepted definition is from the Brundtland Report (1987) which described sustainable development as, 'development that meets the needs of the present without compromising the ability of future generations to meet their own'. It is also widely accepted that sustainability has a triple bottom line: economic, social and environmental (Newport et al., 2003). It is only when demands in all three of these areas are met that sustainable development is achieved (Figure A).

In order to link sustainability with procurement methods, Berry and McCarthy (2011) stated that, under traditional procurement, 'there is little opportunity for the contractor to input into the design or planning phases of the project, resulting in limited opportunities for the contractor or its supplier partners to influence the sustainability of the overall project'. The report added that design and build methods are more desirable for clients who wish to have a project with a high level of sustainability. This premise also corresponds closely with Miller et al. (2009) in their statement 'there is a pent up need to move from traditional procurement delivery models (in their various guises) to new methods that are able to incorporate innovative change processes that are required to address sustainable outcomes'. However, it must be noted that currently there are strong barriers in place that can be detrimental to the benefits achieved through sustainability in construction projects. According to Sourani (2008), integrating sustainability seems far from reach in an industry considered as 'inherently defensive' for change. Progress in this area has been hindered by many barriers, such as the industry's fragmented nature (Egan, 1998), lack of long-term perspective (Lam et al., 2010), lack of clear concept definition of sustainable construction and regulatory constraints (Adetunji et al., 2003) and competitive bidding (NAO, 2005). Adding to these barriers, Bullen and Davis (2003) advocated that sustainable construction requires change to construction methods and the use of resources, but more significantly, the building process will need to change. In order to achieve this, significant change to the organisation, structure and communication channels of the industry will need to be made. They also highlight that the use of traditional procurement processes creates a professional barrier to innovative sustainable requirements. Furthermore, Hamza and Greenwood (2007) stated that under the traditional and design and build procurement arrangements, it may prove to be a very challenging task to design environmentally sensitive buildings as the 'iterations required are at odds with the contractor's incentive to avoid delays and extra cost'. Embracing the principle of sustainable construction, from the government's perspective, will facilitate a real

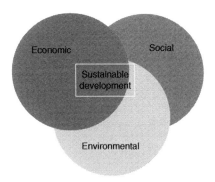

Figure A *Sustainable development.*

cultural change in the construction industry towards the adoption of partnering as a procurement process (Ball and Fortune, 2000).

Finally, there is some debate among authors as to whether other integrated procurement consortia such as PFI are able to achieve sustainable end results. Berry and McCarthy (2011) quoted the PFI as an example of a project where 'contractors and consultants are brought on early in the project, which allows them to use their expertise and influence design and construction methods to increase the overall sustainable performance of the project'. Although not entirely contradicting to this point, Miller et al. (2009) has a different view of PFI procurement in relation to sustainability, stating 'the PFI process fails to take account of how service delivery, and therefore the way in which buildings are used will change over the course of a PFI contract and beyond. This often results in inflexible and unsustainable buildings that may become redundant long before the contract expires. Taking into account the overall lifespan of a PFI project, the sustainability result may not be as promising as originally perceived'.

3.3 Procurement method and supply chain management (SCM)

Kranz (1996) defined SCM as 'the effort involved in producing and delivering the final product from the supplier's supplier to the customer's customer'. While Khalfan (2004) stated that '(SCM) is directed toward the minimisation of transaction cost and the enhancement and transfer of expertise between all parties'. It has been argued by Walker and Walker (2015) that successful SCM should be done under integrated project management, meaning it is centrally coordinated and that the relationship between firms is maintained for the construction duration so that design and delivery are more closely linked. Adekunle et al. (2009) cited partnering and Walker and Walker (2015) cited design and build and partnering as ways of doing this. Indeed, the Egan Report (1998) has challenged the industry to adopt a more collaborative and integrated approach. At that time, the report projected that, 'by the end of 2004, 20% of construction projects by value should be undertaken by integrated teams and supply chains and this should be increased to 50% by 2007'. Subsequently, several supply chain management (SCM) initiatives, such as alliancing/partnering and incentive-based contracting, have been sporadically implemented to ameliorate construction project performance.

There are, however, barriers to supply chain integration. An earlier study by Dainty et al. (2001) suggested that an adversarial culture seems to be ingrained within the industry's operating practices, and there is a general mistrust within the SME companies that make up the construction supply chain. This is due to an overriding belief that existing supply chain management processes seek to enhance main contractor profitability at the expense of other supply chain companies. In response to this, Love et al. (2004) and Ozorhon et al. (2014) both stated that a greater deal of client and project management leadership is required in order to drive the integration process, together with an insistence on transparent and mutually beneficial processes for all parties in the supply chain.

According to Al-Bizri and Gray (2010), current procurement approaches do not create an organisational framework to deal with the cultural issue and fragmentation of the building process. They suggested that grouping by a technology-clusters approach as a way of tackling integration problems. Technology clusters form an organisational framework to deal with the full integration of supply chain for a component-based construction. It is a multi-faceted group collaborating including the client, the designers, the main contractor and the specialist trade contractors to achieve high-value, defect-free assembly of the respective sets of components. In short, it splits the complexity of the whole process into groups of supply chain to deliver complete sets of integrated technologies.

As SCM is a management philosophy, its principles can be applied to any procurement approach, although management-oriented forms of procurement provide a better framework. It is unclear whether the competitive traditional procurement method of design–bid–construct would still be considered suitable for a project that requires an integrated supply chain for a successful delivery. As Forgues and Koskela (2009) put it: 'traditional procurement processes reinforce socio-cognitive barriers that hinder team efficiency. It also illustrates how new procurement modes can transform the dynamic of relationships between the client and the members of the supply chain and have a positive impact on team performance'. In contrast to this, Larsson (2002) and Lohnert et al. (2002) suggested that with the traditional fragmented procurement routes, the design process from sequential to iterative needs to be redefined, while maintaining traditional project lifecycle and procurement modes. Bourn (2001) in his Modernization Construction report recommended design and build, prime contracting, public-private partnership / private finance initiative as the main procurement approaches for team integration. Under a similar philosophy, Oyegoke et al. (2009) put the case forward that procure 21 is an example of a hybrid model that embraces integration, which is a form of design and build that uses an integrated supply chain.

3.4 Procurement methods and innovation

Innovation, in its simplest form, is about applying new sciences and solutions to constructions and it has become essential for construction organisations because of increasing pressures from clients to improve quality, reduce costs and speed up construction processes.

Recently, innovation has attracted many academics and practitioners through a number of popular management publications. According to Man (2008), innovation is 'the process of bringing new creative ideas to reality and implementing them through new work practices, processes, business models and strategic partnerships to produce new products and services which are of value to society'. More broadly, Abbott et al. (2006) classified innovation as product innovation, procurement innovation and process innovation. This innovation is not just limited to the components of the building, but also the organisation of the project and the management of the construction phase.

Other researchers conducted empirical studies to measure the benefits of innovation. For example, Shafik and Martin (2006) analysed two live projects and found that the 'Kincardine O'Neil project' which was constructed under the traditional method, faced limited innovation and skills shortage, despite the fact that the project met the required completion time and budget. Whereas the 'Rothesay Tower project', which was based on a partnership arrangement, resulted in a highly innovative project in both techniques and methods with joint solutions provided.

According to Naoum et al. (2010), the rate of implementing the concept of innovation within the UK construction industry during the 1980s and 1990s was rather slow. This has been largely due to: (a) the attitude of the construction industry; (b) competition in tendering; (c) lack of knowledge and training; (d) perceived risk by the client; (e) fragmentation; and (f) legislation. As a means to solve the innovation barrier in the construction industry, Yuventi et al. (2013) echoed the fact that 'integration' is the key. This involves consolidating vertically or horizontally fragmented supply chains into one company or longitudinal integration through long-term alliances. In addition to such integration, the authors went on to state that:

> [P]roject networks should consider increased use of processes aimed at better managing stakeholder relationships, addressing broken agency, and optimizing system lifecycles, e.g., integrated project delivery, systems engineering, and lean construction. This is especially true with projects such as large-scale Photovoltaic PV system because their development affects stakeholders who are not directly involved in developing or operating the facilities, i.e., energy consumers with regard to the cost of energy.

Despite these organisational barriers to innovation, there has been an improvement in the new millennium to resolving the fragmented structure of the construction industry with significant attempts being made to bring the design and construction together. This is particularly evident in the increases in design and build projects, management contracting and project management as noted in the work of Eriksson and Pesamaa (2007), Hamza and Greenwood (2007), Shafik and Martin (2006), and also on partnering, PPP and PFI as noted by Ng et al. (2002), Kumaraswamy and Dulaimi (2001) and Weisheng et al. (2013). Apart from calls to adopt alternative procurement methods, several authors wrote on specific issues that are associated with innovation. For example, Love et al. (2004) and Sebastian (2010) wrote on technology and methods of construction, Briscoe et al. (2004) on value engineering, Egbu (2004) on managing knowledge, Eriksson et al. (2007), Miller (2002) and Ng et al. (2002) wrote on subcontractors, Love et al. (2008) on conflict, power and mistrust and Kumaraswamy and Dulaimi (2001) wrote on disputes.

3.5 Procurement method and buildability

Arguably, a design that is buildable would lead to saving time, costs and cost of change. The CII (1986) defined 'buildability' as 'the optimum use of construction knowledge and experience in planning, design, procurement and field operations to achieve overall project objectives. It deals with the optimal integration of construction expertise and experience at various project stages to achieve the overall project goals'. In order to connect procurement methods and buildability, Ng et al. (2002) in their paper 'Fuzzy Membership Functions of Procurement Selection' made an attempt to place expert 'value judgments' on what they believe are 'fuzzy' procurement selection criteria. They placed the concept of buildability under the heading of 'quality' as buildability can enhance quality by designing a building to best utilise the expertise of the contractors. On this basis, they confirmed that using an integrated procurement method is beneficial as the contractor is able to contribute to the buildability of the design. This notion is in line with the later work of Miller et al. (2009), who provided evidence that improved constructability due to contractor's input into the design is one of the main advantages of using a design and construct approach to procurement.

Despite the construction industry welcoming initiatives to improve buildability and constructability, it is firmly believed that this entails a fundamental change of attitude and organisational culture.

3.6 Decision-making charts and their limitations

3.6.1 *Previous decision charts*

With the increase in use of alternative procurement methods, a number of researchers have developed decision-making charts in order to investigate the criteria for their selection and their rate of success in terms of time, cost, quality, safety, risk and maintainability during post-occupancy. Among the most popular ones were by NEDO (1985); Skitmore and Marsden (1988); Brandon et al. (1988); Franks (1990); Singh (1990); Bennett and Grice (1990); Naoum (1991); Griffith and Headley (1997); Love et al. (1998); Alhazmi and McCaffer (2000); Chan et al. (1995); Cheung et al. (2001); Chang and Ive (2002); Luu et al. (2003); Seo and Hyan, (2004); Luu and Chen (2005); Li et al. (2005); Heravi and Ilbeigi (2012); Love et al. (2012); and Naoum and Egbu (2016).

3.6.2 *Critical evaluation and limitations of decision charts*

Arguably, these decision-making charts for selecting the appropriate procurement method for the project have certain limitations. The author of this dissertation recognises some of the challenges associated with decision-making models, tool-kits and support systems. They are often seen as not flexible, adaptable and responsive, not taking account of reality and not taking account of the vagaries of contexts and competencies of the decision maker. There are also those who have criticised some of the assumptions underlining some of the decision support systems (Leeuwen and Timmermans, 2006). In addition, there are those who contend that a number of decision support models are steeped in conservatism and err on the side of caution; are too structured and sequential in their orientation; and often see the world as stable.

The author contends that decision-making is not a punctual act. It is often a complex process. The nature of the issue or problem at hand, for which decision is needed, may change during the decision-making process. Effective decision-making demands quality and timely information, and a careful consideration of alternatives, as well as the consequences of the alternatives. The rational model or approach of decision-making often assumes that the decision maker has accurate information and knowledge of the situation, however, it is often the case that decision makers satisfice and make do with the information at their disposal at any one time (Simon, 1956; Kahneman and Tversky, 1984). It is not the intention of this dissertation to argue for or against the rationale or rational approaches to decision-making, as it is a complex area which cannot receive effective and due treatment in this dissertation. The author, however, argues that one of the positives of the developed chart is not to belittle or take away the social embeddedness associated with effective decision-making but to offer decision makers an opportunity to broaden their horizon on the different alternatives that could be considered, and the potential of different alternatives leading to different consequences. This is more so for an up-and-coming decision maker, or one who is newly exposed to a new context. In a way, this is part of exposing the decision maker to other pieces of information for consideration. Galbraith (1973) informed us of the importance of information in effective decision-making, and the role of considering alternatives before a final choice is made.

3.7 Critical appraisal of Chapter 3

This chapter has provided a literature review of the state of the art of procurement methods in the academic field with the aim of establishing a platform for scholars and researchers to obtain more useful insights into concerns of procurement methods. It has identified research trends in procurement methods which may allow research academics and industrial practitioners to appreciate the key concerns in the development of modern concepts and principles such as supply chain, sustainability and innovation.

The sustained implementation of these concepts can go a long way towards combating short-termism and industry fragmentation over time. The view is that this will drive change as clients and their project teams experience the benefits achieved through these concepts. Ultimately, this will equate to a shift towards a more wholly integrated industry where achieving best value and continuous improvement through team integration is of paramount importance. It is difficult to escape the premise that increased collaboration within the industry will be vital to achieve future gains, and for the industry to deliver improvements on the clients' triangulated factors of cost, time and quality. If the industry is to deliver the best value for clients in a changing world, better use and standardisation of information technology is likely to be the solution.

In many areas, however, there seem to be barriers in terms of widespread adoption of modern techniques when considering the procurement route for the project. This is partly due to associated risks and attitude towards change. In order for the construction industry to be able to meet the managerial, technical and social challenges, both the industry and its participants have to welcome 'change' and allow innovative procurement methods to grow. As noted by Ruparathna and Hewage (2013) and indeed by many well-known academic journals, this change needs to be a client-driven process supported by the rest of the building team.

References of this example

Note to students

For references of this example on writing a literature chapter, read the following research paper:

Naoum, S.G. and Egbu, C. (2016) Modern selection criteria for procurement methods in construction: A state-of-the-art literature review and a survey. *International Journal of Managing Projects in Business*, Issue 3/4, April 2016.

Note to students

The preceding example attempts to demonstrate 12 fundamental aspects of a good literature review:

1 A clear literature title.
2 Division of chapters into sections: It starts with 'Scope of chapter' and ends with 'Critical appraisal'. (See Chapter 9, Box 9.6 pp. 157–163 for another example.)
3 Sifting of information. This means that the researchers included materials which are directly related to their study.
4 Clarity in writing: It is precise and clear in presenting other people's work.
5 Clearly appraising the common issues raised by previous writers in the field, as well as the similarities and differences among them.
6 Coherence in writing: The material is presented in an orderly, logical progression to facilitate understanding and good reading.
7 Good grammar and punctuation.
8 Where relevant, the use of accurate linking phrases such as 'in contrast', 'it has been reported by', 'according to', 'there is much debate about', 'another school of thought suggests', 'whereas', 'another view', 'all evidence points towards', 'conflict in opinion was revealed when', ' this is contradicted by', 'two sources, namely … and … admitted that', 'alternatively' and the like.

☞ **Find out more about 'linking words' in Thomas, G. (2017, p. 66).**

9 The inclusion of a diagram, such as the one shown in Figure A to clarify the point to be made as well as to make the reading more interesting. You may also wish to include other interesting exhibits and illustrations such as tables, charts, literature map and so on which were developed by previous writers.
10 Acknowledging the work of others. Good citation and accurate referencing. Naturally, this list of references would be part of the overall referencing list, which would be inserted at the end of the dissertation. However, some students may prefer to include the reference list at the end of each chapter.
11 A good balance of old and new references.
12 A good balance of sources. For example, it includes material published by:
   • refereed journals;
   • conference proceedings;
   • reports;
   • secondary sources such as textbooks;
   • web sites.

Note to students

For more insight into Naoum and Egbu's research paper, please read the following publication:

Naoum, S.G. and Egbu, C. (2016) Modern selection criteria for procurement methods in construction: A state-of-the-art literature review and a survey. *International Journal of Managing Projects in Business*, Issue 3/4, April 2016.

☞ **See more examples of 'writing the literature review' in Laycock et al. (2016, pp. 56–59).**

Summary

The literature review is one of the earliest stages in the research process, and it amounts to a significant proportion of a dissertation content. This review basically searches for material that is relevant to the subject of your dissertation with the intention to describe and analyse what has been written by others. It can take some time to get to grips with. Hence, it is advisable to allow sufficient time to cover the activities involved in undertaking a literature review. These activities are: (1) knowing the sources of information; (2) understanding how the library works; (3) knowing the search engines related to your discipline; (4) organising the literature review; (5) reading and note-taking; (6) designing the contextual framework for your literature review; and (7) appraising and writing up the literature review.

References

Bell, J. (2014) *Doing Your Research Project: A Guide for First-Time Researchers in Education and Social Science*. 6th edn. McGraw-Hill International, New York.

Haywood, P. and Wragg, E. (1982) *Evaluating the Literature*. Rediguide 2, School of Education, University of Nottingham.

Naoum, S.G. and Egbu, C. (2016) Modern selection criteria for procurement methods in construction: A state-of-the-art literature review and a survey. *International Journal of Managing Projects in Business*, 9 (2), pp. 309–336.

Sharp, J., Johns, P. and Howard, K. (1993) *The Management of a Student Research Project*. Routledge, Abington.

Smith, H.W. (1991) *Strategies of Social Research*. Holt, Rinehart and Winston.

Additional reading

Biggam, J. (2014) *Succeeding with Your Master's Dissertation: A Step-By-Step Handbook*. Open University Press McGraw-Hill Education, Berkshire. *Read Chapter 6 (The literature review) and Chapter 7 (Systematic review)*.

Burns, T. and Sinfield, S. (2006) *Essential Study Skills – The Complete Guide to Success at University*. Sage, London. *Read Chapter 3 (How to research and read academically) and Chapter 5 (How to learn creatively)*.

Farrell, P., Sherratt, F. and Richardson, A. (2017) *Writing Built Environment Dissertations and Projects – Practical Guidance and Examples*. 2nd edn. Wiley Blackwell, Chichester. *Read Chapter 3 (Review of theory and the literature)*.

Laycock, E., Howarth, T. and Watson, P. (2016) *The Journey to Dissertation Success for Construction, Property and Architecture Students*. Routledge, Abington. *Read Chapter 5 (Evaluating the existing literature)*.

Northedge, A. (1997) *The Good Study Guide*. The Open University, Milton Keynes. *Read Chapter 2 (Reading and note taking)*.

Thomas, G. (2017) *How to Do Your Research Project – A Guide for Students in Education and Applied Social Sciences*. 2nd edn. Sage, London. *Read Chapter 3 (The literature review)*.

Wallace, M. (2016) *Critical Reading and Writing for Postgraduates*. 3rd edn. Sage, London. *Read Part 2 (Becoming a critical reader and self critical writer)*.

Part II

Research design and methodology

4 Approaches to data collection

Once you have determined the purpose of your study and have completed a thorough literature search, you should be ready to design your research in detail. Research design is an action plan for getting from 'here' to 'there', where 'here' may be defined as the initial set of questions to be answered, and 'there' is some sort of conclusion (answers) to these questions. Between 'here' and 'there', a number of major steps may be found, including the collection and analysis of relevant data (Yin, 2018).

This chapter will review the various approaches to data collection. It first explains the difference between 'quantitative' and 'qualitative' research. Second, it explains the two main approaches to data collection known as 'fieldwork' and 'desk study', and will discuss the survey approach, the case study approach, action research and archival data collection. The contents of Chapter 4 are illustrated in Figure 4.1.

Research strategy

One of the problems of reading about research methods and techniques is the terminology. Writers use terms that may be incomprehensible to other people. In order to avoid confusion, it may be helpful to define the various terms as I go along. Here, research strategy can be defined as the way in which the research objectives can be questioned. There are two types of research strategies, namely 'quantitative research' and 'qualitative research'. Deciding on which type of research to follow depends on the purpose of the study and the type and availability of the information that is required.

Quantitative research

Quantitative research is 'objective' in nature. It is defined as an inquiry into a social or human problem, based on testing a hypothesis or a theory composed of variables, measured with numbers and analysed with statistical procedures, in order to determine whether the hypothesis or the theory holds true (Creswell and Creswell, 2018). Quantitative data are, therefore, not abstract; they are hard and reliable; they are measurements of tangible, countable, sensate features of the world (Bouma and Atkinson, 1995).

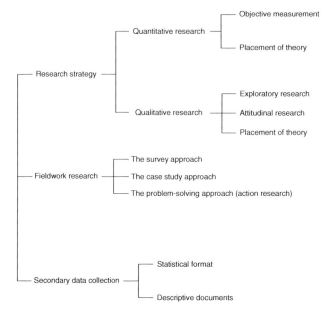

Figure 4.1   *Contents of Chapter 4.*

Quantitative research is selected under the following circumstances:

- when you want to find facts about a concept, a question or an attribute;
- when you want to collect factual evidence and study the relationship between these facts in order to test a particular theory or hypothesis (see Proposal 2 in Appendix 1).

Chapters 6 and 7 provide details of constructing a questionnaire as well as types of measurement. But for now, the following questions show a flavour of the types of quantitative questions related to various disciplines.

Examples of factual questions related to construction:

- What procurement method was used for the project? Design and build, management contracting, traditional, partnering or others.
- What type of contract? JCT, NEC, others.
- What type of tender? Open tender, selected or negotiated tender.
- What type of building? Commercial, industrial, residential, health, others.
- What type of structure? Concrete, steel, mix, innovative, others.
- What was the total built area of the project in sqm?
- What was the estimated total cost of the project and the actual in £?
- What was the programmed schedule of the project and the actual construction in weeks?
- How many variation orders and what was the total value of the orders in £?
- Were there any safety issues throughout the project?

Examples of factual questions related to design and architecture (extracted from Borden and Rüedi, 2003, p. 23)

Questions of production:

- How was this architecture constructed?
- Who was involved?
- When was it built?
- How was it paid for? Who paid for it? Why?
- Has it been altered after its original construction? When? Why?
- What were the main intentions of the architects and other producers?
- Where did these ideas come from?
- What is the function of the architecture?
- Who benefited from this architecture? In what way?

Questions of use:

- What was the intended use of the architecture?
- What was the actual use?
- Who used it? Were there different groups of users? How did they differ from one another?
- When was it used? Did use change over time? How and why? What is the use of the architecture today?

☞ **See the full list of questions in Borden and Rüedi (2003, p. 23).**

Note to students

The techniques and tools that are commonly used in data collection are described in Chapter 5.

Examples of factual questions related to civil engineering:

- What was the designed strength of the in-situ concrete column measured in N/mm sq.?
- What was the actual design strength of the tested cubes measured in N/mm sq.?
- What was the flexural strength of the fibre beam measured in N/mm sq.?
- What was the extension of steel of a reinforced concrete measured in mm?

Qualitative research

Qualitative research is 'subjective' in nature. It emphasises meanings, experiences (often verbally described), descriptions and so on. The information gathered in qualitative research can be classified into two categories of research, namely attitudinal and exploratory.

Attitudinal research

Attitudinal research is used to 'subjectively' evaluate the 'opinion', 'view' or the 'perception' of a person, towards a particular object. The term 'object' is referred to as an 'attribute', a 'variable', a 'factor' or a 'question'. Chapters 6 and 7 provide examples of questionnaire construction as well as types of measurements. But here are some specimens of subjective questions:

- Do you think that 'lack of workers' motivation' is a factor that can significantly affect productivity on-site?
  Yes / No / Difficult to say.
- Safety officers should have the power to stop operatives from work if they see them working in an unsafe manner, such as without a helmet. Please express your level of agreement.
  1. Strongly agree, 2. Agree, 3. Neither agree nor disagree, 4. Disagree, 5. Strongly disagree.
- Please indicate which of the following factors in Table 4.1 is most important to motivate operatives to work harder on-site, which comes next in importance, which is third and so forth.

Exploratory research

Exploratory research is used when you have a limited amount of knowledge about your topic. Here, the interview technique is usually selected as a method of data collection (see Chapter 5). The purpose of exploratory research is intertwined with the need for a clear and precise statement of the recognised problem. Researchers conduct exploratory research for three interrelated purposes: diagnosing a situation, screening alternatives and discovering new ideas (Zikmund, 2000). For instance, personnel research managers often conduct exploratory research as a diagnostic tool to point out issues of employees' concern or to generate possible explanations for motivational patterns. For example, preliminary interviews with employees may be utilised to learn current 'hot' issues, as well as concerns about bread-and-butter issues such as wages, working conditions and career opportunities.

The raw data provided in exploratory research will be exactly what people have said (in interview or recorded conversation) or a description of what has been observed. The following ideas for a qualitative study may prove helpful:

- Begin the research questions with the word 'What' or 'How'. Tell the reader that the study will do one of the following: discover, explain or seek to understand, explore a process, describe the experiences.

Table 4.1   *Example of an attitudinal question into the ranking of factors that motivate operatives to work harder on-site*

Job security	1st rank, 2nd, 3rd, 4th, 5th
Money	1st rank, 2nd, 3rd, 4th, 5th
Work condition	1st rank, 2nd, 3rd, 4th, 5th
Job interest	1st rank, 2nd, 3rd, 4th, 5th
Prosperous job	1st rank, 2nd, 3rd, 4th, 5th

- Pose questions that use non-directional wording. These questions describe, rather than relate variables or compare groups. Delete words that suggest or infer a 'quantitative' study, words with a directional orientation, such as 'affect', 'influence', 'impact', 'determine', 'cause' and 'relate'.
- Expect the research questions to evolve and change during the study, a thought also consistent with the assumption of an emerging design. Often in qualitative studies, the questions are under continual review and reformulation.
- Use open-ended questions without reference to the literature or theory unless otherwise dictated by a qualitative design type.

The following is an example of exploratory research questions (Goodman and Adler, 1985, p. 2, cited by Creswell and Creswell, 2018, p. 72).

Example – explaining or seeking to understand

How are (these) conceptions of social studies played out – or not played out – in classroom practice? (A grand tour question) ... How is each setting organised? (The beginning of sub-question) ... What kind of interpersonal dynamics exist? ... How do the students, co-operating teachers, faculty members and pupils act? ... What activities occur in each setting? What topics are discussed, and what information, opinions and beliefs are exchanged among the participants?

Comparing quantitative and qualitative research

From that discussion, you may have noticed a number of contrasting features of quantitative and qualitative research. The difference between quantitative research and qualitative research is rather like the difference between counting the shapes and types of design of a sample of greenhouses against living in them and feeling the environment. The difference between each one may be somehow quantifiable but such measurements will not convey the importance and the special impact of some over others.

Bryman (1988) provides a useful list of differences between the two research strategies. Table 4.2 includes some of the important dimensions. Naturally, the focal point of any research is its outcome. Although Table 4.2 shows distinctive features of the two strategies, the relationship between theory/concept and research strategy in terms of verifying the theory or concept, rather than expecting a theory to emerge from the data, is not as clear-cut as is sometimes implied.

The concept of a theory and building up your theoretical/conceptual framework

In this section, I will explain in detail how your research questions and objectives can be grounded in a theoretical framework (step-by-step). But first, I would like to discuss the term 'theory'. A theory is:

> [A] set of interrelated constructs (variables or questions), that presents a systematic view of phenomena by specifying relationships among variables, with the purpose of explaining natural phenomena. Here, the systematic view

might be an argument, a discussion, or a rationale that helps explain (or predict) phenomena that occur in the world

*(Kerlinger, 1979, cited by Creswell and
Creswell, 2018, p. 73)*

A theory can be introduced as:

- *A series of hypotheses/sub-hypotheses in the form of 'if … then' logic statements i.e. the cause-and-effect relationship.* For example, a proposition that the more money you offer to operatives, the more productive they become is a theory.
- *A hunch.* For example, a hunch about the quickest method (method A or method B) to build a building of type X is a theory.

These hunches and hypotheses are derived from the literature review that you have read and analysed (see Chapter 3). Afterwards, you would need to build up your own theoretical framework (step-by-step). Sometimes the term 'conceptual framework' is used instead of, or interchangeably with, a 'theoretical' but I will stick with the term theoretical framework throughout this book.

Note to students

In quantitative studies, one tends to use a theory deductively and places it towards the beginning of the plan for a study: the objective is to test or verify a theory. One thus begins the study advancing a theory, collects data to test it and reflects on whether the theory was confirmed or unconfirmed by the results in the study. The theory becomes a framework for the entire study, an organising model for the research questions or hypotheses and for the data collection procedure (Creswell and Creswell, 2018). (Proposal 2 in Appendix 1 is an example of theoretically based research.)

In qualitative research, the use of a theory is less clear than in quantitative design because there is no standard terminology or rules about placement. A theory may be placed at the beginning of the research or emerge during the data collection and analysis phase, or be used relatively late in the research process as

Table 4.2   *Some differences between quantitative and qualitative research (Bryman, 1998)*

	Quantitative	*Qualitative*
1 Role	Fact-finding based on evidence or records	Attitude measurement based on opinions, views and perceptions measurement
2 Relationship between researcher and subject	Distant	Close
3 Scope of findings	Nomothetic	Idiographic
4 Relationship between theory/ concepts and research	Testing/confirmation	Emergent/development
5 Nature of data	Hard and reliable	Rich and deep

Note to students: The data gathered under the qualitative research can later be 'quantified' to some extent, but a qualitative approach tends to value the data as 'qualitative' (Coolican, 1993).

a basis for comparison with other theories. However, the placement of theory in qualitative research usually tends to be towards the end of the study. Therefore, the end product of qualitative research will be throwing up hunches and hypotheses which can be tested more rigorously by further quantitative research.

Creswell and Creswell (2018) identify some principles to observe about using a theory in the qualitative approach: (a) employ it in a manner consistent with the type of qualitative design; (b) use it inductively so that it becomes not something to test, but rather something to develop and be shaped through the process of research; (c) create a visual model of the theory as it emerges; and (d) if used at the end of the study, compare and contrast it with other theories.

Steps for building up your theoretical framework

Step 1. The first step to build up your theoretical framework is to establish the initial hunches and the dependencies of the variables or factors. The term 'hunch' is normally used at the early stage of the research (proposal stage) and should be converted to the term 'hypothesis' later. For example, suppose you had established a simple hunch that the larger the project is, the more difficult it becomes to control the construction operations and, subsequently, the project will overrun its schedule. This first step relationship should be drawn as shown in Figure 4.2.

In Figure 4.2, the size of project is an independent variable and overrun on time is the dependent variable. The terms 'independent' and 'dependent' variables mean that there is the 'cause' and 'effect' relationship. This is basic to the logic of a hypothesis (Bouma and Atkinson, 1995). The element that does the causing is called an 'independent variable'. The element which is acted upon, produced or caused by the independent variable is called a 'dependent variable'.

Step 2. After further reading, you established that time overrun is not determined solely by the size of the project. Projects can also overrun because of the selection of an inappropriate procurement method or type of tender, client variation orders, client inexperience, environmental factors such as weather and industrial factors such as strikes and the like. Each of these causes will have a greater or lesser effect depending on its strength. Therefore, you would need to take further steps to complete the build-up of your theoretical framework. Using the example mentioned, the framework in Figure 4.3 is possible.

In Figure 4.3, the three variables – client experience, project complexity and size of project – are the 'independent' variables and are related to the 'dependent' variable, time overrun. One of the independent variables is seen to be negatively related and the other two are positively related to the dependent variable.

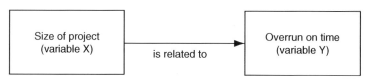

Figure 4.2   *A diagram showing the relationship between an independent variable (size) and the dependent variable (overrun on time).*

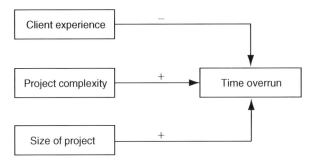

Figure 4.3   *A diagram showing three independent variables and one dependent variable.*

Here, the negative sign means that the more experienced the client is with the building process, the less chance there is that the project will overrun on time.

Step 3. A further step in building up your theoretical framework would be to include an 'intervening' variable as shown in Figure 4.4.

The variables in Figure 4.4 are related in such a way that client experience, project complexity and size of project affect the selection of procurement method, which in turn affects time overrun. Here, procurement method is working as an 'intervening variable' (sometimes called a 'process variable' or a 'moderating variable'). An intervening variable is a process that helps to explain linkages between the dependent and independent variables and can cause the relationship between them to change.

Bouma and Atkinson (1995, p. 45) comment that the possibilities of such diagrams/models are endless. They write:

> While the most complex theories can be diagrammed, most research projects deal with only one small aspect of the whole diagram. It is often a useful discipline to diagram more than you plan to study in order to show where the proposed research fits in the larger frame of reference.

Step 4. Carry on to build these relationships of 'independent', 'moderating' and 'dependent' variables until you complete the theoretical framework of your research. Figure 4.5 shows the final theoretical framework of this example which is related to Proposal 2 in Appendix 1 (Figure 4.5).

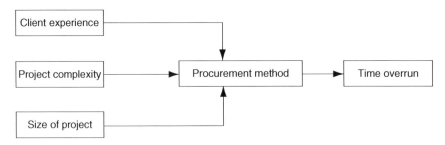

Figure 4.4   *A diagram showing three independent variables, one intervening variable and one dependent variable.*

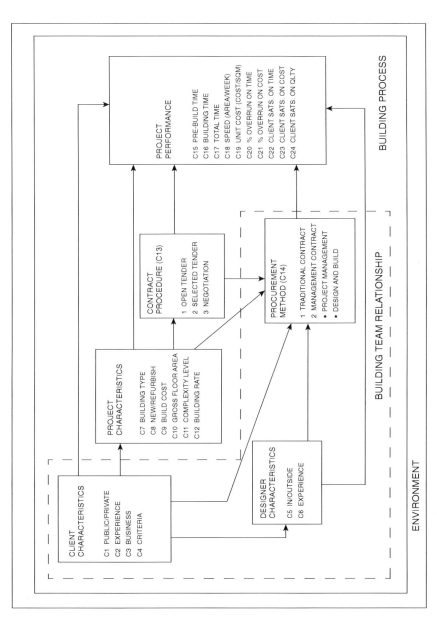

Figure 4.5 *Example of a complete theoretical framework related to Proposal 2 in Appendix 1.*

Note to students

The theoretical framework can:

- Be a self-designed framework which can be formed as a result of a literature search coupled with informal interviews with persons who have a wealth of knowledge about the subject area. The aforementioned four steps of building up a theoretical framework serve as an example and you might need to take more steps to build yours.
- Be based on a previous theoretical framework.
- Modify an existing framework.

EXERCISE

Suppose you are conducting a dissertation in architecture, building surveying, town planning, civil engineering or any other built environment subject and you have analysed the relevant literature review and established your hunches. You then designed your 'contextual' framework of your literature (like the one shown in Figure 3.2, page 42). Following the four steps in the previous section, make an attempt to construct your own 'theoretical' framework for your research topic.

☞ **Also read Chapter 4 in Farrell et al. (2017, pp. 67–106)** – *Research goals and their measurement.* Particularly useful are the following tables and figures in the book by Farrell et al.:

Table 4.1 – Shows example of performance variables measured in construction.
Table 4.2 – Shows example of environmental variables measured in construction.
Figure 4.2 – Shows a time frame: the relationship between the independent variable and the dependent variable.
Figure 4.3 – Shows examples in intervening variables.
Table 4.3 – Shows examples of intervening variables.
Tables 4.4 and 4.5 show examples of a relationship between variable 'age of site managers' and 'profitability'.

Approaches to data collection

The approach to be adopted for conducting the research depends on the nature of the investigation and the type of data and information that is required and available. For the student reading this book, there are two approaches to data collection, namely fieldwork (primary data collection) and desk study (secondary data collection), both of which are described next.

Fieldwork research

In this book, the term 'fieldwork research' refers to the methods of primary data collection used by the researcher and must not be confused with the definition of field research as 'the study of people acting in the natural courses of their daily lives'. Here, fieldwork can be associated with four practical approaches:

1   The survey approach.
2   The case study approach.
3   The problem-solving approach (action research).
4   The experiment (mainly for civil engineering research).

Note to students

Other approaches, such as observational, are also useful to know, but they are of very limited use to the level of students reading this book. They usually require long periods of time in the 'field' and emphasise detailed evidence.

The survey approach

Surveys are used to gather data from a relatively large number of respondents within a limited time frame. A survey is thus concerned with a generalised result when data are abstracted from a particular sample or population (see Chapter 5, 'Sampling', page 76). There are two types of surveys available: the descriptive survey and the analytical survey.

1   The descriptive survey aims to answer such questions as: 'How many?' 'Who?' 'What is happening?' 'Where?' and 'When?' It deals with counting the number of respondents with certain opinions/attitudes towards a specific object. The counting can be analysed later to compare or illustrate reality and trends; for example, the number of respondents in the survey that answered 'Yes' to the question, 'Should safety officers have the power to stop operatives from work if they see them working in an unsafe manner?' or the number of contractors that have more than five site accidents each year.
2   The analytical survey aims to establish relationships, correlations and associations between the attributes/objects of your questionnaire, i.e. how often an attribute is associated with another attribute within the sample questionnaire. For example, you might find that most of the respondents who answered 'Yes' to the question whether 'workers' motivation affects site productivity' are operatives, and the majority who answered 'No' are site managers. In this sense, you may conclude that site managers are not aware of how important motivation can be to improve site productivity. Here, it is strongly advised to build up your theoretical framework as explained in the previous sections.

Note to students

There are situations when you need to explain why a particular phenomenon is taking place. For example, in analysing the results of accidents on-site, you may find a drop, over a period of time, in the number of accidents that the contractors have recorded in their books. You may need to explore why this is happening. Is it the contractor's policies with regard to safety which made the record go down, or is it the provision of new health and safety regulations? The answers to these types of questions, although they can be assumed by the researcher and they are acceptable at the level of students reading this book, may not be totally adequate. Therefore, the 'why' questions and the 'cause-and-effect relationship' can be better explained and interpreted by designing an 'analytical case study using a theoretical framework'.

The case study approach

Case studies are used when the researcher intends to support his/her argument by an in-depth analysis of a person, a group of persons, an organisation or a particular project. As the nature of the case study focuses on one aspect of a problem, the conclusion drawn will not be generalised but, rather, be related to one particular event. This is not to say that the case study approach is of limited value. On the contrary, it provides an in-depth analysis of a specific problem.

There are three types of case study design:

1   The descriptive case study, which is similar to the concept of the descriptive survey (i.e. counting), except it is applied on a detailed case(s).
2   The analytical case study, which is similar to the concept of the analytical survey (i.e. counting, relationships, correlations and associations), except it is applied on a detailed case(s).
3   The explanatory case study, which is the theoretical approach to the problem. It explains causality and tries to show linkages among the objects of the study. It asks why things happen the way they do. It also suggests that a single cause can have a specific effect. In other words, the researcher collects facts and studies the relationship of one set of facts to another, with the hope of finding some causal relationship between them.

Note to students

If the sample is large, then the relationship can be tested statistically. If the sample is small, then the relationship can only be discussed 'intellectually', which is acceptable for the level of students reading this book.

Problem-solving approach (action research)

With the survey and the case study approach, the researcher tends not to affect or interfere with what is being studied. In the problem-solving approach (also named action research), the researcher reviews the current situation, identifies the problem, gets involved in introducing some changes to improve the situation and, possibly, evaluates the effect of his/her changes. This type of research is more attractive to practitioners, industrialists and students from particular professional backgrounds who have identified a problem during the course of their work and wish to investigate and propose a change to improve the situation.

Examples of problem-solving research include changing organisation policy towards promotion, designing a new information flow system, recommending a new system for measuring the quality management of the organisation and the like (see Proposal 3 in Appendix 1, as an example).

It has to be stressed that whatever idea is to be recommended, it must be original and practical. Moreover, the dissertation project must be structured and written as an academic piece of research and not as a project report.

The experiment (mainly for civil engineering research)

An experiment research is a procedure that will be carried out to support, refute or validate a hypothesis or test a theory about how physical processes work under particular conditions (e.g. whether a particular engineering process can produce a desired material strength). Here, an experiment can be associated with three practical descriptions:

1 It provides insight into cause-and-effect by demonstrating what outcome occurs when a particular factor is manipulated.
2 It varies greatly in goal and scale but always relies on repeatable procedure.
3 It expresses a logical analysis of the results. In other words, an experiment aims to answer a 'what-if' question, without a specific expectation about what the experiment reveals, or to confirm prior results. If an experiment is carefully conducted, the results usually either support or disprove the hypothesis.

According to some philosophies of science, an experiment can never 'prove' a hypothesis, it can only add support. On the other hand, an experiment that provides a counter-example can disprove a theory or hypothesis, but a theory can always be salvaged by appropriate ad hoc modifications at the expense of simplicity. An experiment must also control the possible confounding factors – any factors that would mar the accuracy or repeatability of the experiment or the ability to interpret the results. Confounding is commonly eliminated through scientific controls and/or in randomised experiments, through random assignment.

Secondary data collection

The data collected using the three approaches discussed (surveys, case studies, problem-solving) are called 'primary' data because they are obtained first-hand. The data collected using the desk study approach are called 'secondary' data because the data are obtained from other sources. Secondary data can be stored in either a statistical or a descriptive format. Secondary information has some distinctive advantages over primary data collection effort. Stewart and Kamins (1993, p. 37) note:

> The most significant of the advantages of the secondary data are related to time and cost. In general, it is much less expensive to use secondary data than it is to conduct a primary research investigation. This is true even when there are costs associated with obtaining the secondary data. When answers to questions are required quickly, the only practical alternative is to consult secondary sources. If stringent budget and time constraints are imposed on primary research, secondary research may provide higher quality with a new research project. Secondary data also may provide a useful comparative tool. New data may be compared with existing data for purpose of examining differences or trends.

Statistical format

In construction-related research, the word 'statistical' refers to official statistics collected by the state and its agencies. These statistics are available in all public libraries and in most university libraries. The sources that publish this official information include institutions such as:

- British Research Establishment (BRE).
- Her Majesty's Stationery Office (HMSO).
- Chartered Institute of Building (CIOB).
- Royal Institute of British Architects (RIBA).
- Royal Institute of Chartered Surveyors (RICS).
- Construction Industry Research and Information Association (CIRIA).
- Health and Safety Executive (HSE).

Generally speaking, these institutions assemble the data in two ways, namely through registration or self-survey. As far as the registered information is concerned, all construction-related companies are required to provide information to the government by law. Therefore, the researcher can at any time make use of this data to show 'what is happening'. On the other hand, government bodies conduct their own routine surveys to collect data and publish them at regular intervals, say every year. For example, in the fourth proposal shown in Appendix 1, the student intended to look in depth at the type of accidents within the construction industry and compare them with other industries. He, therefore, brought together empirical evidence related to accidents on-site gathered from several sources. For instance, the student used the statistical data provided by the Health and Safety Executive (Statistical Services Unit) in Liverpool to analyse figures and present them in graphs. This method allowed the student to make a critical examination of the data (see Table 8.5 on page 121 for further details on analysis).

Descriptive documents

The other method for conducting secondary data research is to analyse and critically appraise the contents of an archival document. This is similar to appraising previous literature and can include diaries, newspapers, observations and so on.

Secondary data are usually processed before the researcher starts to make use of them. Therefore, the researcher should take absolute care when using them. Here are some questions that ought to be considered when using secondary data:

- Is the material factually accurate?
- Is the material reliable? Would it have been the same if it had been collected by anyone else?
- Is it systematic, providing a complete account of what it describes? What is lacking?
- Why was it collected?
- Is the material representative?

Of course, there is no way that the researcher can answer any of these questions with certainty, but they are worth bearing in mind. Nevertheless, most of these questions have to be asked when collecting primary data as well.

After gathering the information that is required for your investigation, you will then need to analyse it. Chapter 8 explains various methods of data analysis.

Summary

This chapter reviewed the various approaches to data collection in construction. It first distinguished between quantitative and qualitative research. Quantitative research is an objective measurement of the problem, investigating facts and trying to establish relationships between these facts, whereas qualitative research is a subjective assessment of a situation or problem, and takes the form of an opinion, view, perception or attitude towards objects. An object is referred to as an attribute, variable, factor or question. The concept of a theory and building up a theoretical framework is also explained.

This chapter also explained the approaches to data collection that are suitable for the level of students reading this book. It explained the survey approach, the case study approach, action research and archival data collection approach.

References

Bouma, G. and Atkinson, G. (1995) *A Handbook of Social Science Research: A Comprehensive and Practical Guide for Students*. Oxford University Press, Oxford.

Bryman, A. (1988) *Quantity and Quality in Social Research*. Unwin Hyman, Michigan.

Coolican, H. (1993) *Research Methods and Statistics in Psychology*. Hodder & Stoughton, London.

Creswell, J. and Creswell, D. (2018) *Research Design: Qualitative, Quantitative Approach and Mixed Methods Approach*. 5th edn. Sage, London.

Goodman, J. and Adler, S. (1985) Becoming an elementary social studies teacher: A study in perspectives. *Theory and Research in Social Education*, 13 (2), 1–20.

Kerlinger, F.N. (1979) *Behavioral Research: A Conceptual Approach*. Holt, Rinehart, and Winston, New York.

Stewart, D. and Kamins, M. (1993) *Secondary Research: Information Sources and Methods*. 2nd edn. Sage, London.

Yin, R. (2018) *Case Study Research and Applications: Design and Methods*. Sage, London.

Zikmund, W. (2000) *Business Research Methods*. 6th edn. Dryden Press, New York.

Additional reading

Farrell, P., Sherratt, F. and Richardson, A. (2017) *Writing Built Environment Dissertations and Projects – Practical Guidance and Examples*. 2nd edn. Wiley Blackwell, New York. *Read Chapter 4 (Research goals and their measurement)*.

Borden, I. and Rüedi, K. (2006) *The Dissertation: An Architecture Student's Handbook*. 2nd edn. Architectural Press, Elsevier, Oxford.

5 Techniques for data collection

After you have decided on the type of data to be collected (quantitative, qualitative or both), and have also decided on the research approach (survey, case study, action research or analysing archival data), you will be in a position to think seriously about the technique for collecting the data. This chapter will explain the main features of two major research techniques available to elicit data and information from respondents. These are the postal questionnaire and the personal interview. It has to be stressed, however, that data collection does not necessarily depend on one method or technique. Some research depends solely on one method of data collection, but others do not. In other words, it is possible for you to conduct a postal questionnaire and a case study, or to conduct interviews in addition to a postal questionnaire, or whatever you choose. It is also possible that your dissertation questionnaire includes quantitative questions as well as qualitative ones. Your decision will depend on your judgement as to which method or techniques will best obtain the information you need in order to achieve the purpose of your study. Whatever decision you make, you need to consult your supervisor before going ahead with it. The contents of Chapter 5 are illustrated in Figure 5.1.

Postal questionnaire

The postal questionnaire is probably the most widely used data collection technique for conducting surveys. It is most suited to surveys whose purpose is clear enough to be explained in a few paragraphs of print, in which the scheme of questions is not over-elaborated. Postal questionnaires have been widely used for descriptive and analytical surveys in order to find out facts, opinions and views on what is happening, who, where, how many or how much. Almost all postal questionnaires have 'closed-ended' questions that require a specific response such as 'Yes' or 'No' or ranking the importance of factors (see Chapter 6 for details).

The main advantages of postal questionnaires are:

• *Economy*. Postal questionnaires are perceived as offering relatively high validity of results because of their wide geographic coverage. As a result, they are more suited to assembling a mass of information at a minimum expense in terms of finance, human and other resources.

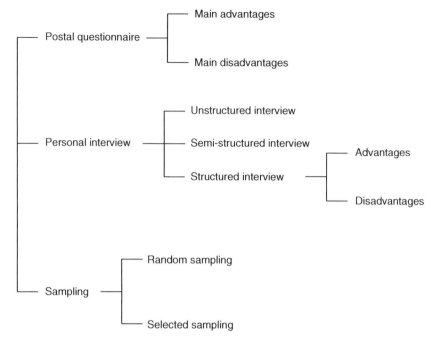

Figure 5.1 *Contents of Chapter 5.*

- *Speed.* Postal questionnaires are certainly a quick method of conducting a survey. If administered properly, the bulk of the returns will probably be received within 2 weeks. However, time must be allowed for late returns and responses to follow-up attempts. For example, if there is a lack of response to the first return of replies (beginning about 2 weeks after initial posting), a reminder needs to be sent to those who have not yet returned the questionnaire. Therefore, a period of about 4 weeks needs to be allowed in your programme of work from the date of the initial mailing to the commencement of the final analysis.
- *Consultation.* In certain cases, respondents may not have the information to hand, particularly when the questions are of a quantitative nature, and the respondent may need to consult a document or a colleague in order to give accurate answers. Examples are questions such as 'When was the project built and what was its building cost?' or 'How many fatal accidents has your organisation been involved in over the past 5 years?' Such questions may have to be answered in the respondent's own time, rather than provided on the spot as is usually associated with interviews. However, such a problem can be overcome in the interview if the questionnaire is posted to the respondent in advance of the interview.

The main limitations of postal questionnaires are:

- *Must contain simple questions.* The postal questionnaire is suitable only for simple and straightforward questions which can be answered with the aid of easy instructions and definitions. The questions should be very carefully worded and free from faults such as ambiguity, vagueness, technical expressions and difficult questions. These faults can affect the results of the postal questionnaire even more seriously than when conducting an interview (see the following section, 'Personal interview').

- *Inflexible technique.* Postal questionnaires are inflexible in the sense that they do not allow the opportunity for probing. In other words, the answers have to be accepted as final, and there is no opportunity to clarify ambiguity or to appraise the non-verbal behaviour of respondents, though the latter can sometimes create bias.
- *Accuracy.* Respondents may answer generally when you are seeking a response on a specific level of analysis. People may also answer according to what they think you want to hear. They may answer according to their public profile rather than the underlying corporate reality.
- *No control over respondents.* This means that, although you state in your questionnaire that a particular person should complete the questionnaire (such as the marketing director, managing director or site agent), there is no guarantee that this statement will ensure that the right person completes the questionnaire. However, this is less of a problem than not getting a response at all, given the fact that response rates for postal surveys usually range between 40 and 60 per cent.
- *Industry fatigue.* Companies receive a steady stream of questionnaires and the pressures of modern business mean that, for many organisations and individuals, students' questionnaires have a lower priority.

Note to students

Some of the limitations of the postal questionnaire can be overcome by supplementing it with personal interviews.

The SurveyMonkey tool

SurveyMonkey is a free online survey tool that provides a quick data collection and data analysis. Conducting original primary research is a core component of your dissertation and using surveys will give credence and credibility to your dissertation. It makes your research conclusions stronger and more compelling as well as providing direct evidence to support or refute your theory. By using research questionnaires, researchers can answer questions and test hypotheses about opinions, attitudes and behaviours in a range of domains including research in the built environment. To know more about how to use this tool, visit the following link:

☞ **https://www.surveymonkey.com/. This site states:**

Sending surveys online makes it easy to reach more respondents and eliminates the hassle of entering data from a pencil and paper survey, saving you both time and money. And with a paid SurveyMonkey plan, your data can be downloaded directly to Excel or SPSS. This means that it offers tools that calculate statistical significance for your survey results, using a standard 95% confidence level. This makes it easy to see segment one group's answers from another group's answers to see if the results are reliably different, which helps you with your data analysis. (Chapter 7 provides you with a detailed explanation of what is meant by statistical significance.)

SurveyMonkey highlights three tips for academic research surveys to ensure that you collect reliable and actionable data. These are:

1 *Keep surveys short and engaging*
   Plan out the goal of your survey before you start creating it. Be mindful of survey takers' time and write clear questions. Generally, your survey should take no more than 10 minutes to complete.
2 *Pre-test your survey*
   Before launching a larger project, it's a good idea to send a shorter survey with more open-ended questions to obtain rich qualitative data. It can help you resolve any inconsistencies or unexpected interpretations of questions before launching the project to your entire audience.
3 *Test to find your target population*
   What's the best way to reach the people you want to survey? Via mail or email? Are they regular internet users? Do they use smartphones? Are they on social networks? With this information, you can obtain your sample quicker, cheaper and easier.

☞ **Visit https://www.surveymonkey.com/r/millennialemployees for complete examples of a SurveyMonkey.**

Personal interview

The personal interview is another major technique for collecting factual information as well as opinions. It is a face-to-face interpersonal role situation in which an interviewer asks respondents questions designed to elicit answers pertinent to the research hypothesis. The questions, their wording and their sequence define the structure of the interview (Nachmias et al., 2014). The interview technique is suitable under the following circumstances:

- When the people being interviewed are homogeneous and share the same characteristics.
- When you know enough about your interviewee so you ask only what is important and know how to ask it.
- When interpersonal contact is essential to explain and describe the questions.
- When a case study needs to be investigated in detail asking questions such as how and why things had happened the way they did.
- When the research requires an explanation of why the respondents are answering or feeling the way they do, that is more than a 'Yes' or 'No', or 'Agree' or 'Disagree' answer.

Interviews can take three forms: unstructured, structured and semi-structured. Some research may require one form of interview, although others may require a combination of the three forms. There are many other terms in use to distinguish between what are called here structured and unstructured interviews. For example, there are formal and informal, inflexible and flexible, standardised and unstandardised, controlled and uncontrolled interviews.

Unstructured interview

This form of interview uses 'open-ended' or 'open' questions and the questionnaire is often pitched at a very general level so that the researcher can see in what direction the interviewee takes things in their response. It is usually conducted with qualitative research (see 'Qualitative research' in Chapter 4).

Unstructured interviews can also be conducted at the beginning of any research (also known as exploratory interviews) when the researcher knows little about his/her subject area. However, in this type of interview, you need to have a clear research outline that you are familiar enough with to carry the general points around in your head. Here, there is no set order or wording of questions, no schedule and you are not looking for the same information from each person. It is purely an exploratory exercise. For example, suppose you are studying the factors that affect job satisfaction for construction operatives and you wish to explore your thinking around this research outline through informal interviews. On your first interview, the operative may focus his/her discussion around salary, job security and promotion as motivating factors affecting his/her satisfaction with the job. On your informal interview with the second, third or fourth operatives, you will seek to find out whether the same factors apply to them as well, and if there are other factors that need to be added. For instance, other operatives may add leadership, working environment and the organisation itself. At the end of the unstructured interviews, you will probably end up with a list of ten factors which you will then examine on a wider sample through structured interviews or a postal questionnaire.

Note to students

Some students rely solely on two or three exploratory unstructured interviews. This is not enough from which to draw firm conclusions.

Semi-structured interview

This is more formal than the unstructured interview in that there are a number of specific topics around which to build the interview. This form of interview uses 'open' and 'closed-ended' questioning but the questions are not asked in a specific order and no schedule is used. Your task is to discover as much as possible about the specific issues related to your subject area. Merton and Kendal (1946) state four distinguishing characteristics of the semi-structured interview or, as they named it, a 'focused interview':

1   It takes place with respondents known to have been involved in a particular experience.

2 It refers to situations that have been analysed prior to the interview.
3 It proceeds on the basis of an interview guide specifying topics related to the research hypotheses.
4 It is focused on the respondents' experiences regarding the situations under study.

Semi-structured interviews start by asking indirect questions in order to build up a rapport with the respondent and then explore the specific issues that the interviewer has in mind. Suppose you are investigating the factors which cause conflict between managers and the site agents. You may start by asking the site agents 'What sort of problems do site agents have in getting along with their managers?' and 'What sort of disagreement do you have with your site manager?' You can then move on to ask more formalised questions such as 'Have you ever had any disagreement with your manager over the following: (a) allocation of resources, (b) scheduling, (c) overtime pay, (d) promotion?'

In the semi-structured interview, the interviewer has a great deal of freedom to probe various areas and to raise specific queries during the course of the interview. For example, the first question just mentioned can be probed by asking 'In what way do site managers try to restrict your work?' or 'Do any of your colleagues have the same problem?'

Structured interview

In the structured interview, questions are presented in the same order and with the same wording to all interviewees. The interviewer will have full control of the questionnaire throughout the entire process of the interview. In this technique, the questioning may start with some 'open' questions but will soon move towards a 'closed' question format. Nachmias et al. (2014) cited three assumptions of the structured interview:

1 That for any research objective, the respondents have a sufficiently common vocabulary so that it is possible to formulate questions which have the same meaning for each of them.
2 That it is possible to phrase all questions in a form that is equally meaningful to each respondent.
3 That if the meaning of each question is to be identical for each respondent, its context must be identical and, since all preceding questions constitute part of the context, the sequence of questions must be identical.

The main advantages of the structured interview therefore are:

- The answers can be more accurate.
- The response rate is relatively high (approximately 60–70 per cent), especially if interviewees are contacted directly.
- The answers can be explored by finding out 'Why' the particular answers are given.

Note to students

There is another data collection technique, which is known as the 'telephone interview'. The rules and techniques that are applied to telephone interviews are similar to face-to-face interviews. It incurs high cost, but it is a quicker way to find a respondent to interview. It may not be as detailed as face-to-face interviewing; however, technological changes and improvements in communication equipment have made telephone interviewing easier, especially when researchers use random-digit dialling and computer-assisted telephone interviewing.

☞ **See Table 7.6 in Laycock et al. (2016, p. 121) on forms of interview.**

Also, see examples of structured interview open-ended questions in Chapter 6 of that book by Farrell et al. (2017).

Sampling

Once you have decided on the technique for collecting your fieldwork data and have thought about what you want to ask, you should be ready to decide on the characteristics of the respondents. In all cases, a sample has to be drawn from its population. The term 'sample' means a specimen or part of a whole (population) which is drawn to show what the rest is like. For instance, if you are conducting a postal survey then you need to obtain a list of respondents which is known to fall into the category of your survey (survey sample). If you are conducting case studies interviews, then a relatively small number of cases (interview sample) is used for inferences to all cases (a population).

Selecting the research sample is very important and great care must be taken when choosing the type of sample design. The researcher has to ensure that the characteristics of the sample are the same as its population and act as representative of the population as a whole. Usually, drawing a representative sample is done either randomly or non-randomly. The term 'random' means selecting subjects (respondents) arbitrarily and without purpose.

Designing the research sample can take many forms, each of which is suitable for a particular situation. Listed below are some of the types of sampling designs available to the researcher:

* Non-random accidental sampling.
* Non-random purposive sampling.
* Simple random sampling.
* Systematic random sampling.
* Stratified random sampling.

Detailed description of these types of sampling design is beyond the scope of this book. Students conducting MPhil or PhD research should know about these types and ought to consider reading the appropriate parts of the references on sampling procedures provided on page 100. However, for the purpose of this book, you need to know that there are two types of sampling: random sampling and selected sampling.

Random sampling

This type of sampling can be used when specifics about the characteristics of the sample are not essential, such as the background of the respondents, size of the company and type of work. However, there are two main criteria that you need to take into consideration when selecting your sample. First, what do you want to know? Second, about whom do you want to know it? Both of these questions can be answered by referring back to the purpose of your study, that is your aim, objectives and hypothesis (or key questions).

In order to draw a random sample, you need to follow two steps:

1   Identify the population from which the sample is to be drawn. This means obtaining a list of names and addresses of, say, top contractors operating in the Greater London area. Such names and addresses can be obtained from your direct personal contacts or from organisations and references such as the Building Federation, Chartered Institute of Building, Chartered Institute of Building Surveyors and Royal Institute of British Architects.
2   If the list is small, you may be able to send your questionnaire to all the names identified in your list. If the list is long, you then need to devise a method of random selection which ensures that each subject (in this case, contractor) has the same probability (chance) of selection. In other words, adopt a random numbering technique to select a sample. For example, if you have a list of 400 contractors and you want a sample of 80, you might select every fifth name on the list.

Selected sampling

This type of sampling is usually chosen with the interview approach. It begins by choosing a list of names and addresses of participants with specific characteristics, for instance, the top contractors who are offering alternative procurement methods and undertaking refurbishment work for commercial clients. All other contractors should be excluded from the survey. For example, consider the following interviews with clients to obtain their views on and experience with management contracts when compared with the traditional form of contracts. A structured interview questionnaire is recommended to be used to obtain the clients' view of management contracting and to compare the management contracting system with the traditional form of contract, having in mind clients' needs in terms of function, cost, speed and aesthetics. This section is not intended to be a thorough treatment of questionnaire construction and administration, as this is covered in Chapter 6. However, it is important to show you a flavour of an interview questionnaire in order to follow the discussion. Table 5.1 demonstrates an example of interviewing ten clients:

Note to students

•   In the example shown in Table 5.1, the names of clients and their addresses can be obtained from the management contractors (as they are the type of contractors related to this type of investigation).

- Names of persons who were suitable to participate in the research can be identified through telephone conversations with the client organisations.
- Ideally, the clients to be selected for the interviews should be homogeneous and share similar characteristics, as people who are of different characteristics, philosophy and experience would likely interpret the questions differently. The answers, therefore, may be ambiguous for the subject under investigation. However, this does not mean that you are not permitted to have a sample of different characteristics. Your research design may require you to compare the views of two groups of people who have different backgrounds; for example, comparing the views of quantity surveyors and architect clients on the concept of value management technique. This would be an interesting research design.

  For example, the interviewees should all be of similar size organisations, experienced with the building process and, most importantly, they should all have undertaken different types of work under different contractual arrangements. It would be ideal if you can find a sample as homogeneous as this, but in reality, this may be rather difficult. Therefore, you need to discuss with your supervisor as to what characteristics of clients would be reasonable to select. For example, you might be selecting a mixture of privately and publicly funded organisation or engaging in different type of business, etc.

- The structured interview questionnaire should be designed and posted prior to the interview.
- The interviews will provide some freedom to probe certain areas and raise specific queries during the course of the interview. More specifically, 'Why do you feel that way?' and 'Why do you hold that view?' or 'How did this happen?'

Table 5.1 *Structured interview questions to clients on their experience with two types of procurement methods, namely, Management Contracting (MC) versus Traditional Contracting (TC)*

Questions	Yes	Same	No
Is MC riskier to clients than TC?			
Is MC more profitable to the contractor?			
Does MC involve fewer claims?			
Is MC more flexible to variations?			
Does MC allow an earlier start on-site?			
Is MC quicker during construction?			
Is MC more reliable in predicting the build time?			
Is MC cheaper?			
Is MC more reliable in estimating the building cost?			
Does MC provide more control over subcontractors?			
Does MC exercise more control over construction tasks?			
Does MC provide a better building design?			

Summary

This chapter discussed the main features of the postal survey and the personal interview together with showing the advantages and disadvantages of both techniques (see Table 5.2 for a summary). The postal questionnaire is an impersonal survey technique that is most suitable for a descriptive or analytical survey. Its main advantages are cost-effectiveness, speed of process and that respondents can consult others for information. Its main limitations are that it must contain simple questions, it is inflexible, and it gives no control over respondents.

The personal interview is a face-to-face situation that is most suitable for case study research and studies that require respondents with homogeneous characteristics. Interviews can take three forms: unstructured, semi-structured and structured. The main advantages of personal interview are knowing the identity of

Table 5.2 *Comparison between a postal survey and interview technique*

Features	Interviews	Postal questionnaire / SurveyMonkey
1 Identity of respondents	Known	Unknown
2 Interaction between interviewer and respondent	Close	Distant
3 Time involving the researcher	Long time to go through the interview	Short time
4 Cost	High	Significantly lower than the interviews
5 Sample	Small	Large
6 Quality of information	Deep and detailed	Rich
7 Skill and experience	The interviewer needs to have the skill to ask questions and, if necessary, to probe	No skill required
8 Control of the process	High	Low
9 Flexibility	Allows great flexibility to reword questions and clarify terms that are not clear	Rigid. The answers are accepted as they are
10 Analysis of the results	Difficult and becomes complicated in the unstructured interviews	Easy to analyse
11 Interviewer bias	The flexibility of interviews allows for bias. Sometimes the non-verbal communication or behaviour of the interviewee may mislead the interviewer to incorrect judgement	If sample is selected appropriately, there should be no bias

respondents, interaction between interviewer and respondent, that it allows probing, that the quality of information is deep and detailed, and that the interviewer
has a high level of control over the interview process. The main limitations of the
personal interview are high cost, long process time, that the sample can be small,
and difficulty in analysing the information.

References

Laycock, E., Howarth, T. and Watson, P. (2016) *The Journey to Dissertation Success for Construction, Property, and Architecture Students.* Routledge, London.
Merton, R. and Kendal, P. (1946) The focused interview. *American Journal of Sociology,* 51, 541–557.
Nachmias, C., Nachmias, D. and DeWaard, J. (2014) *Research Methods in the Social Sciences.* 8th edn. Worth, New York.

Additional reading

Barnett, V. (1991) *Sample Survey Principles and Methods.* Arnold, London.
Bouma, G. and Atkinson, G. (1995) *A Handbook of Social Science Research: A Comprehensive and Practical Guide for Students.* Oxford University Press, Oxford.
Farrell, P., Sherratt, F. and Richardson, A. (2017) *Writing Built Environment Dissertations and Projects – Practical Guidance and Examples.* 2nd edn. Wiley Blackwell, New Jersey. *Read Chapter 5 (The methodology chapter; analysis, results and findings, Review of theory and the literature). Also the list of appendices of that book.*
Jolliffe, F. (1986) *Survey Design and Analysis.* Ellis Horwood, Amsterdam.
Stewart, D. and Michael, K. (1993) *Secondary Research: Information Sources and Methods.* 2nd edn. Sage, London.

6 Questionnaire construction

Chapter 5 introduced several techniques for gathering information. As discussed, the selection of the technique depends largely on your choice of research approach. For instance, if your research requires you to conduct case studies, then the interview technique is more appropriate than the postal questionnaire, and if your study seeks to survey the opinion of top contractors operating in London, then the postal questionnaire will be more appropriate and feasible than interviews. After deciding on the technique, your next step is to construct your questionnaire.

The foundation of all questionnaires, whether to be mailed or to be used for interviewing, is the questions. At first, the order and wording of the questions are not crucial. Your aim is to list the ideas which can be developed into a questionnaire at a later stage. The principles that you need to follow in constructing your questionnaire are shown in Figure 6.1.

Figure 6.1 shows that, during the research process, the research objectives are translated into specific questions. Therefore, while thinking what item or question to include in your questionnaire, you should ask yourself the following:

- Which objective is the question related to?
- Is the question relevant to the aim of the study?
- Is the question relevant to the research hypothesis?
- Can the answer be obtained from other sources?

This chapter describes the stages for questionnaire construction and administration. It describes and illustrates (through examples) the types of questions, question formats and typical questionnaires. It also provides criteria for writing the questions. The contents of Chapter 6 are illustrated in Figure 6.2.

Note to students

A typical questionnaire format can be seen in Appendix 2.

How to construct a questionnaire

There are three fundamental stages in constructing your questionnaire:

1 Identifying the first thought questions.
2 Formulating the final questionnaire.
3 Wording of questions.

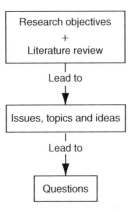

Figure 6.1   *A diagram showing that during the research process, research objectives are translated into specific questions.*

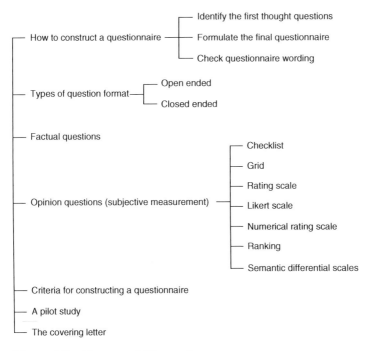

Figure 6.2   *Contents of Chapter 6.*

Stage 1 – Identifying the first thought questions

Before constructing your questionnaire, you should go back to your proposal and the literature file and start formulating the 'first thought' list of questions. At this stage, the order and wording of the questions are not crucial. Your aim is to write down all possible questions (say, 20–30 questions) which are related to your research (you will edit and order them later). Suppose you are investigating whether the characteristics of site managers have an effect on project performance. You will be thinking of asking certain types of questions and not others. Whatever questions you intend to ask, they should not be arbitrary and need to be based on your literature review. For example, you may not include in the first thought questions a question about the site manager's favourite location of work, but you are expected to include a question about his/her educational achievements. The reason for this is either that you are assuming that location of work has nothing to do with time overrun but that educational achievement has, or that previous studies in other fields have supported the second assumption. Moreover, should you ask a question about the site manager's personal life? This may just be relevant. But if you start to cover every aspect, then you will end up with a very lengthy questionnaire which could be rather hopeless. Therefore, it is absolutely important that, at the proposal stage, you need to have the purpose of your study specific, narrowly defined and stated clearly. This should provide you with more focused research and help you to formulate the final questionnaire more easily.

Stage 2 – Formulating the final questionnaire

After you have identified the first thought questions, you will be ready to construct your final questionnaire. To do that, you need to introduce a number of sections or categories for the questionnaire (say, four to six sections) and try to fit the first thought questions in these sections. Give these sections a title or a theme which should correspond closely with the objectives. For example, in Proposal 1 (in Appendix 1), there were two objectives. The first objective was to survey large private house-building companies and investigate the company business philosophy, organisational structure, marketing information and marketing policy. The second objective was to relate the companies' marketing philosophy with their financial performance. From these objectives, the student began to think of what to ask and what not to ask. He constructed the questionnaire with six sections to correspond with his objectives. The first section of the questionnaire was named 'General Information'. The second section was named 'Overall Business Philosophy' and here he listed six issues that he thought important and relevant to ask. These six issues were:

1 Type of business.
2 Business philosophy.
3 Management philosophy on products.
4 Marketing plan.
5 Management philosophy on the market.
6 Management success criteria.

These items or ideas were not introduced arbitrarily but were based on his background literature review (see Table 6.1).

Table 6.1 *Section of a questionnaire related to marketing*

Please respond to the following questions by ticking beside the option (letter) which best fits your company

SECTION – OVERALL BUSINESS PHILOSOPHY

1   What business are you in?
   (a)   We build houses.
   (b)   We build homes.
   (c)   We market homes.

2   In the house-building cycle, what action best describes your firm's business philosophy?
   (a)   We first determine customers' wants; and then design the product types and packages to satisfy those wants.
   (b)   We first start to build the estate; and then work out how best to sell the product.

3   What is the management's philosophy on products and markets?
   (a)   Management primarily thinks in terms of selling current and new products to whoever will buy them.
   (b)   Management thinks in terms of serving a wide range of markets and needs with equal effectiveness.
   (c)   Management thinks in terms of serving the needs and wants of well-defined markets chosen for their long-term growth and profit potential for the company.

4   Does management develop different offerings and marketing plans for different segments of the market?
   (a)   Yes.
   (b)   Sometimes.
   (c)   No.

5   Which of the following best describes top management's philosophy guiding the firm's current marketing effort?
   (a)   Customers will favour those products that are affordable and therefore the main task of management is to pursue improved production.
   (b)   Customers will not buy enough of the organisation's products unless the organisation makes a substantial effort to stimulate their interest in its products.
   (c)   The key to achieving organisational goals consists of the organisation's determining the needs and wants of target markets and adapting itself to delivering the desired satisfactions more effectively than its competitors.

6   Top management's focus is on _____ (please print a, b or c)
   (a)   Cost (i.e. how to do things cheaply and well).
   (b)   Sales volume (i.e. maximise sales targets).
   (c)   Profit (i.e. maximise profit).

Stage 3 – Wording of questions

After deciding what to ask, you should then check how you have asked them. The last section of this chapter gives details on criteria for constructing the questionnaire, but here is a summary:

- Your questions/questionnaire should be short but comprehensive.
- Avoid leading questions.
- Avoid double questions.
- Avoid presuming questions.
- Avoid hypothetical questions.
- The questions must not be ambiguous.
- The questions should be logical in their sequence.
- The questionnaire must be attractive in appearance.

Note to students

Examining other questionnaires to identify possible clues, through which you can construct yours, is essential at this stage. This means that you should look at good questions or questionnaires in books, journals, dissertations, theses and so on and try to copy the ideas. Remember, authors of past work have given their research a great deal of thought, and you can frequently benefit from their thinking when designing your questionnaire. For instance, question 3.2 of section 3 in Appendix 2 is a modification of a similar research project which was conducted in the manufacturing industry. The student fine-tuned the wordings to suit his field of investigation. Provided that you make a reference to other people's work, you will not be penalised.

Types of questions

Questionnaires are classified into two types: the 'open' form or unrestricted type, and the 'closed' form or restricted type. Open questions seek to encourage the respondent to provide free responses. For instance, the question 'What do you personally feel are the most important factors that make workers work harder?' is an open-ended question designed to study people's opinion. Oppenheim (1996, p. 112) notes:

> Open or free-answer types of questions are not followed by any kind of choice, and the answers have to be recorded in full. In the case of a written questionnaire, the amount of space or the number of lines provided for the answer will help to determine the length and fullness of the responses we obtain. Inevitably, some of this richness is lost when the answers are classified later, but it is useful to report a few such answers in the final report to give the reader some of the flavour of the replies. Statistical tabulations are important and must remain our first aim, but they make dull reading.

The main advantages of the open type of questions are therefore:

1 They give the respondent the opportunity to express his/her views. Once the respondent understands the theme of the investigation, he/she can let the thoughts roam freely, unencumbered by a prepared set of replies.
2 They are easy to ask.
3 They are more appropriate to construct with interview questionnaires but can also be used in postal surveys. During the interview, the interviewer has a great deal of freedom to probe various areas and to raise specific queries during the course of the interview.
4 They are useful to adopt when sensitive information is required from the respondent.

Open questions can, however, present problems. As the open question offers no direct clues and is broad based, predictably this type of questionnaire is more difficult to analyse and interpret. Therefore, some form of content analysis is required for open questions (see Chapter 8).

By contrast, closed questions often require a short response in the form of Yes or No, Agree or Disagree, Important or Not Important, and so on. Closed-ended questions are easy to ask and quick to answer, they require no writing by either respondent or interviewer, and their analysis is straightforward (Nachmias and Nachmias, 1996). Their major drawback, however, is that they may introduce bias, either by forcing the respondent to choose from given alternatives or by offering the respondent alternatives that might not have otherwise come to mind.

The appropriateness of either a closed-ended or open-ended question depends on a number of factors. Paul Lazarsfeld (1944) suggested the following considerations to determine appropriateness of which type of question to ask:

• The objective of the questionnaire.
• The respondent's level of information about the topic in question.
• The extent to which the topic has been thought through by the respondent.
• The ease with which respondents can communicate the content of the answer or the extent to which respondents are motivated to communicate on the topic.

Factual questions

This chapter has so far discussed the type of questions. The rest of the chapter will explain and illustrate the different formats for asking the questions. I will start with the factual questions.

Factual questions are mostly designed to elicit information related to the following:

1 Facts related to the background of an individual or organisation. Most questionnaires, whether for descriptive or analytical purposes, almost certainly begin by asking factual questions such as:
   a What is your position within the organisation?
   b How many professional employees work within the organisation?

   c   Which type of projects is your firm specialised in?

   d   What is the annual turnover of your organisation?

2   Facts related to events or projects. For instance, the questionnaire in Table 6.2 contains questions which are designed to find facts about the characteristics of projects and their performances. In this example, the researcher's aim was to investigate the difference in performance of projects delivered by a management contract and the traditional form of contracting. A theoretical model was formulated as shown in Figure 4.5 in Chapter 4 of this book on page 63 of which a number of sub-hypotheses were proposed. In order to test the sub-hypotheses, factual data were collected from previously completed projects and the performance of these projects was measured objectively.

Note to students

It is extremely difficult to determine causality in such studies unless a detailed case study is undertaken or a controlling variable system is used. This means you ought to be selective in your sample. For example, you may need to study certain categories of clients or projects and exclude others. In this way, you will be limiting the variables that determine causality. Nevertheless, at the level of students reading this book, if some kind of relationship is established between the variables, then that should be sufficient. For MPhil/PhD level, an in-depth investigation to causality is necessary; for example, follow-up interviews should be conducted with those involved in the study to explain how and why certain events took place. Otherwise, causality can be best studied in an experimental type of research such as laboratory and social behaviour research. As mentioned earlier, these are outside the scope of this book. They basically involve validating the hypotheses under real test.

3   Facts gathered from secondary data. As mentioned in Chapter 5, secondary data are available in two formats: statistical and descriptive. For example, in Proposal 4 shown in Appendix 1, the student examined and analysed the type of accidents within the construction industry using material which was published by the HSE Statistical Services Unit in Liverpool (see the HSE record in Appendix 4 as a typical example). From these statistics, the student compared the accident rate of the construction industry with four other major industries within the UK. He also took the accident statistics for the construction industry and separated them into their elements and components to show their type and relation to employees. Analysis of these factual records was then presented in graphical forms (see Figure 8.2 on page 122).

Open-ended questionnaire (subjective measurement)

This is a face-to-face interview between the researcher and the respondents in which an interviewer asks respondents questions designed to elicit answers pertinent to the research aim, objects and hypothesis. Following are examples of ten open-ended interview questions that were conducted and prompted with two site managers, by Farrell et al. (2017):

Q1 What is the approximate proportion of subcontractors and directly employed labour currently working in the development? Here, one more question was prompted.

Q2 How would you describe your working relationship with your workforce? Here, six more questions were prompted.

Q3 How would you describe your working relationship with your contract manager? Here, three more questions were prompted.

Q4 In what way do you believe your building programme influences your ability to build houses to an adequate standard of quality? Here, one more question was prompted.

Q5 Based on your experience, what would you say are the main reasons for sometimes being unable to build houses to an adequate standard of quality? Here, one more question was prompted.

Q6 Describe how the build quality is controlled by this company? Here, six more questions were prompted.

Q7 How would you compare customer satisfaction within the private housing sector to, say, five years ago? Here, three more questions were prompted.

Q8 To what extent do customers exhibit a willingness to recommend this company to family and friends? Here, two more questions were prompted.

Q9 What awards for quality have you or any other site managers at this company been nominated for or received?

Q10 Finally, would you say that the opinions you have voiced in answers to these questions are commonly held by other site managers currently working for this company?

☞ **See Appendix E2 in Farrell et al. (2017, p. 309) for full interview questions and prompts with the two site managers A and B.**
☞ **Also see Appendix E3 in Farrell et al. (2017, p. 310) on verbatim transcripts of interviews with the two site managers A and B.**

Opinion survey questions (subjective measurement)

There are several formats in which opinion type of questions can be asked in a survey:

- Checklist.
- Grid.
- Rating scale.
- Likert scale.
- Numerical rating scale.
- Ranking.
- Semantic differential scales.

Table 6.2 *Examples of factual questions related to construction project management*

The research theme: Procurement methods for the project.

The problem/rationale for the research: Evidently, a large number of projects overrun on time and cost in the UK.

Possible cause: Selecting the inappropriate procurement method and contract for the project.

Research hunch/assumption: The traditional form is not suitable for large and complex projects (costing over £5 million)

Focus of the research: Compare the performance of Traditional and Management Contracting procurement methods.

Method of investigation: Case studies.

The sample: 30 traditionally procured projects (15 projects < £5m, 15 projects > £5m) and 30 management contracts (15 projects < £5m, 15 > £5m).

Type of project: Offices of similar type of construction.

The ultimate aim and goal: To design a decision-making chart for selecting the appropriate procurement method for the project based on client and project characteristics. *(Note to students: This chart should be inserted in the conclusion chapter.)*

The research impact: To offer decision makers an opportunity to broaden their horizon on the different alternatives that could be considered, and the potential of different alternative procurement methods leading to different consequences.

Questions	Possible answers (Facts from documents and interviews with participants)	Rationale for the question and comments
Section 1 – Questions related to client characteristics		
1 How was the project funded?	Privately funded	This is to find out whether the type of client influences the selection method and, in turn, its performance.
2 What type of business?	Commercial	This is to find out whether the type of business influences the selection method and performance.
3 How many projects has the client built before?	5 projects	This is to measure how experienced the client was and whether the selected method depends on it and its performance.
4 What were the main criteria for the project?	Speed and maintenance cost	This is to find out whether client criteria and priorities influenced the selection method.
Section 2 – Questions related to project characteristics		
5 What type of building?	Office, high rise, air-conditioned	Seven floors

(*continued*)

Table 6.2 *(Continued)*

6 Was it a new-build project, refurbishment or both?	New build	This is to find out whether the performance of the method selected depends on whether the project is a new build or a refurbishment.
7 What was the type of construction?	Innovative mix of concrete and steel	This is to find out whether the type of construction influences the selection method and in turn its performance.
8 What was the total built area of the project in meter sq.?	3000 square meters	This is to find out whether the size of the project influences the selection method and in turn its performance.
9 What was the cost per square meter?	£2,000	
10 How many sub-contractors were involved in the project?	6 main sub-contractors	This is to find out the level of complexity of the project. (Note that a yardstick was designed to measure complexity based on this information.)
11 How much was the value of work constructed per week	£116.000 per week	This ratio was used as an indication of how complex the project was and whether this data was related to the method selected and its performance. (Note that a yardstick was designed to measure complexity based on this date.)

Section 3 – Questions related to the design and professionals

12 Was the project designed by an in-house professional?	No	This is to find out whether the client is sophisticated and had their own team of professionals.
13 How many similar projects had the quantity surveyor been involved in before?	6	This is to measure how experienced the QS was and whether the selection method depends on it and in turn on its performance.
14 In how many projects had the designer been involved with similar buildings before?	4	This is to measure how experienced the designers were and whether the selection method depends on it and in turn on its performance.
15 Was the BIM tool used?	No	This is to identify whether advanced technology was used for the project.
16 Was VE applied?	No	This is to identify whether an independent multi-disciplinary team was appointed to value engineer the project.

(continued)

Table 6.2 *(Continued)*

Section 4 – Questions related to tendering and method of procurement adopted

17 Which procurement method was used for the project?	Traditional form of contract	Method was selected based on the architect's advice. This question is the main 'focus' of this research.
18 What type of contract?	JCT/SBC/2016 (with quantities)	
19 What type of tender?	Selected tender	4 main contractors were selected for this project and the pre-qualification questionnaire was used to evaluate the tenders.

Section 5 – Questions related to project performance

20 What was the estimated total cost of the project and the actual?	Estimated £6M and the actual £6.4M	Overrun by £400,000. This is to find out whether the facts in sections 1–4 above are linked with cost performance.
21 What was the programmed project duration and the actual (in weeks)?	The programmed was 50 weeks but completed in 55 weeks.	Overrun on time by 5 weeks. However, 3 weeks were authorised because of client's variation orders. This is to find out whether the facts in sections 1–4 above are linked with time performance.
22 How many variation orders and what was the total value of the orders?	3 variation orders, totalling £200,000. 2 variation orders were authorised.	Extension was added to the project. This is to find out whether there is a link between the method selected for this project and variation orders.
23 Where there any defects when the project was completed?	No	This is to find out whether there is a link between the method selected for this project and defects.
24 Were there any claims?	Yes	The client claimed compensation from the contractor in the form of a liquidated damages according to clause 2.32.2 of the signed JCT contract. This is to find out whether there is a link between the method selected for this project and claims.
25 Were there any disputes?	Yes	This is to find out whether there is a link between the method selected for this project and disputes. A form of ADR was successfully applied for this project.
26 Were there any safety issues throughout the project?	Two minor injuries	Dealt with by first aid. This is to find out whether there is a link between the method selected for this project and safety performance.

Checklist

This type of question is essentially a list of items, about themselves, an organisation or an event, that respondents are offered to mark or tick. It is a straightforward means of collecting information and the data can be analysed easily. For example, a question may be a list of management techniques and the respondent is asked to tick which of these techniques are used by his/her organisation. It may be a list of motivational factors and respondents are asked to tick which of these apply to them, and so on.

The checklist questions are specially designed for a group of respondents who have accurate information and can answer the questions with a high degree of certainty. For example, a respondent may be asked a question on a specialised area, such as: 'Over the next 5 years or so, do you expect the use of value management to:

1   Increase a lot.
2   Increase a little.
3   No change.
4   Decrease a little.
5   Decrease a lot?

The checklist format is a quick format but can be rather rigid. The response to each item does not have a degree of intensity, but a dichotomy. As an attribute, it is either applicable or not. Two examples of checklist questions are illustrated in this chapter. Table 6.1 was an exhibit of a checklist of questions taken from a dissertation topic on marketing related to Proposal 1 in Appendix 1. Table 6.3 is another exhibit in which a checklist is used to find out the level of knowledge people have on a particular subject.

Grid

A grid is an elaboration of the checklist format, except it provides answers to two or more questions at the same time (see example in Table 6.4).

Table 6.3   *Which of the following problems do you think need to be overcome in relation to the project management system?*

Please tick one or more of the following	
No universally accepted definition of project management.	☐
No standard form of project management.	☐
Defining responsibilities of members of the project management team.	☐
Controlling the work packages of the project.	☐
Associated problem of communication.	☐
Higher cost associated with the project management system.	☐
Attitude of personnel involved in the project management project.	☐
Others (please state).	☐

Table 6.4 *Here are some well-known procurement methods that can be used to deliver projects according to client criteria. Please tick those procurement methods that you think are best to achieve each criterion listed*

Criterion	Procurement method		
	Traditional	Design and build	Management fee
Speed of total process			
Building complexity			
Building quality			
Cost of change			
Degree of price certainty			
Functionality			
Buildability			

Rating scale

The rating scale is one of the most common formats for questioning respondents on their views or opinions of an object, event or attribute. Like the grid, rating scales can be regarded as an elaboration of the checklist format, except the respondent has the choice to express his/her degree of agreement or disagreement on a particular scale. The response categories of such questions are called quantifiers: they reflect the intensity of the particular judgement involved. The following are some common sets of response categories:

1 Strongly agree (5 points)	1 Of great importance	1 More	1 Too little
2 Agree (4 points)	2 Of some importance	2 Same	2 About right
3 Neither/nor (3 points)	3 Of no importance	3 Less	3 Too much
4 Disagree (2 points)	4 Do not know		
5 Strongly disagree (1 point)			

1 Very satisfied	1 Very favourable	1 Very bad
2 Fairly satisfied	2 Favourable	2 Bad
3 Fairly dissatisfied	3 Not favourable	3 Would not matter
4 Very dissatisfied		4 Fairly good
		5 Very good

The numerical number shown beside the first category represents the intensity of the response. These are not usually shown in the questionnaire but are included here for your own use at the analysis stage.

Table 6.5 shows an extract from a questionnaire which was designed to investigate the views of the industry on factors affecting productivity on construction sites. Respondents were asked to rate various factors they considered important. This type of rating is also called 'matrix rating'.

Table 6.5 *Here are a number of factors which can have an impact on site productivity. From your experience, please express your opinion on how important each factor can be on influencing productivity. (Please tick the appropriate box)*

Factors influencing site productivity	Of great importance	Of some importance	Of no importance

1 Head office factors

- Delegation of responsibilities
- Integration of project information
- Project planning
- Scheduling of project activities
- Level of authority
- Supervision of subordinates
- Communication between head office and site
- Involvement of site managers in contract meetings
- Characteristics/attitude of site personnel
- The decision-making process

2 Resource management effectiveness

- Procurement of materials
- Site programme
- Accuracy of the technical information
- Appropriateness of tools to be used for the tasks
- Knowledge of project technology
- Management interference on workmanship
- Site layout

3 Motivational factors

- Promotion of employees
- Resentment regarding company policy
- Incentive schemes for good performance
- Opportunities to exercise skill/knowledge
- Management response to settle employee's grievances
- Workers' uncertainty about career prospects
- Work environment

4 Education and training

- Experience of employees
- Contract administration skill
- Knowledge of scientific techniques
- Training on new technology
- Availability of multi-skilled project personnel

With the rating scales, it is your task to decide the number of scale points to use. Moser and Kalton (1993, p. 359) write:

> If the scale is divided too finely the respondents will be unable to place themselves within the scale, and if too coarsely the scale will not differentiate adequately between them. Often five to seven categories are employed, but sometimes the number is greater. The choice between an odd or even number depends on whether or not respondents are to be forced to decide the direction of their attitude; with an odd number there is a middle category representing a neutral position, but with an even number there is no middle category, so that respondents are forced to decide to which side of neutral they belong. Another factor to take into account in fixing the number of categories is that respondents generally avoid the two extreme positions, thus effectively reducing the number they choose between.

Likert scale

This type of scaling is similar to the rating scale, except the questions consist of attitudinal statements on the survey object (say attitude to job satisfaction) ranging from one extreme of favourableness to the other. Table 6.6 on page 116 is an exhibit of a Likert scale questionnaire extracted from Mullins's (2010) book, *Management and Organizational Behaviour.*

☞ **Also see Figure 5.3 in Farrell et al. (2017, pp. 121–22) for another example of a Likert scale question titled 'leadership of bosses and motivation of workers'.**

Numerical rating scale

The numerical rating scale is another common questionnaire format. In this format, respondents are asked to give scores on an analogy, a service or an event. The rating may be out of 100, out of 10, out of 5 and so on. Examination marking is a typical example of a numerical rating scale. Table 6.7 on page 118 and 6.8 on page 119 are exhibits of a subjective way to tell the respondent's opinion on the criteria that are used in assessing a case study / project performance / organisational effectiveness and the like.

☞ **Also see Table 4.6 and Table 5.1 in Farrell et al. (2017) for other examples of rating scale questions.**

Table 4.6 in Farrell et al. (2017) provides an example of a foreman who is required by 'his' employer to rate the quality of work of bricklayers based on eight criteria.

Table 6.6 *The following statements are related to job satisfaction at work. Please indicate your reaction to each statement by ticking the appropriate cell*

Job satisfaction factors	Strongly agree	Agree	Neither agree nor disagree	Disagree	Strongly disagree
1 Special wage increases should be given to employees who do their jobs well					
2 Better job descriptions would be helpful so that employees will know exactly what is expected of them					
3 Employees need to be reminded that their jobs are dependent on the company's ability to compete effectively					
4 Supervisors should give a good deal of attention to the physical working conditions of their employees					
5 Supervisors ought to work hard to develop a friendly atmosphere among their people					
6 Individual recognition for above-standard performance means a lot to employees					
7 Indifferent supervision can often bruise feelings					
8 Employees want to feel that their real skills and capacities are put to use in their jobs					
9 The company retirement benefits and share programmes are important factors in keeping employees in their jobs					
10 Almost every job can be made more stimulating and challenging					
11 Many employees want to give their best in everything they do					
12 Management could show more interest in the employees by sponsoring social events after hours					
13 Pride in one's work is actually an important reward					

(continued)

Table 6.6 *(Continued)*

14 Employees want to be able
   to think of themselves as the
   best at their own job
15 The quality of the
   relationships in the informal
   work group is quite important
16 Individual incentive
   bonuses would improve the
   performance of employees
17 Visibility with upper
   management is important to
   employees
18 Employees generally like to
   schedule their own work
   and to make job-related
   decisions with a minimum of
   supervision
19 Job security is important to
   employees
20 Having good equipment to
   work with is important to
   employees

Source: Mullins (2010, pp. 514–16).

Table 5.1 in Farrell et al. (2017) provides an example of rating ten criteria for the disability access provision on a (0–10) scale. In that example, ten criteria were evaluated against five buildings (Building A, B, C, D, E). These ten criteria were based on Building Regulations in Practice. They are:

a   Quality of disabled toilet provision.
b   Level access entrance.
c   Provision and proximity of disabled car parks.
d   Staff support.
e   Allocated seating area.
f   Circulation space area.
g   Door widths.
h   Braille signage.
i   Tactile surfaces.
j   Communication aids.

Ranking

The ranking format is used when the respondent is asked to place a set of attitudes or objects in ranking order indicating their importance, priorities or preferences. For example, in a survey on the level of job satisfaction, respondents were

Table 6.7 *On a scale out of 10, how would you rate the achievements of the following 13 policies of the NPPF to your local town plan? 10 (Highly achieved), 0 (Not achieved at all)*

Policy no.	Description of the policy	Scale of achievement out of (10)
1 Building a strong, competitive economy.	In this policy, the government is dedicated to supporting the planning system towards economic growth, the planning side should be enthusiastic to sustain economic growth. Therefore, local planning authorities must comply with the new developments and needs of businesses to equip an economy suitable for the coming future.	
2 Ensuring the vitality of the town centres.	The planning policies should support the competitiveness of the town centres and the environment around the surrounding area. They should manage the growth of the centres over a period of time. They should be able to follow policies in order to work successfully and ensure the vitality of the town.	
3 Supporting a prosperous rural economy.	The planning policy should encourage economic growth within rural regions, to make it easier to generate more jobs and prosperity. Whilst having the support of sustainable new development.	
4 Promoting sustainable transport.	In this section, the transport policy plays a vital role in the action of sustainable development. Therefore, there must be a variety of ways people can travel. It states that encouragement should be provided regarding different sustainable transport, to decrease and prevent congestion within the region and carbon emissions. Transport must be safe and accessible for people to reach and use efficiently in the area.	
5 Supporting high-quality communications infrastructure.	In this policy, the local planning authority should encourage the more extensive networks regarding the increase of speed in broadband and telecommunications, as they play an essential role in increasing the supply of services to the local community. This policy focuses on having the high-quality means of communication within the infrastructure as a necessity for the development of a sustainable economy.	
6 Delivering a wide choice of high-quality homes.	Within this policy, it states how the government has a perspective of the way the local planning organisation should provide suitable housing in order to increase the supply of housing.	
7 Requiring good design.	In this policy, the government makes great efforts over the design of the built environment. As they believe that having an efficient design is vital in ensuring sustainable development, with increasing positivity to producing a better area for occupants. The design of the town planning should be strong when developed to enable a clear quality of development that is presumed for the region.	

(continued)

Table 6.7 *(Continued)*

8 Promoting healthy communities.	Within this policy, the planning systems should make it easier to create a healthy community. Therefore, the planning policy aims to promote and encourage a gathering of community members together by having community centres as well as having a safe environment to live in and to decrease crime within the area.
9 Protecting Green Belt land.	The government makes the Green Belt a significant policy to follow, as one of the Green Belt policy visions is to avert urban sprawl from making the open area of land open for a long-term period. An extremely important feature of the Green Belt is its openness and stability.
10 Meeting the challenge of climate change, flooding and coastal change.	Planning a strategy to combat the effects of climate change is crucial; if this principle is ignored, people are more vulnerable to disasters such as flooding and rising sea levels. The NPPF has established policies to reduce carbon emissions and support renewable and low carbon energy infrastructure; finding solutions and making clean energy more accessible is on the local authority's management.
11 Conserving and enhancing the natural environment.	This principle focuses primarily on protecting the natural and local environment; this includes geological, biodiversity and environmental conservation.
12 Conserving and enhancing the historic environment.	In this particular policy, it states how planning authorities should set a strategic plan in regard to conservation of the historic environment. Therefore, they should identify that heritage is a valuable resource that they will need to safeguard in an effective way.
13 Facilitating the sustainable use of minerals.	Minerals are essential for infrastructure, buildings, energy and goods. The extraction of minerals must go according to the NPPF policies. This means that the practices carried out in the extraction of minerals must be transported according to safeguard policies and regulations. Moreover, planned rail links to quarries are necessary, materials that can be recycled support a sustainable practice and avoid unacceptable impacts on the natural and historic environment, human health or aviation safety.

Note to students

The 13 principles in Table 6.7 have been extracted from the NPPF document and are summarised in the table.

asked to rank various dimensions they considered important about being in their jobs (see Table 6.9 on page 119). There are, however, particular limitations to the number of rankings most people can be expected to carry out. Under normal survey conditions, to put ten objects in rank order is probably as much as can be asked (Oppenheim, 1996). Therefore, for a large number of objects you need to ask the respondents to rank for you a number of factors (say five factors) out of many factors as in the example shown in Table 6.10 on page 101.

Table 6.8 *The following are a number of criteria which are commonly applied by clients of the building industry in assessing the performance of their projects. Please give a rating from 0 to 10 to each criterion according to the magnitude of importance each would be to your organisation (10 = very important)*

Criteria	Rating out of 10
1 Early start on site	
2 Reliability of the estimated design time	
3 Reliability of the estimated construction time	
4 Minimising the construction time	
5 Reliability of the estimated construction cost	
6 Obtaining a building at the cheapest cost	
7 Obtaining a building with low maintenance cost	
8 Obtaining a building with high aesthetic quality	
9 Obtaining a functional building to fit its purpose	
10 Input from the contractor related to buildability	
11 To have confidence in the contractor	

Table 6.9 *Would you please indicate, in priority order, which of the following factors you find important in being satisfied with your job. Please indicate which factor is first in importance, which is second, which is third and so forth (please circle the appropriate figure on the right-hand side)*

1	A well-paid job (having a good income and being able to afford the good things in life)	1 2 3 4 5 6 7 8
2	A prosperous job (having a good opportunity to develop myself)	1 2 3 4 5 6 7 8
3	An important job (a job full of achievement that brings me respect and recognition)	1 2 3 4 5 6 7 8
4	A secure job (making certain that I have steady work and steady wages)	1 2 3 4 5 6 7 8
5	Relationship with fellow workers (getting along well with the people I work with)	1 2 3 4 5 6 7 8
6	Relationship with superiors (getting along well with my supervisor)	1 2 3 4 5 6 7 8
7	Job interest (good chance to do work of my interest)	1 2 3 4 5 6 7 8
8	Working condition (working within a good physical job condition)	1 2 3 4 5 6 7 8

☞ **Note to students: Also see Figure 5.2 in Farrell et al. (2017, p. 130) for another example of a ranking type about 'Factors that keep sites safe'.**

Semantic differential scales

Diagrammatic rating scales is another means of measuring intensity of judgement and the semantic differential is the most popular form of this type of scaling. The technique was developed by Osgood (1956) to investigate the perceived meaning of various concepts. In this method, the respondent is asked to indicate his/her position on a seven-point bipolar scale defined with contrasting adjectives at each end. It can best be applied when the perceptions of different groups on

Table 6.10 *In your view, what are the most serious factors causing accidents on construction sites? (Please select no more than five and number them 1, 2, 3, 4, 5 in order of seriousness)*

_____	Age (very young or too old)	_____ Lack of experience to execute the task
_____	Lack of background safety training	_____ Paying operatives danger money
_____	Lack of personal care for safety	_____ Poor enforcement of safety laws and regulations
_____	Lack of safety training on-site	_____ Bad supervisor's safety behaviour
_____	Bad workmates' safety behaviour	_____ Bad subcontractors' safety behaviour
_____	Mishandling of dangerous material	_____ Improper fixing of scaffolding
_____	Improper erection of steel	_____ Lack of inspection for safety
_____	Insufficient skill to operate plant	_____ Lack of provision of safety clothing
_____	Improper use of safety clothing	_____ Improper use of safety equipment
_____	Not issuing of safety booklet	_____ Lack of trade union involvement
_____	Lack of site safety representative	_____ Lack of safety policy
_____	Lack of safety talk by management	_____ Not displaying safety posters
_____	Untidy site	_____ Badly planned and disorganised site

a particular matter need to be compared. Examples could be good/bad, strong/weak, satisfied/dissatisfied.

The seven-point bipolar scale can be presented in numerical dimensions such as:

Good	—	—	—	—	—	—	—	Bad
	3	2	1	0	–1	–2	–3	

or can be presented on a descriptive dimension like that shown in Table 6.11 on page 102. Numerical values can be assigned to the descriptive dimensions, and comparisons can be made between items of various groups in terms of mean scores.

Criteria for constructing a questionnaire

The characteristics of a good questionnaire are summarised by (Wood, 1991; cited in Naoum, 2016, pp. 18–20) as follows:

1   It must deal with a topic of some significance that is important enough to the respondent to merit a response.

2   It must seek information not obtainable from other sources. You should not ask people to do your data gathering for you, especially when the data are readily available elsewhere.
3   It should be as short as possible but comprehensive enough to allow you to derive what you need without alienating the respondent.
4   It should be attractive in appearance, well laid out and well reproduced (see Appendix 2).
5   Where it contains directions, they must be clear and complete.
6   Unless there is a very good reason for another format, questions should be arranged in categories which allow easy and accurate responses.
7   Questions must be as objective as possible without offering leading questions. For example, a question such as 'Do you not agree that site managers should have the right to have a say in finalising the building design?' is leading. Here, it might be difficult for site managers to answer 'No' in response to that question.
8   In their sequencing, questions should run from the general to the specific, from simple to complex, and from those that will create a favourable impression upon the respondent to those that may be sensitive.
9   Bearing in mind point (8) above, you should avoid questions that may annoy or embarrass the respondent.
10   The questionnaire must provide for ease of tabulation and/or interpretation and should be designed accordingly.

Table 6.11   *Think of your leader and describe him/her by completing the following scale. Place an 'X' in one of the eight spaces according to how well the adjective fits your leader. Look at the words at both ends of the line before placing your 'X'*

	8	7	6	5	4	3	2	1	
Pleasant	—	—	—	—	—	—	—	—	Unpleasant
Friendly	—	—	—	—	—	—	—	—	Unfriendly
Rejecting	—	—	—	—	—	—	—	—	Accepting
Helpful	—	—	—	—	—	—	—	—	Frustrating
Unenthusiastic	—	—	—	—	—	—	—	—	Enthusiastic
Tense	—	—	—	—	—	—	—	—	Relaxed
Distant	—	—	—	—	—	—	—	—	Close
Cold	—	—	—	—	—	—	—	—	Warm
Cooperative	—	—	—	—	—	—	—	—	Uncooperative
Supportive	—	—	—	—	—	—	—	—	Hostile
Boring	—	—	—	—	—	—	—	—	Interesting
Quarrelsome	—	—	—	—	—	—	—	—	Harmonious
Self-assured	—	—	—	—	—	—	—	—	Hesitant
Efficient	—	—	—	—	—	—	—	—	Inefficient
Gloomy	—	—	—	—	—	—	—	—	Cheerful
Open	—	—	—	—	—	—	—	—	Guarded

The ten points illustrate the importance and the role of the questionnaire to the survey's success. The design of the questionnaire also requires careful attention, and consideration should be given to:

- Examining other questionnaires to identify possible clues.
- Obtaining as much help as possible in order to make sure it is easy to be understood by different audiences.
- Allowing for a pilot stage at the draft phase in order to get valuable responses and to detect areas of possible shortcomings.
- Close liaison with the supervisor and making sure that he/she has seen and approved the questionnaire.
- Trying different question orders at the pilot stage. This may assist in finding the best approach.
- Experimenting with different types of questions, both open and closed.
- Collecting the most relevant information and obtaining the maximum number of respondents by making sure that:
  a You identify the sender and the person who receives the returned questionnaires.
  b You know the purpose of the research and the questionnaire.
  c There is an incentive for the respondent to complete the questionnaire.
  d You reassure the respondent of the confidentiality of the questionnaire.
  e You allow the respondent the opportunity to provide some personal insight not contained elsewhere.

Note to students

When trying to design the questionnaire, you need to ask yourself a number of questions such as:

- Are you using quantitative or qualitative measures?
- Is your study a comparative or a singular investigation?
- If it is a comparative study, how many survey groups are you investigating and who are they?
- How do the groups differ in their characteristics?
- What is the depth of the investigation? Is it a specific problem or a generalised one?
- How many responses or cases do you need in order to answer your questions and achieve your objectives?
- If you are testing a theory, are you using control variables and why?

Once you have answered the aforementioned questions and designed the questionnaire, you can then invite the respondents to fill out the questionnaire or rate them or do whatever is required. It is absolutely essential to do a complete pilot study before you collect the final data for your main study.

A pilot study

Whenever you construct a questionnaire, it is advisable to complete a pilot study before you collect the final data from the whole sample. A pilot study provides a trial run for the questionnaire, which involves testing the wording of the question, identifying ambiguous questions, testing the technique that you use to collect the data, measuring the effectiveness of your standard invitation to respondents, and so on. Bell (1996, p. 84) described a pilot study as:

> [G]etting the bugs out of the instrument (questionnaire) so that subjects in your main study will experience no difficulties in completing it and so that you can carry out a preliminary analysis to see whether the wording and format of questions will present any difficulties when the main data are analysed.

Bell (ibid.) went further and noted that you should ask your guinea pigs the following questions:

1   How long did it take you to complete?
2   Were the instructions clear?
3   Were any of the questions unclear or ambiguous? If so, will you say which and why?
4   Did you object to answering any of the questions?
5   In your opinion, has any major topic been omitted?
6   Was the layout of the questionnaire clear/attractive?
7   Any comments?

You will probably be amazed by how much you will learn from a pilot study. The little extra time it takes to complete a pilot study test will be well spent.

Covering letter

After constructing your questionnaire, your next step is to write a covering letter to accompany your questionnaire. The letter should explain the purpose of the survey or questionnaire in order to encourage a high response. The content of the covering letter is particularly important in postal questionnaires and other survey tools such as the SurveyMonkey. It is important because the covering letter is the only way you can persuade the subjects to respond to your questionnaire. Nachmias and Nachmias (1996, p. 20) write:

> A cover letter must succeed in overcoming any resistance or prejudice the respondent may have against the survey. It should (1) identify the sponsoring organization or the persons conducting the study, (2) explain the purpose of the study, (3) tell why it is important that the respondent answer the questionnaire, and (4) assure the respondent that the information provided will be held in strict confidence.

An example of a covering letter that can be used with a SurveyMonkey is presented in Figure 6.3.

Dear Sir/Madam:

You are invited to participate in my research survey using the SurveyMonkey tool.

Re: Dissertation – BSc Construction Management

I am currently undertaking a Bachelor of Science Degree in Construction Project Management at the University of West London. In fulfilment of this degree, I am required to research a topic within the area of Construction Management and write a dissertation on it. The topic that I have chosen is 'Design and Build as a Method of Building Procurement'and I am investigating the following aspects of its use:

1   The criteria which clients feel important in the selection of Project Management contracts.
2   The types of building for which Design and Build is used and the dominant reasons for the selection of this type of procurement path for these buildings.
3   The types of clients who are predisposed to use Design and Build and their satisfaction.

The survey questionnaire is structured under 3 main sections containing 30 questions in total. The questions are related to the above 3 aspects and they require your degree of agreement to a variety of relevant statements to the topic by ticking the appropriate box.

If you are willing to participate in this study, I would be very grateful if you could complete the survey on the link below. Needless to say, the information provided will be treated with strict confidence and individual firms will not be identified.

https://www.surveymonkey.com/Reference *(To students – See page 92 for more details).*

Do you wish to continue? **(By clicking yes, you will be directed to the questions)**

Yes   [O]
No   [O].

Figure 6.3   *Example of a SurveyMonkey covering letter.*

Summary

This chapter described the stages for constructing a questionnaire together with types and question formats. The foundation of all questionnaires, whether mailed or to be used for interviewing, is the questions. The principle that you need to follow in constructing your questionnaire is to go back to your dissertation proposal and start to ask specific questions related to the aim, objectives and hypothesis of your study.

Questions can be of two types: open-ended and closed-ended. Open-ended questions have the advantage of giving an opportunity to respondents to express their views on the subject, but it can be rather difficult to analyse the results later. By contrast, closed-ended questions require a short response and their analysis is straightforward. However, you need to have sufficient knowledge on the subject of your investigation in order to offer respondents a set of response categories from which they should choose the one that most represents their opinions, views, attitudes or perceptions.

Questions can be either factual or an opinion type. Factual questions are designed to obtain objective data whereas opinion questions are designed to elicit subjective information. The questions can be formulated in various ways. The most common formats are the checklist, grid, rating scale, Likert scale, numerical rating scale, ranking and semantic differential scales. These formats are described in this chapter with examples. It is advisable to conduct a pilot study to test the wording of the questions, check the length of the questionnaire and make sure that the questions are not ambiguous. Finally, you need to write a covering letter to accompany your questionnaire stating who you are and the purpose of your study, ensuring confidentiality and perhaps offering an incentive to respond.

References

Bell, J. (2005) *Doing Your Research Project: A Guide for First-Time Researchers in Education and Social Science.* 4th edn. Open University Press, McGraw-Hill International, New York.

Farrell, P., Sherratt, F. and Richardson, A. (2017) *Writing Built Environment Dissertations and Projects – Practical Guidance and Examples.* 2nd edn. Wiley Blackwell, Chichester.

Lazarsfeld, P. (1944) The controversy over detailed interviews: An offer for negotiation. *Public Opinion Quarterly,* 8, 38–60.

Moser, C. and Kalton, G. (1993) *Survey Methods in Social Investigation.* Dartmouth, UK.

Mullins, L. (1996) *Management and Organizational Behaviour.* Pitman, New York.

Mullins, L. (2010) *Management and Organizational Behaviour.* Pitman, New York.

Nachmias, C. and Nachmias, D. (1996) *Research Methods in the Social Sciences.* 5th edn. Arnold, London.

Naoum, S.G. (2016) *Dissertation Guide: Instructions for Preparation, Control and Presentation of the Dissertation.* School of Built Environment and Architecture, London South Bank University, London.

Oppenheim, A. (1996) *Questionnaire Design, Interviewing and Attitude Measurement.* Pinter, London.

Osgood, C.E. (1956) *Method and Theory in Experimental Psychology.* Oxford University Press, Oxford.

Additional reading

Farrell, P., Sherratt, F. and Richardson, A. (2017) *Writing Built Environment Dissertations and Projects – Practical Guidance and Examples.* 2nd edn. Wiley Blackwell, Chichester. *Read Chapter 3 (Review of theory and the literature) and Chapter 5 (The methodology: analysis, results and findings).*

Part III

Analysis and presentation of the results

7 *Measurements and probability*

Measurement is a procedure in which a researcher assigns numerals (numbers or other symbols) to empirical properties (variables) according to rules. It is closely linked to the research approach and questionnaire construction, which were discussed in Chapters 4 and 6, respectively. There are four levels of measurement: nominal, ordinal, interval and ratio. In some cases, your research involves a search for a measure that is already developed and in other cases, you need to design a measure. This chapter focuses on these levels of measurements in order to prepare the ground for the next exciting chapter: analysis of the results. This chapter also provides a statement of probability, which is an important term to understand in testing your research hypothesis. The contents of Chapter 7 are illustrated in Figure 7.1.

Note to students

The term 'measurement' is mainly used to quantify quantitative questions. I prefer to use the terms 'evaluation' and 'assessment' to process exploratory questions. Analysis of both quantitative and exploratory questions is discussed in Chapter 8.

Level of measurement

In order to be able to select the appropriate method of analysis, you need to understand the level of measurement. For each type of measurement, there is an appropriate method (or more than one) that can be applied and others that cannot.

Measurement is a procedure in which a researcher assigns numerals (numbers or other symbols) to empirical properties (variables) according to rules. Suppose you invited five contractors (A, B, C, D and E) to tender for building your project. Having found that the difference in price among five tenderers is minute, you decided to make the selection on the basis of which contractor best meets the following criteria: speed, quality and safety. These three criteria vary. For example, one contractor may deliver the project earlier and have a safety programme, but the quality of the finished product may be unsatisfactory. Accordingly, you decide to rank each of the three criteria on a scale from 1 to 5, where 1 indicates total dissatisfaction and 5 stands for complete satisfaction. You then evaluate the five tenderers. After examining the scores, you may decide to appoint contractor B because it received the highest score on the three counts. The numbering process

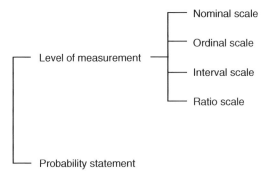

Figure 7.1   *Contents of Chapter 7.*

just discussed is a crude example of explaining the nature of measurement. However, it conveys the basic idea expressed in the definition of measurement, that is, you assigned numerals to properties according to rules. The following section will explain the four principal levels of measurement, namely nominal, ordinal, interval and ratio. Your primary data collection should fall within one or more of these levels.

Nominal scale

Nominal numbering implies belonging to a classification or having a particular property and a label. It does not imply any idea of rank or priority. Nominal numbering is also conventional integers, that is, positive and whole numbers (this may well be because most statistics are analysed by a computer, which, as you know, handles numbers more easily than letters or strings). For example, if you conducted a survey to investigate the use of a particular project management software in the construction industry, you would count the number of companies using the package and categorise them as shown in Table 7.1.

The numbers given to the categories in Table 7.1 are nominal (i.e. name only). For example, number 1 (contractors) is not half of number 2 (architects) or in any way prior to or less than the others in quantity. The numbers are simply convenient but arbitrary labels for identifying each type of company. You could have used the label A instead of 1, B instead of 2, C instead of 3 and so on. The numbers within each category are called frequencies. The frequency distribution and the terms associated with it will be discussed in Chapter 8.

Table 7.1   *Categorisation table of companies using project management*

Category				
1 (contractors)	2 (architects)	3 (quantity surveyors)	4 (engineers)	5 (others)
20	70	35	40	10

Ordinal scale

This is a ranking or a rating of data which normally uses integers in ascending or descending order. An example of an ordinal is when you ask an attitudinal question. For instance, you may want to measure your respondents' attitude to a motivational statement such as 'individual incentive bonuses would motivate people to work harder and in turn improve the performance of employees'. Here, the respondent is asked to mark a number representing his/her degree of agreement or disagreement with this statement. Table 7.2 illustrates a possible coding frame between the numbers and the answers. The numbers assigned to the agreement scale (5, 4, 3, 2, 1) do not indicate that the intervals between the scales are equal, nor do they indicate absolute quantities. They are merely numerical labels.

Another example of an ordinal scale is when respondents are asked to rank items by their own preference. For instance, if we asked eight people to rank the quality of a particular product in order of their preference, we might obtain Table 7.3.

Similarly to the previous example, the numbers in Table 7.3 do not indicate that the interval between the ranks is equal. Although the numbers are equally spaced, it does not imply that the property each represents is also equally spaced. If two respondents have the rank 8 and 6 and two others are ranked 7 and 5, it does not mean that the differences between the two pairs are equal. Notice the

Table 7.2   *Ordinal ranking scale*

	Strongly agree (5)	Agree (4)	Neutral (3)	Disagree (2)	Strongly disagree (1)
Site managers	4	3	5	5	0
Head office personnel	0	1	1	9	6
Operatives	7	5	4	1	0

Table 7.3   *Quality of product scores*

Person	Score	Rank of score
1	13	5.5
2	20	7
3	9	1
4	13	5.5
5	10	3
6	10	3
7	10	3
8	24	8

tied ranks in Table 7.3. In this example, the score of 9 was given the first rank. As three people share the score of 10, you need to share the ranking, such as:

$$\frac{2+3+4}{3} = \frac{9}{3} = 3$$

For subjects 1 and 4 this means ranks 5 and 6 are shared, that is:

$$\frac{5+6}{2} = \frac{11}{2} = 5.5$$

Interval scale

The numbering system in the ordinal and nominal measurement is purely an arbitrary label for identifying each type of person. If you have a set of observations or data where the distance between each observation is constant, then this type of measurement is called an interval level of measurement. Often-used examples are minutes, kilograms, number of words recalled in a memory test and percentage marks in the exam. The interval between 20 and 30 minutes is the same as between 50 and 60 minutes. When it comes to numerical scores, such as numbers of items recalled per minute, you are dealing with numbers and you can assume that the distances between scores are the same. This type of measurement is another example of interval measurement because it assumes equal intervals between the data on a continuous scale.

Ratio scale

The ratio scale is similar to the interval scale except it involves the kind of numerical scale which has a natural zero, such as age, salary, time and distance. However, you do not need to bother about the difference between interval and ratio scales. For the level of statistics described in this book, both measurements are treated in exactly the same way.

☞ **Also see Table 4.9 – Variables to measure in construction at the categorical/nominal, ordinal and interval level in Farrell et al. (2017, p. 96).**

Probability statement

The subject of probability is important to understand when you start to analyse your results. Statistical probability will tell you whether any differences in scores are due to your manipulation of the variables, as predicted by your research hypothesis or, alternatively, only due to chance fluctuations as stated in the null hypothesis. You do not need to be bothered now about the term 'null hypothesis'; it is discussed later, in Chapter 8.

We use the word 'probably' almost every day to express our views on certain things. Consider the following statements:

- It will probably rain next week.
- I will most probably visit my friend tomorrow.
- I will definitely pass my maths exam.

In the first statement, you are giving a certain degree of chance that it will rain tomorrow. This chance is normally measured as a percentage out of 100. It could be 1 per cent, 5 per cent, 20 per cent, 50 per cent and so on. In the second statement, you are making a more assured statement by saying 'most probably'. Again this could be any percentage out of 100, but rather towards the upper limit of the scale. It could be an 80 per cent, 90 per cent, 95 per cent chance and so on, but not 100 per cent. In the third statement, you are making a more certain statement by using the word 'definitely' (i.e. 100 per cent). But on what basis have you made these statements or judgements? The second statement may be based on your experience, but the first and third statements are based on historical records. For example, your past record shows that you never failed the maths test in the past; hence, you are eliminating the chance of failing this time.

The term 'probability' can, therefore, be defined as the percentage that an event occurs in a number of times. In observational or experimental studies, if 1000 tosses of a coin result in 529 heads, the relative frequency of heads is $529/1000 = 0.529$. If another 1000 tosses result in 493 heads, the relative frequency in the total of 2000 tosses is $(529 + 493)/2000 = 0.511$. According to the statistical definitions, by continuing in this manner we should ultimately get closer and closer to a number which we call the probability of a head in a single toss of the coin. From results so far presented this should be 0.5 to one significant figure. To obtain more significant figures, further observations/experiments must be made.

Similarly, scientific and attitudinal research, related to the built environment, can be based on primarily probabilistic or indicative explanation. For example, a researcher might state that traditional contracts will most probably overrun on cost. His/her rationale is that, from past project records, in 8 out of 10 occasions the project exceeded the budget when using the traditional form of contract. But how significant is your result, that is, how confident or sure are you of arriving at this concluding remark? The answer to this is: you have to apply statistical tests to determine the direction of your research. Chapter 8 provides details of the most popular statistical tests for the level of students reading this book.

Note to students

The statistical tests discussed in Chapter 8 will provide you with a probability that allows you to judge whether your results are significant or are due to chance. Later, you will find out that all the given examples will end up by stating the probability figure of the statistical test. For instance, you will come across an expression $P < 0.05$. This means that the probability of a result being due to chance is less than 5 per cent, or 5 in 100. Another, $P < 0.01$, means that the probability of a result being due to chance is less than 1 per cent, or 1 in 100, and so on. Therefore, the lower the probability figure the more confident you can be in concluding that there is a significant difference applied to your data.

The conventional level at which you can reject the null hypothesis and conclude that the results are significant is $P < 0.05$. Otherwise, the results of your test are not significant and you have to accept the null hypothesis of no relationship or association between the research variables.

Summary

This chapter discussed the level of data measurements and explained the term 'probability'. Measurement is a procedure in which you assign numerals (numbers or other symbols) to empirical properties (i.e. variables) according to rules. There are four levels of measurement and the data that you will collect should fall within one or more of these levels. The four levels are known as nominal, ordinal, interval and ratio. The nominal level implies belonging to a classification or having a label and does not imply any rank or priority. The ordinal level refers to data that are ranked or rated in ascending or descending order. The interval level is when you have a set of observations in which the distance between each observation is constant (e.g. minutes, kilograms and exam results). The ratio level is similar to the interval except it involves a natural zero.

The term 'probability' is defined as the percentage that an event occurs in a number of times. It is calculated to determine the direction of your study. The statistical tests that are explained in Chapter 8 will allow you to establish the confidence level of your research by testing the hypothesis. The probability figure, which is calculated using the statistical tests, will give you a level of significance by which you can judge whether to approve or disprove your research hypothesis.

Additional reading

Farrell, P., Sherratt, F. and Richardson, A. (2017) *Writing Built Environment Dissertations and Projects – Practical Guidance and Examples.* 2nd edn. Wiley Blackwell, Chichester. *Read Chapter 4 – Sections 4.15 (Examples of ordinal data in construction) and 4.16 (Examples of interval and ratio data in construction).*

8   *Analysis of the results*

Once you have collected the data, you will be ready to analyse the results to determine the direction of the study. You will be gathering a lot of information, which makes it difficult to present every bit of it. Therefore, it is expected that you give a summary of the data which highlights main trends and differences in the most appropriate manner. At this stage of your research study, you will ask yourself a number of questions. For example, will I use a frequency distribution table or a bar chart to analyse each question in the questionnaire? Will I use a total score or should I analyse the data separately for each item in the questionnaire or rating scale? Which is the most appropriate test to use with the data: the *t*-test or the chi-square test? Should I compute some rank order correlation? Once you and your supervisor are satisfied with the answers to these questions, you can apply the statistics to find out if there are significant results.

This chapter describes, with examples, the methods of analysis that are commonly used to summarise and organise the data in a most effective and meaningful way. The chapter will cover the following:

- exploratory data analysis (open-ended questions).
- the descriptive method of analysis, including measurement of central tendency, the normal curve and the frequency distribution.
- the inferential statistical method of analysis, including the *t*-test, chi-square test, Spearman 'rho' ranking correlation and the product–moment correlation coefficient.

The contents of Chapter 8 are illustrated in Figure 8.1.

Exploratory data analysis (open-ended questions)

As discussed in Chapter 4, exploratory research is a type of qualitative research and can be described as social or organisational behaviour research which produces results that are not obtained by statistical procedures or other methods of quantification. This type of data analysis refers to research about people's lives, their stories and behaviour, and it can also be used to examine organisations, relationships and social movements. Some of the data may be quantified afterwards, but the analysis is qualitative.

Research carried out in this way produces descriptive data such as people's own spoken or written words or observable behaviour. (Note that observational

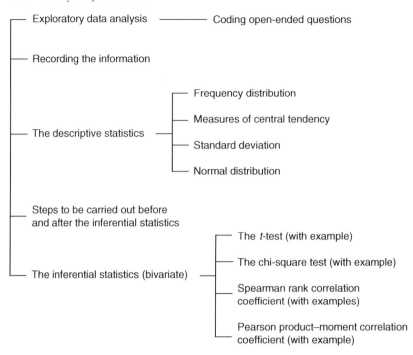

Figure 8.1   *Contents of Chapter 8.*

and experimental studies are not covered in this book.) The instrument or tool that is often used to collect exploratory research data is the open-ended type of questionnaire. The following section explains the procedure for processing open-ended questions.

Coding open-ended questions

Open-ended questions can be used in postal questionnaires as well as in interviews. The usual reason for using open-ended questions is that the researcher has no clear hypotheses regarding answers, which will be numerous and varied. Analysis of the open-ended questions can be rather complicated and not as straightforward as structured closed-ended questionnaires. It also requires great skill to accurately report the information.

The best way to analyse open-ended questions is to code the information in terms of ideas and themes. The purpose of coding such questions is to reduce the large number of individual responses to a few general categories of answers that can be assigned a numerical code. In order to analyse open-ended questionnaires, the following steps can be taken:

1   Place all similar answers in a general category and assign them a code. For example, individual clients asked about the use of construction management for their projects might give the following answers:

a   We build large and complex projects.
b   We want to have good control on the project.
c   It is quicker.
d   Construction management provides high integration.

   All of these answers can be categorised under 'favourable to construction management'. Other clients might give the following answers:

a   We build housing projects.
b   We are not sophisticated clients.
c   It is too risky.
d   It is not a straightforward process as with the JCT contract.

   All of these answers can be categorised under 'unfavourable to construction management'.

2   After establishing the general categories, you then need to divide them into, say, two to four sub-categories, and assign them a code. Coding is the process of identifying and classifying each answer with a numerical score or other character symbol. It usually involves entering the data for analysis or for computer storage. The coding categories should be exhaustive and provide for all possible responses. They should be mutually exclusive and independent so that there is no overlap among categories. On highly structured questionnaires, the categories may be pre-coded. With open-ended questions, the answers are post-coded. This means that the categories are assigned after the data have been collected. The categories must be assigned according to your judgement. It is better to assign too many categories than too few because it is easier to collapse several categories into one than to increase the number of categories (Zikmund, 1997). Table 8.1 shows an example of constructing categories and sub-categories to an open-ended question and devising their coding scheme. These categories are for clients' responses to a question that asked for comments about the use of construction management for their projects.

3   After establishing the coding, choose the method of analysis which you think is suitable for your data (descriptive and/or inferential method). These methods are described later in this chapter. The suitability of each method depends on the nature of data, the type of measurement and your sample size.

Recording the information

Recording the information is an important step in the research process. Before starting any form of analysis you need to devise a data summary sheet for your data. The actual process of transferring the data from the questionnaire or data collection form (after the data have been collected) into a data summary form is called the 'recording scheme' or 'production coding'. Table 8.2 is an example of a data summary form. (See also section 3 in Appendix 5: SPSS data entry.)

   The first column of the data summary form is usually designated for the respondent's number. The rest of the columns represent the coded answers to the questions in the questionnaire. For example, question 1 in Table 8.2 may

Table 8.1   *Example of coding open-ended questions*

Favourable to construction management

Sub-category 1 – Team relationship code	Sub-category 2 – Project control code
10 Smooth running project	20 High control on subcontractors
11 Right attitude of team members	21 High control on safety
12 Contract of trust	22 Good control on variations
13 High integration	23 Good control on quality
14 Good communication	24
15	25
…	…
19 Other team relationship	29 Other project control
Sub-category 3 – Project outcome code	**Sub-category 4 – Miscellaneous code**
31 Would not change the project objectives	41 Good for complex projects
32 High certainty on programme time	42 Architects recommended
33 High certainty on project cost	43 Concentrates on client needs
34 Safer project	44 Would not cut corners
36	46
…	…
30 Other project outcome	49 Other miscellaneous

Unfavourable to construction management

Sub-category 5 – Team relationship code	Sub-category 6 – Project control code
50 Too complicated	61 Difficult to control the programme
51 Does not eliminate 'them and us' attitude	62 Does not control subcontractors
	63 Difficult to control supervisors
52 Conflict with the professionals	64
53	65
54	…
…	69 Other project control
59 Other team relationship	
Sub-category 7 – Project outcome code	**Sub-category 8 – Miscellaneous code**
71 Expensive method	81 Do not like the concept
72 Not economical for small projects	82 Use what our architect recommends
73 Too risky to clients	83 No universal accepted contract
74	84 The concept comes in different formats
75	85 Difficult to define and agree the work packages
…	…
79 Other project outcome	89 Other miscellaneous

be an opinion question requiring the respondent to indicate strong agreement (coded 3), neither agreement nor disagreement (coded 2) or strong disagreement (coded 1). Question 2 may require a response of 'Yes' (coded 1) or 'No' (coded 2) and so on.

☞ **Also see Table 4.6 in Farrell et al. (2017, p. 92) on an example of 'scoring judgements for ten bricklayers based on eight criteria; scoring range 1 to 5 with 1 as the best score'.**

Table 8.2 *Example of a data summary form (see also section 3 in Appendix 5: SPSS data entry)*

	Question 1	Question 2	Question 3	Question 4...	Question 30
	Code number	Code number	Code number	Code number	Code number
Respondent number	1 2 3	1 2	1 2 3	1 2 3	1 2 3
1	3	1	1	2	3
2	3	2	3	3	3
3	2	2	1	3	3
4	2	2	3	3	3
5	3	2	3	3	3
6	3	2	3	3	3
...					
37	1	2	2	1	2

Notes to students

- The principle of the data summary form can be applied to open-ended questions (post-coded) as well as to closed-ended questions (pre-coded).
- The data summary form is usually inserted in the appendix of your dissertation because the data it includes are known as 'raw data'.

After recording the information, the field of statistics can be applied to the raw data so that some kind of interpretation and discussion can be made on the results. There are two methods you can use to analyse your data: the descriptive statistics method and the inferential statistics method (also known as bivariate statistical analysis). Both are explained next.

The descriptive statistics method

The descriptive statistics method is the simplest method of analysis, which provides a general overview of the results. It gives an idea of what is happening. The descriptive method will either analyse the responses in percentages (as in the case of a large sample) or contain actual numbers (as in the case of a small sample). In this section, I shall introduce three formal terms which are used to describe aspects of a group of data: these are 'frequency distribution', 'measurement of central tendency' and 'measurement of dispersion'.

Frequency distribution

When summarising large numbers of raw data, it is often useful to distribute the data into categories or classes and to determine the number of individuals or cases belonging to each category. This is called 'category frequency'. It can be presented in the form of tabulation, a bar chart, a pie chart or a graph.

Tabulation

Tabulation is the simplest way to show the frequency of observations of each response to each variable under investigation. To conduct a frequency distribution you simply list the categories of the variable and count the number of observations in each. Table 8.3 shows the frequency distribution of the results related to 'an investigation of the marketing philosophy of private house-builders'. In this example, out of the 37 house-builders, eight respondents fall into category A and 29 respondents fall into category B. The frequencies can then be converted into percentages of the total number. Therefore, about 20 per cent of the house-builders believed that their firm's business philosophy is to 'first build the estate and then work out how best to sell the product' (i.e. category A), whereas 80 per cent believed that they 'first determine customers' wants and then design the product types and packages to satisfy those wants' (i.e. category B).

The other type of frequency is when two or more different categories of people respond to the questionnaire and the sample is small. For example, Table 8.4 shows results of clients' satisfaction on the performance of time of construction management contracts.

Notice that Table 8.4 shows only the actual frequencies with no percentages. It is important to use actual numbers when the sample is small as in the case of limited interviews. This is because a statement on the aforementioned figures, such as '80 per cent of public clients were highly satisfied with the time of construction management', is factually accurate but can be misleading as the reader will assume a much larger total number of public clients than five.

Table 8.3 *Frequency distribution of marketing philosophy*

Question	No. of respondents in Category A: 'We first build the estate and then work out how best to sell the product'	%	No. of respondents in Category B: 'We first determine customers' wants and then design the product'	%
In the house-building cycle, which action best describes your firm's business philosophy?	8	20	29	80

Table 8.4 *Level of clients' satisfaction on the performance of time of construction management contracts*

	High	Low	Total
Public clients (n = 5)	4	1	5
Private clients (n = 10)	7	3	10
Total	11	4	15

n, number of sample.

Table 8.5 is an example of a frequency distribution applied for analysing secondary data collection. In this particular example, the data are the frequency of accidents record, published by the HSE, of 12 occupations.

Bar charts/histograms

Horizontal or vertical bar charts can be used with the frequency distribution table or as an alternative method of presentation in the dissertation. Figure 8.2 is a bar chart for the data presented in Table 8.5. The variable 'worker occupation' is placed on the horizontal axis and the percentage frequency on the vertical axis. The actual frequencies are included at the top of the bars and the total frequency of $n = 1798$ for major accidents and $n = 9375$ for minor accidents is stated in the conventional format. The height of the bars indicates the proportion of the frequency.

Pie charts

Another method of presentation that is widely used is the pie chart. The areas of the pie chart represent the proportion of the respondents and are usually presented as percentages. Figure 8.3 is a pie chart representing the percentages of alternative contractual arrangements as part of a survey.

Note to students

The method of presentation chosen (tabulation, compound bar chart, component bar chart, graph or pie chart) depends on your judgement of which presentation is the clearest. Remember, always consult your supervisor.

☞ **Find out more about 'how to create charts' in the *Journey to Dissertation Success for Construction, Property and Architecture Students* by Elizabeth Laycock, Tim Howarth and Paul Watson (2016, Chapter 8, pp. 166–183).**

Table 8.5   *An example of a typical frequency distribution of injuries to employees in the construction industry based on secondary data gathered by the HSE's Field Operations Division (see raw data in Appendix 4)*

Worker occupation	No. of major accidents	%	No. of minor accidents	%
Bricklayer	72	4.0	550	5.9
Carpenter/joiner	136	7.5	1127	12.1
Electrician	108	6.0	330	3.5
Ground worker	58	3.2	139	1.5
Pavior	39	2.2	443	4.7
Scaffolder	62	3.5	222	2.4
Road worker	64	3.6	195	2.1
Driver	120	6.7	539	5.7
Labourer	316	17.6	1659	17.7
Maintenance	60	3.3	294	3.1
Manual production	104	5.8	548	5.8
Other	659	36.6	3329	35.5
Total	1798	100.0	9375	100.0

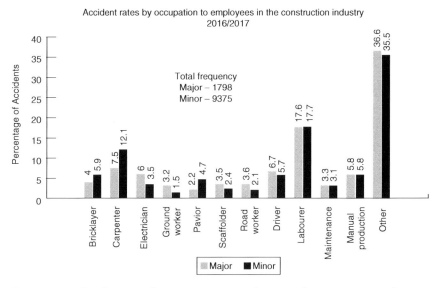

Figure 8.2   *Accident rates by occupation to employees in the construction industry.*

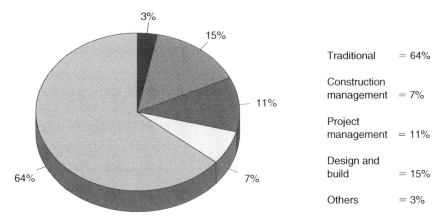

Figure 8.3   *Breakdown of procurement methods in the UK.*

Measurement of central tendency

This type of analysis is applied when you have a group of data and you wish to find the most typical value for the group, or the score which all other scores are evenly clustered around. These statistics are known as the 'mean', the 'median' and the 'mode'.

The mean

This is the average of all the values in a set of data. The mean is calculated by adding all the values in the group and then dividing by the number of values.

Hence, the arithmetic mean of the cost per square metre of five contracts £564, £505, £556, £445 and £530 is taken as:

$$\frac{564+505+556+445+530}{5} = \frac{2600}{5} = £520$$

The median

The median of a set of numbers arranged in order of magnitude (i.e. in an array) is the middle value or the arithmetic mean of the two middle values. To establish the median you need to arrange the set of data in an array. Hence, the array of the same set of numbers is 445, 505, 530, 556, 564 and the median is, hence, 530.

The mode

The mode of a set of numbers is the value which occurs with the greatest frequency (i.e. the most common value). The mode may not exist, and if it does exist it may not be unique. For example:

1 The set 220, 220, 500, 700, 900, 900, 900, 1000, 1000, 1100, 1200 has mode 900.
2 The set 300, 500, 800, 1000, 1200, 1500, 1600 has no mode.
3 The set 200, 300, 400, 400, 400, 500, 500, 700, 700, 700, 900 has two modes, 400 and 700.

Measurement of dispersion based on the mean

This type of analysis can show you the degree by which numerical data tend to spread about an average value, known as 'variation' or 'dispersion'. This is represented by the formula:

$$\text{Mean deviation} = \frac{\Sigma(X - \bar{X})}{N}$$

Hence, if the cost per square metre of five projects was taken and the results were £505.00, £557.00, £465.00, £458.00 and £530.00, the mean deviation can be calculated as follows:

Arithmetic Mean = £503.00

$$\frac{|505-503|+|557-503|+|465-503|+|458-503|+|530-503|}{5} = \frac{141}{5} = 28.2$$

Standard deviation

The standard deviation is another measure of the degree in which the data are spread around the mean. The theoretical basis of the standard deviation is complex and need not trouble the ordinary user (most scientific calculators have a function to calculate the standard deviation). However, a practical point to note is that the data should fall approximately into a so-called 'normal distribution'. When it does so, the standard deviation provides a useful basis for interpreting the data in terms of probability (see 'Probability statement' in Chapter 7).

The formula for the Standard Deviation (SD) is:

$$SD = \sqrt{\frac{\Sigma(X - \bar{X})}{N}}$$

Hence, the SD for the five-unit cost is £35.70.

Normal distribution

Normal distribution is an important expression in the field of statistics because the selection of some inferential statistics depends on whether or not the data are normally distributed. The normal distribution curve can tell you a great deal about the scatter or distribution of the data (see Figure 8.4). The principal properties of the normal distribution curve are as follows (Nachmias and Nachmias, 1996):

- It is symmetrical and bell-shaped.
- The mode, the median and the mean coincide at the centre of the distribution.
- The curve is based on an infinite number of observations.
- A single mathematical formula describes how frequencies are related to the value of the variable.
- In any normal distribution, a fixed proportion of the observations lies between the mean and fixed units of the standard deviation. A range covered by one standard deviation above the mean and one deviation below ($X \pm 1SD$) includes about 68 per cent of the observations. A range of 2 standard deviations above and 2 below ($X \pm 2SD$) includes about 95 per cent of the observations. And a range of 3 standard deviations above and 3 below ($X \pm 3SD$) includes about 99.73 per cent of the observations. Consequently, if you know the mean and standard deviation of a set of observations, you can obtain some useful information by simple arithmetic. By putting 1, 2 or 3 standard deviations above and below the mean you can estimate the ranges that would be expected to include about 68 per cent, 95 per cent and 99.7 per cent of the observations.

The inferential statistics method (also known as bivariate statistical analysis)

Many survey analyses entail the comparison of results for different parts of the sample, for example, the proportion of traditional contracts that overrun on time versus the proportion of design and build contracts that overrun on time. In this case, one might carry out a statistical significance test of the difference between the proportions. Statistical tests vary in their applications. Some tests are appropriate for testing differences in scores; other tests are suitable for assessing whether

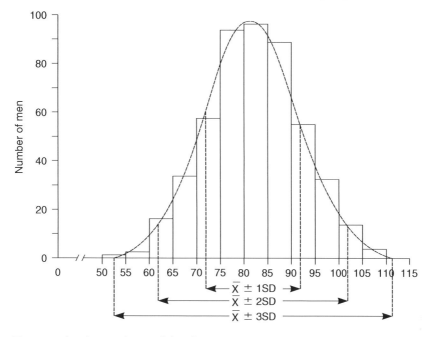

Figure 8.4 *A typical normal distribution curve.*

two sets of scores are correlated. For example, if you have two samples of normally distributed data and you want to find out whether there is a significant differ-ence in the mean between the two samples, then you choose the *t*-test. If you have two or more categories of people and you want to find out whether there is significant difference in their attitude towards certain issues, then you use the chi-square test. If two groups of people are ranking a range of criteria and you want to know whether the differences in their ranking are significant, you will apply a ranking correlation (rho) and so on. The following sections will describe these tests in detail. Other statistical tests are also available but they are left for you to review. However, before describing these tests, there are five steps that you need to consider.

Steps to be carried out before and after the inferential (bivariate) statistical tests

Step 1: Formulate your research hypothesis in terms of the predicted results (like the one stated in your proposal)

See examples in Appendix 1.

Step 2: State the null hypothesis

The null hypothesis is a statement that you make which is the antithesis of your research hypotheses. It is usually an expression of no difference or no relationship between the variables. Suppose that the research hypothesis (H_1) states: 'Projects delivered under the traditional contracts are more expensive than similar projects delivered under the design and build contracts'. With the mean score for the cost of projects delivered under the traditional contracts designated as X_1 and in the design and build contracts as X_2, the research hypothesis, symbolised by H_1, will be:

$$H_1 : X_1 > X_2$$

The null hypothesis, symbolised by H_0 will be:

$$H_0 : X_1 > X_2$$

This means that your null hypothesis states: 'There is no significant difference in the mean cost between traditional contracts and the design and build contracts'. After applying the appropriate test you will find out whether your null hypothesis is true or false.

Step 3: Decide which test to use

Choose the appropriate statistical test for your data to determine the direction of your investigation. There are two main kinds of statistical tests that you can apply, known as 'parametric' and 'non-parametric' tests. A parametric test is a statistical test based on several assumptions about the parameters of the population from which the sample was drawn. To apply a parametric test, your data must comply with certain conditions. Among the most important conditions are the assumptions that the observations must be drawn from a normally distributed population and be of an interval scale (see the earlier discussion of normal distribution) whereas a non-parametric test does not specify the normality condition. There are certain assumptions associated with most non-parametric tests; however, they are weaker than those associated with parametric tests. I will introduce the rationale, the rules and the steps to apply for each test as I go along.

When deciding the significance of your results, also include tests for correlation. These kinds of tests measure the strength of the relationship between two or more variables and are usually applied on analytical studies. I will introduce the 'Spearman rank correlation' and 'Pearson product–moment correlation', as they are the most common tests and suitable for the level of students reading this book.

Step 4: Calculate and obtain the test statistics

After you decide on the test, you need to carry out the appropriate calculations on your research data. There are two ways in which you can carry out the calculations:

1 Manually.
2 Using a software package such as SPSS, Minitab or Statsmaster. These packages are easy to learn and, once you get the hang of using them, you will find

it very easy to analyse your data in a matter of seconds. All you need to do is to input your data from the data summary form (see Table 8.2) into the software spreadsheet and then select the appropriate statistics to carry out the calculations. Details of the SPSS package are described in this book on page 147 and also in Appendix 5.

Step 5: Decide whether the result is significant (depending on significant level set)

Whichever type of statistical test you use, you will end up with a figure which is calculated earlier in Step 4. You then need to look in the statistical tables appropriate to that particular test to find out where your calculated figure falls. Each statistical table contains critical values against which the calculated figure can be compared. If your calculated figure is less than the critical value, then the results of your research are not significant and you should therefore accept your null hypothesis. If your calculated figure is equal to or more than the critical value in the statistical table, then the results of your research are significant; therefore, reject the null hypothesis.

Appendix 3 gives four different statistical tables which correspond to the four statistical tests that will be described later. In certain statistical tables, such as the *t*-distribution and the chi-square, you will find the expression 'df'. This means 'degrees of freedom'. Degrees of freedom is a dimension that is used to find the critical value in the statistical tables. Sometimes it is determined by the number of subjects (respondents), sometimes by the number of subjects minus 1, and sometimes by the number of categories. However, you need not worry too much about the notion of degree of freedom or how to use the statistical tables. You will be guided on exactly what to do whenever degrees of freedom come up in connection with a statistical test.

There is one further point about the statistical inferential method and that is whether the research hypothesis is 'one tailed' or 'two tailed'. The point is that for a hypothesis which predicts a difference in only one direction (one tailed), there is a specified percentage probability that the difference might occur by chance but, if your research hypothesis makes a prediction that a difference might occur in either direction (two tailed), then there is double the probability that such differences might occur by chance. In the two-tailed condition, there is the probability that a difference might occur in one direction plus the probability that a difference might occur in the other direction. However, you do not need to worry too much about the one-tailed and two-tailed notions; you can always use the probability level of the one-tailed direction.

Note to students

The following statistical tests discussed will provide you with a probability that allows you to judge whether your results are significant or are due to chance. Later, you will find out that all the worked examples will end up by stating the probability figure of the statistical test. For instance, you will come across the expression $P < 0.05$. This means that the probability of a result being due to chance is less than 5 per cent, or 5 in 100. Another, $P < 0.01$, means that the probability of a result being due to chance is less than 1 per cent, or 1 in 100, and so on. Therefore, the lower the probability figure the more confident you can be in concluding that there is a significant difference applicable to your data.

The conventional level by which you can reject the null hypothesis and conclude that the results are significant is $P < 0.05$. Otherwise, the results of your test are not significant and you have to accept the null hypothesis of no relationship or association between the research variables or issues under investigation.

Parametric test (the t-test)

The *t*-test is a parametric test which is used to compare the difference between the mean scores of two samples.

Example

Table 8.6 gives results of the unit cost of two samples of projects completed over the same period of time and they were of a similar type. All projects were office blocks, reinforced concrete structure and of medium-sized projects, costing between £5 million and £10 million. However, one sample was taken from projects delivered using the design and build method of contracting and the other sample was taken from projects delivered using the traditional method of contracting. The aim of the research was to determine whether unit costs of Sample 1 (design and build projects) differ significantly from those of Sample 2 (traditional projects). Following the directions given in the previous section, the following steps were taken:

1   Formulate the research hypothesis: 'The unit cost of projects delivered under the traditional form of contract (X_1) is higher than similar projects delivered under the design and build contracts (X_2)'. H_1 states that $X_1 > X_2$.
2   By implication, the null hypothesis is: 'There is no significant difference in the unit cost between the two samples'. H_0 states that $X_1 = X_2$.
3   The *t*-test is the most suitable test for this type of problem. The rationale for using this test is that: (a) The data are of an integer type (see definition in Chapter 7). (b) The problem is to compare the mean of two samples. (c) The samples are normally distributed. Note that, for the level of students reading this book, normality is not a strict condition.
4   Carry out the calculation (if not using the SPSS software package). In order for the mean unit cost of the two samples to be significant, the calculated value of *t* has to be equal to or larger than the critical values of *t* given in Table A in Appendix 3. There are a number of formulas by which *t* can be calculated. This depends on whether the sample is small or large and whether it covers related or unrelated subjects. To simplify matters for students reading this book, *t* will be calculated by applying the following formula:

$$t = \frac{\overline{X}_1 - \overline{X}_2}{\sqrt{\dfrac{(SD_1)^2}{n_1} + \dfrac{(SD_2)^2}{n_2}}}$$

where

$\overline{X}_1$ = mean for sample 1	$\overline{X}_1$ = 512.6
$\overline{X}_2$ = mean for sample 2	$\overline{X}_2$ = 528.5
SD_1 = standard deviation for sample 1	SD_1 = 50.8
SD_2 = standard deviation for sample 2	SD_2 = 61.9
n_1 = number of subjects in sample 1	n_1 = 10
n_2 = number of subjects in sample 2	n_2 = 10

The standard deviation can be calculated using the formula given in the previous section. However, most calculators can work out the SD in a matter of seconds so you can use one here. Therefore, in this example:

$$t = \frac{512.6 - 528.5}{\sqrt{\frac{(50.8)^2}{10} + \frac{(61.9)^2}{10}}} = 0.63$$

5   Look up the significance of *t* in Table A of Appendix 3, taking into account the degrees of freedom, to see whether your result is significant.

For the *t*-test,

$$df = (n_1 - 1) + (n_2 - 1)$$
$$= (10 - 1) + (10 - 1) = 18$$

Look down the left-hand column of Table A to find the df (in this example 18). Then look along the row to see whether the calculated value of *t* is larger or equal to the critical values in the statistical table. In this example *t* = 0.63, which is much smaller than the critical value of 2.10.

Table 8.6 *Cost per square metre obtained from design and build projects and traditional projects*

Sample 1 (design and build projects) Unit cost (£) (X_1)	Sample 2 (traditional projects) Unit cost (£) (X_2)
564.00	505.00
521.00	557.00
445.00	465.00
560.00	458.00
480.00	530.00
540.00	480.00
585.00	665.00
426.00	525.00
530.00	605.00
475.00	495.00
X_1 = £512.60	X_2 = £528.50

From these findings, one can say that the null hypothesis (of no difference) has to be accepted and conclude that there is no significant difference in the unit cost between projects delivered using the design and build contracts and those using the traditional form of contracts.

Note to students

If the calculated value falls between two critical values in the statistical table, say $t = 2.4$, you should use the expression $0.05 < P < 0.02$ for a one-tailed hypothesis.

Non-parametric test (the chi-square test)

The chi-square (symbolised as χ^2) is a test of association between two sets of data and can be used only when the data are nominal or ordinal. It predicts how many subjects in each group will fall into certain categories. Therefore, you have to test quite a number of subjects to make sure that a sufficient number of subjects turn out to be allocated to each category. Most statisticians consider 20 subjects to be the minimum number required in order to apply the chi-square test.

Example

This example is related to Proposal 1 in Appendix 1, that is, to find out whether companies that performed well financially also had a business philosophy different from those that performed badly financially. Table 8.7 shows the data that were gathered from 37 companies. Financial performance was categorised as high

Table 8.7 *Business philosophy and company performance*

Company	Business philosophy	Financial performance	Company	Business philosophy	Financial performance
1	1	2	20	1	2
2	2	2	21	2	2
3	1	2	22	2	1
4	2	2	23	2	2
5	1	2	24	1	1
6	2	2	25	1	1
7	1	1	26	1	1
8	2	1	27	2	1
9	2	2	28	2	2
10	2	2	29	1	1
11	2	2	30	1	1
12	2	2	31	1	1
13	1	2	32	1	1
14	2	2	33	2	2
15	2	2	34	1	1
16	2	2	35	2	2
17	2	1	36	2	1
18	2	1	37	2	2
19	2	2			

(given numerate 2) or low (given numerate 1). The measurements of high and low were based on the annual profit of the companies. On the other hand, the business philosophy of each of the 37 companies was categorised as marketing oriented (given numerate 2) or production oriented (given numerate 1). The question at issue here is whether business philosophy and financial performance 'go' together or there is no association between the two variables. Following the direction just given, the following steps were taken.

1   Formulate the research hypothesis: 'The type of business philosophy can have an effect on the financial performance of the private house-builders'.
2   By implication, the null hypothesis is: 'The financial performance of private house-builders that have a marketing-oriented philosophy does not differ from those that have a production-oriented philosophy'.
3   The chi-square test is appropriate for this kind of problem. The rationale for using this test is that:
    a   The data are nominal (see definition in Chapter 7).
    b   The research subjects (private house-builders) can be allocated into categories. In this example, there are two categories.
    c   The sample is quite large (37 subjects).
4   Carry out the calculation (if not using a computer). In order for the financial performance of the two categories to differ significantly, the calculated value of χ^2 has to be equal to or larger than the critical values of χ^2 given in Table B of Appendix 3. To calculate χ^2 manually you need to take the following steps:
    a   From the data summary sheet in Table 8.6, allocate the replies into one of the two categories, high financial performance or low financial performance. The results are shown in the form of a 2 × 2 table known as a 'contingency' table. The cells representing each of the categories are numbered 1 to 4 in Table 8.8. Remember that the figures in the table represent the number of subjects that fall into each category; they are not scores or percentages. For example, in the first top right cell, the number 6 means that in the sample there are six companies that performed low financially and also have a marketing-oriented philosophy (check the rest by yourself).

Note to students

The rationale of the chi-square test is that it compares the 'observed' frequencies (O) in each of the squares (cells) of the contingency table with the 'expected' frequencies (E) for each cell if the differences are due to chance, as stated in the null hypothesis. In other words, the test compares the actual numbers of subjects (private house-builders) that fall into each cell as against the numbers of subjects we would expect to fall into each cell if there were, in fact, no differences between the financial performance of the two types of subjects (i.e. the marketing-oriented companies and the production-oriented companies). The observed frequencies are already known from the investigation (as shown in Table 8.8). Therefore, the expected frequencies need to be calculated. If the observed frequencies are close to the expected frequency, then the results are not significant. However, if

Table 8.8 *Contingency table between business philosophy and financial performance*

	High financial performance (2)	Low financial performance (1)	Total
	1	2	
Marketing oriented (2)	17	6	23
	$E = 13.67$	$E = 9.32$	
	3	4	
Production oriented (1)	5	9	14
	$E = 8.32$	$E = 5.67$	
Total	22	15	37

Chi-square = 5.67.

the differences between the observed frequency and the expected frequencies are large, then the research hypothesis is supported. Therefore, the larger χ^2, the more significant are the results, so the computed value of χ^2 should be equal to or larger than the critical values in Table B of Appendix 3.

b   To calculate the expected frequency (E) for each cell, follow this procedure:
  i   Add the total observed frequencies for the rows and columns. In this example, they are equal to 23, 14, 22, 15. Here, the grand total is 37 (23 + 14 for rows) and (22 + 15 for columns) – see Table 8.8.
  ii   Multiply the two relevant marginal totals for each cell and divide by the total number of subjects N. Therefore, for Cell 1: the expected frequency (E) = 22 × 23/37 = 13.67, Cell 2: E = 15 × 23/37 = 9.32, Cell 3: E = 22 × 14/37 = 8.32, Cell 4: E = 15 × 14/37 = 5.67.
  iii   Find the value of chi-square from the formula

$$\chi^2 = \sum (O - E)^2 / E$$

where O = observed frequencies for each cell (as shown in Table 8.8) E = expected frequencies for each cell (as calculated earlier) Σ = add up the results of $(O-E)^2/E$ calculated for each cell. Chi-square = 5.26. Therefore,

$$\chi^2 = \frac{(17-13.67)^2}{13.67} + \frac{(6-9.32)^2}{9.32} + \frac{(5-8.32)^2}{8.32} + \frac{(9-5.67)^2}{5.67}$$

$$= 0.81 + 1.18 + 1.32 + 1.95 = 5.26$$

5 Look up the significance of χ^2 in Table B of Appendix 3, taking into account degrees of freedom, to see whether your result is significant.

6 For the χ^2, the degree of freedom (df) = $(r-1)(c-1)$, where r = number or rows in contingency Table 8.8 ($r = 2$)c = number of columns in contingency Table 8.8 ($c = 2$). Therefore, df = $(2-1)(2-1) = 1$.

Table B gives critical values against which the calculated value of χ^2 can be compared. The level of significance depends on the degrees of freedom (df). In this example, df = 1 so we should look along that row in Table B. Since our calculated value of χ^2 is 5.26 and so is larger than the critical value of 3.84 for $P < 0.05$, the results of this research are significant.

From this finding, one can say that the null hypothesis (of no difference) has to be rejected and conclude that there is a significant difference in the financial performance between house-builders that had a marketing-oriented philosophy and those that had a production-oriented philosophy.

Notes to students

- In this example, the calculated value of χ^2 falls between two critical values in the statistical table (between 0.05 and 0.02). In this case, we use the expression $0.02 < P < 0.05$.
- Remember, it is absolutely essential to make comments on and interpretations of your findings after the analysis. What do your findings tell you? What do they mean? Do they correspond closely with previous studies or not? Chapter 9 provides you with guidance on how to comment and interpret your results.

Spearman rank correlation coefficient

The Spearman rho correlation is a non-parametric test for measuring the difference in ranking between two groups of respondents scoring a number of issues, attributes or factors. The test can be applied when:

- The question is requesting a ranking value like that in Table 6.9 page 100 and Table 6.10 on page 101.
- The question is requesting a scoring value and the scores are then converted into rankings like that in Table 6.7 on page 98 and Table 6.8 on page 100.
- The question is requesting rating values and the ratings are converted into rankings like those in Table 6.5 on page 94 and Table 6.6 on page 96.

Example 1

Consider the question in Table 8.9 on page 135. The researcher sent the questionnaire to site operatives of two different industries: to 50 workers in Indonesia and to 50 workers in the UK. The student wanted to find out whether there is a difference in perception between the two groups towards the factors that can affect job satisfaction. Forty-two replies were received from UK workers and 44 replies from Indonesian workers. Table 8.9 shows the data obtained. Column 1 represents the average rank for UK workers and column 2 represents the average rank for the Indonesian workers. Columns 3 and 4 represent the difference in ranks and their squares respectively. The following steps were taken to apply the appropriate test:

1   Formulate the research hypothesis: 'The factors that satisfy workers with their jobs differ between Indonesian workers and UK workers'.
2   By implication, the null hypothesis is: 'There is no significant difference in the ranking of job satisfaction factors between the two industries'.
3   The Spearman rank correlation is an appropriate test for this type of problem. The rationale for using this test is that:
    a   The attitude is measured on an ordinal scale (see definition in Chapter 7).
    b   The problem is to measure the amount and significance of a correlation between people's rank on a number of issues.
4   Carry out the calculation (if not using a computer). Here, the prediction is that, if there is a high positive correlation in opinions between the two groups, then the low ranking of one item by the UK operatives should correspond to low ranking by operatives in Indonesia and vice versa. However, if there is no correlation (as stated by the null hypothesis) the average ranks will be mixed up since one group could have a high ranking on the eight-point scale whereas the other may have a low ranking for the same item. To calculate rho you need to apply the following simple formula:

$$\rho = 1 - \frac{6 \sum d_i^2}{N\left(N^2 - 1\right)}$$

where di = the difference in ranking between each pair of factors, N = number of factors. Therefore, in this example,

$$\rho = 1 - \frac{6(60)}{6(64 - 1)}$$

$$= 1 - \frac{396}{504} = 0.21$$

5   Look up the significance of rho in Table C of Appendix 3, the calculated rho value of 0.21 against the value N (number of factors); in our example $N = 8$, is less than the critical value of 0.643 for $p < 0.05$ in the one-tailed test. Therefore, you can conclude that there is no correlation between the attitudes of the two groups, and the null hypothesis should be accepted. This means that most of the factors that are considered very important to satisfy the UK worker are less important to workers in Indonesia and vice versa.

Note to students

The value of N will be taken as 'number of subjects' if the question or the investigation is of a different format, as in the case of an experimental study. In construction, an example could be when 30 people are asked to rate two different attributes; N will be calculated as the number of subjects that took part in the research, which, in this case, is 30 (see example in section 9.3 of Green and D'Oliveirs's 1993 book).

Example 2

In this example, I will discuss a situation when the question is requesting a rating value and the ratings are converted into ranks (see Table 8.10 on page 136). Here, the student asked two groups of people, namely head office personnel and site managers, to respond to a number of questions by ticking their opinions on a three-point scale. Thirty-six fully completed questionnaires were returned, 19 from contract managers working at head office and 17 from experienced site managers. After receiving the data and recording the information in the data summary sheet, the student assigned scores to the ratings. Highly important = 3 points, moderately important = 2, and less important = 1. Table 8.10 shows results of the survey. Here, the student applied simple arithmetic to convert the average ratings into percentages of actual scores. Hence, Table 8.10 was constructed calculating the maximum possible scores, actual scores and percentage of actual scores for head office respondents and site managers. The maximum possible score for each factor relating to head office respondents is $3 \times 19 = 57$ and for site managers is $3 \times 17 = 51$. For example, ten of the head office personnel thought

Table 8.9 *Average ranking of UK workers and Indonesian workers to factors influencing job satisfaction*

Job satisfaction factor	UK ranks (1)	Indonesia ranks (2)	di(3)	di^2(4)
1 A well-paid job (having a good income and being able to afford the good things in life)	3	1	2	4
2 A prosperous job (having a good opportunity to develop myself)	1	5	4	16
3 An important job (a job full of achievement that brings me respect and recognition)	4	7	3	9
4 A secure job (making certain that I have steady work and steady wages)	2	2	0	0
5 Relationship with fellow workers (getting along well with the people I work with)	8	6	2	4
6 Relationship with superiors (getting along well with my supervisor)	6	4	2	4
7 Job interest (good chance to do work of my interest)	5	3	2	4
8 Working condition (working in a good physical job condition)	3	8	5	25
Total di^2				66

Table 8.10 Ranking of head office personnel and site managers to factors influencing site productivity

Productivity factor	Head office actual scores (%)	Rank (A)	Site managers actual scores (%)	Rank (B)	di (A–B)	di²
1 Delegation of responsibilities	58	24	70	14.5	9.5	90.2
2 Integration of information	77	5	83	3	2.0	4.0
3 Project planning	82	1	85	1	0	0
4 Scheduling of project activities	75	9	75	14.5	5.5	30.2
5 Level of authority	53	27.5	52	29	1.5	2.2
6 Supervision of subordinate	75	9	73	11	2.0	4.0
7 Communication	60	22	78	8.5	13.5	182.0
8 Senior managers' role in contract meetings	75	9	73	11	2.0	4.0
9 Attitude of site personnel	75	9	64	20	11.0	121.0
10 The decision-making process	75	9	64	20	11.0	121.0
11 Procurement of materials	77	5	83	3	2.0	4.0
12 Site programme	77	5	78	8.5	3.5	12.2
13 Accuracy of technical information	67	14.5	81	6	8.5	72.2
14 Fitness of tools for tasks	67	14.5	70	14.5	0	0
15 Knowledge of technology	67	14.5	81	6	8.5	72.2
16 Interference on workmanship	67	14.5	73	11	3.5	12.2
17 Site layout	63	20.5	62	24.5	4.0	16.0
18 Promotion of employee	53	27.5	64	20	7.5	56.2
19 Resentment of company policy	65	18	64	20	2.0	4.0
20 Incentive for good performance	55	26	62	24.5	1.5	2.5
21 Opportunities to exercise skill	39	29	68	17	12.0	144.0
22 Response to employee grievances	58	24	62	24	0	0
23 Uncertainty about career	72	12	70	14.5	2.5	6.25
24 Work environment	81	2	83	3	1.0	1.0
25 Experience of employees	79	3	81	6	3.0	9.0
26 Contract administration skill	65	18	64	20	2.0	4.0
27 Knowledge of techniques	63	20.5	62	24.5	4.0	16.0
28 Training on new technology	58	24	59	27.5	3.5	12.2
29 Availability of skilled personnel	65	18	59	27.5	9.5	90.2
Total di²						1092.7

Note: $\rho = 1 - \dfrac{\sum d_i^2}{N(N^2 - 1)} = 1 - \dfrac{6 \times 1092.7}{29(841 - 1)} = 0.73$, hence, $P < 0.005$

that 'project planning' can highly affect productivity, eight thought moderately and one did not think it has any effect at all.

The actual scores of head office personnel to 'project planning' have then been calculated as:

$$(10 \times 3) + (8 \times 2) + (1 \times 1) = 47$$

Therefore, the percentage of maximum scores was:

$$47 / 57 \times 100 = 82$$

Table 8.10 shows the complete results. The ranking of the 29 factors between the two groups was tested using Spearman's rho, with the correlation found to be significant at $P < 0.005$ (see calculation for rho = 0.73 in the note to Table 8.10). This indicates that high ranking for one productivity factor by one sample, in most cases, corresponds to high ranking by the other sample and vice versa. The research hypothesis, therefore, can be rejected, and the null hypothesis can be accepted, concluding that the difference in opinion between head office personnel and site managers towards factors influencing productivity is not significant.

Pearson product–moment correlation coefficient

The correlation coefficient (r) is a parametric test which is used when you have two sets of scores and you want to calculate whether there is a strong relationship between them. Whereas the Spearman test can be used with any data, the Pearson requires the research data to be measured on an 'interval' scale and to meet the other assumptions for parametric tests. With the Pearson correlation, the relationship can be either positive or negative and the strength of the relationship is measured on a scale that varies from +1 through 0 to −1. When one variable increases as the other increases, the correlation is positive; when one decreases as the other increases, it is negative. The variable can be either factual or perceptional. For example, we would say that the speed of construction is correlated with the unit cost of the building. Since one increases with the other, the correlation is called positive. In contrast, there is a negative correlation between complexity of the building and speed of construction. In other words, the more complex the project, the slower the rate of construction.

After you collect the data, it is best to draw a scatter diagram, which is a graph with axes X and Y corresponding to the two variables being measured. The two variables can represent two dependent factors, two independent factors, or one dependent factor and one independent factor. The scatter diagram should show at a glance whether or not a relationship is likely to exist. Figure 8.5 shows a number of examples.

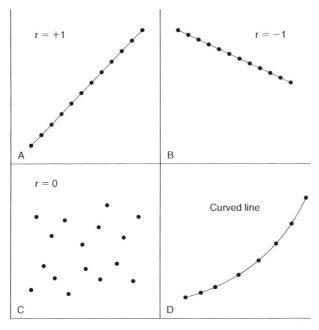

Figure 8.5   *Examples of correlation scatter diagrams.*

Example 1 of Pearson correlation coefficient (manual calculation)

Let us assume that Table 8.11 is a set of data collected by the researcher and he/she wants to assess whether there appears to be a correlation between the two measurements labelled X and Y. For instance, X could be the mathematics marks of the students out of 100 per cent, Y could be the physics marks out of 100 per cent. The question at issue is to find out whether maths performance and being

Table 8.11   *Scores on variables X and Y for 12 subjects*

Number of subject	Variable X	Variable Y	(X) × (Y)	X^2	Y^2
1	65	68	4420	4225	4624
2	63	66	4158	3969	4356
3	67	68	4556	4489	4624
4	64	55	3520	4096	3025
5	68	69	4692	4624	4761
6	62	66	4092	3844	4356
7	70	68	4760	4900	4624
8	66	65	4290	4356	4225
9	68	71	4828	4624	5041
10	67	67	4489	4489	4489
11	69	68	4692	4761	4624
12	71	70	4970	5041	4900
Total	800	801	53467	53418	53649

good at physics 'go' together or there is no connection between the two kinds of ability.

In order to calculate the significance of the correlation, the following steps should be taken:

1 Formulate the research hypothesis: 'Students who are good at maths are also good at physics, students who are average at maths are also average at physics and students who are poor at maths are also poor at physics'.
2 By implication, the null hypothesis is: 'There is no significant relationship between the maths results and physics results'.
3 The Pearson product–moment correlation is an appropriate test to apply. The rationale for using this test is that:
   a The data are of an interval type (see definition in Chapter 7).
   b The problem is to establish a relationship between two variables.
   c The sample is normally distributed. Note that, for the level of students reading this book, normality is not a strict condition.
4 Carry out the calculation of the correlation coefficient (if not using the computer). In order for the scores for the two variables to be highly correlated, the calculated value of r has to be equal to or larger than the critical values of r given in Table D in Appendix 3. The correlation coefficient (r) can be calculated from the following formula:

$$r = \frac{N\sum XY - \sum X \sum Y}{\sqrt{\left[N\sum X^2 - \left(\sum X\right)^2\right]\left[N\sum Y^2 - \left(\sum Y\right)^2\right]}}$$

5 Looking up the significance of r in Table D of Appendix 3, the correlation coefficient of 0.59 indicates a positive correlation between variable X (maths marks) and variable Y (physics). Looking up for significance in Table D of Appendix 3, for df = $(10 - 2)$, the calculated value of 0.59 exceeds the critical value 0.5494 for $P < 0.05$ (one tailed) and therefore the researcher can conclude that there is a significant relationship between the two variables. This means that there is less than 5 per cent probability that it was due to a chance distribution of scores. However, in interpreting correlation it is important to remember that 'correlation is not causation'. There may or may not be a causal connection between the two correlated variables. However, for the level of students reading this book, it will be enough to comment on what was stated in your research hypothesis. In this example, you can say that the research hypothesis is valid and, therefore, reject the null hypothesis, concluding that 'Students who perform well in maths also perform well in physics'. If your dissertation contains a number of findings such as these, then it can be said that your dissertation has substance.

Data analysis using the SPSS (Statistical Package for the Social Sciences) software

SPSS is one of the most widely used statistics analysis packages in providing detailed and comprehensive statistics analysis on various types of data. It can perform all of the statistical tests discussed in this chapter: the *t*-test, chi-square test, Pearson correlation coefficient, ranking correlation, regression analysis and many more tests of significance. The spreadsheet-like interface allows users to enter data easily and to conduct in-depth data analysis.

SPSS is often used in research as a tool to analyse survey/questionnaire feedback. Although the graphics output may not have the level of customisation offered by Excel, it is often used in conjunction with Excel to provide full statistical analyses and professional presentation of data in research reports and dissertations.

Appendix 5 gives a full explanation of the SPSS package.

Worked example of Pearson correlation coefficient (calculated using the SPSS package)

This example is based on research that was conducted at London South Bank University by Tim Whitworth in 2010; the result was later published in the 6th International Structural Engineering and Construction Conference (ISEC – 6) in Zurich, 21–26 June 2011 (see Naoum et al., 2011).

Title of research

Is there a relationship between the lean concept and productivity rate of construction projects?

Aim

To demonstrate in a graphical format the relationship between implementing a lean management initiative and productivity rate of construction projects.

Brief research methodology

Data were collected from 37 randomly selected construction projects across commercial, residential, retail, industrial, health and education sectors through project managers/directors who were members of the Chartered Institute of Building.

Respondents were asked to select answers to 37 questions, which translate into scoring of between 0 (no leanness) and 4 (total leanness). The questions were grouped under nine areas of leanness identified by Taj (2008): project activities, team approach, processes, maintenance, layout, supply chain, start-ups, quality and schedule. An average leanness in terms of percentage is calculated for each area and the final project leanness is assessed based on the average of leanness score for all nine areas, in the same way as computed by Taj (2008) in lean assessment.

Productivity-related data for each project were collected from the same respondents in order to compute the productivity level for a project. In this research, productivity is defined as the output quantity with respect to the input quantity, which is evaluated as the gross floor area (m^2) constructed per week divided by the number of workers involved.

Result

The leanness and productivity scores for all 37 projects are shown in Table 8.12.

Calculating the strength of the relationship using the SPSS package

In order to calculate the significance of the correlation, the following steps were taken:

1 The research hypothesis: 'Projects that implement lean management initiatives will result in a higher rate of productivity on-site'.
2 The null hypothesis is: 'There is no significant relationship between lean construction and productivity rate'.
3 The Pearson product–moment correlation is an appropriate test to apply. The rationale for using this test is the same as in Example 1.
4 Carry out the calculation of the correlation coefficient using the SPSS package as shown in Appendix 5.

Figure 8.6 presents the scatter plot of productivity and leanness for all 37 projects. Pearson correlation analysis shows that there is a strong positive linear relationship between leanness and productivity with r = 0.91 (P < 0.005).

The result signifies a less than 0.5 per cent probability that the relationship was due to a chance distribution of scores. For the purpose of this study, the research hypothesis is proven to be valid, and therefore the null hypothesis can be rejected.

Statistics of the 37 projects were compared with those derived from the manufacturing projects in Taj's study (2008). The leanness score for the 65 manufacturing projects in Taj's research yielded an average score of 55.3 per cent. This represents a moderate level of leanness overall for the manufacturing sector. The expectation that the construction industry is not far behind is evident, as a mean leanness score of 53.5 per cent is obtained from this study. A two-tailed, independent-sampled *t*-test was conducted using SPSS to test the hypothesis that there is no significant difference between the mean leanness scores of manufacturing and construction projects. Levene's test of equality of variances shows that F = 16.6 is significant (p < 0.05) and results from the 'equal variances not assumed' section are used in the comparison of means. A *t*-value of 0.49 at P = 0.63 indicates there is no significant difference between the mean leanness score of construction projects surveyed in this research and that of the manufacturing projects in Taj's study.

Concluding comments of this worked example

Although the focus of construction is heading in the same direction as manufacturing, literature is more advanced in the manufacturing industry. With the trend

Table 8.12   *Construction leanness scores and productivity data*

Project no.	Leanness score (%)	Productivity (m²/man week)
1	39.0	0.21
2	80.6	0.74
3	37.5	0.13
4	35.1	0.14
5	37.3	0.22
6	66.1	0.24
7	60.9	0.51
8	71.0	0.64
9	35.4	0.10
10	60.4	0.53
11	50.0	0.33
12	79.9	1.23
13	70.2	0.63
14	38.8	0.24
15	49.9	0.22
16	80.0	0.83
17	74.7	0.61
18	44.7	0.31
19	43.6	0.13
20	39.7	0.22
21	56.9	0.44
22	28.0	0.21
23	31.9	0.20
24	39.9	0.23
25	82.6	0.94
26	53.4	0.41
27	39.4	0.21
28	42.3	0.23
29	72.7	0.91
30	91.6	1.22
31	54.7	0.30
32	11.0	0.01
33	35.8	0.22
34	25.3	0.12
35	72.9	0.62
36	86.0	0.84
37	60.5	0.43

proving the same and no assessment tool available in the construction industry, the review highlighted that it is viable to transfer the same methodology. In hindsight, more research needs to be carried out in the construction industry in order to investigate in more detail the key assessment areas of lean in construction rather than adapting manufacturing ones.

The research sample provided the study with a broad scope of project, size, type and cost, which resulted in varying degrees of productivity output. The data proved conclusively that there is a strong relationship between a high lean implementation

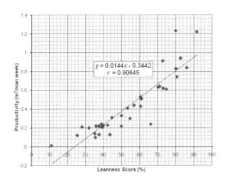

Figure 8.6 *Regression analysis and Pearson product–moment correlation coefficient.*

and high productivity on UK construction sites. The results proved that the probability of a result being due to chance is less than 0.5 per cent, which proves that there is a significant relationship between the two variables.

Lab experiment in civil engineering

If you have conducted a laboratory experiment in civil engineering, this section of the dissertation should show what you have found in your experiment. Your data is manipulated to be presented nicely and explained. Tables, graphs, phonographs and equations (in variable forms) should be used to summarise the results. You need to link equations and visuals together with narrative, like a story. Ben Adams and Professor Will Durfee (2009) provided the following tips in their guide to students on how to write a lab report:

Process tips

- Be concise.
- It is more important you are clear and direct than to follow formatting rules.
- The report organization doesn't follow the way you need to think about it to write it. To help, write a report in the following order: Methods, Results, Discussion, Intro and Abstract.
- Use visuals. Engineering is more than prose writing.
- Be concise. Extra words actually detract from meaning.
- Think of a report as a big string of visuals, linked together by narrative sentences.
- Graphs, Figures, Tables and Equations are all worthy of their own line.
- Avoid showing actual calculations in the body of the report—they are difficult to understand. Keep everything in variable format and show numerical calculations in the appendix.
- Some instructors require more rigorously formatted reports; check with them if you have any questions.

☞ **For more details on how to write a lab report, visit the following site: http:// www.me.umn.edu/education/undergraduate/writing/MESWG-Lab.1.5.pdf**

☞ **For worked examples of presenting laboratory experiments in civil engineering, see section 6.12 in Farrell et al. (2017, pp. 154–163).**

Summary

This chapter explained the methods by which you can analyse the results of your investigation. It explained first the descriptive method and then the inferential method with worked examples.

The descriptive method of analysis includes the frequency distribution, measurement of central tendency and measurement of dispersion. With the descriptive method, you can apply a straightforward calculation to show how the respondents are distributed on all the items of the investigation. For example, 20 per cent of the house-builders believed that their firm's business philosophy is to 'first build the estate and then work out how best to sell the product', whereas 80 per cent believed the opposite. Such breakdowns of percentages or the numbers of observations that fall into each of several categories are termed 'frequency distribution'. The frequency distribution can be illustrated in a table, bar chart, graph or pie chart, all of which are demonstrated in this chapter.

Measures of central tendency are applied when you have a group of data and you wish to find the most typical value for the group or the score which all other scores are evenly clustered around. These statistics are known as the mean, mode and median.

Measurement of dispersion is a type of analysis that can show you the degree by which numerical data tend to spread about an average value. This spreading is called variation, dispersion or standard deviation.

The inferential method of analysis concentrates on the nature of the relationship between two variables and on the construction of measures of relationship. Four types of tests were explained with examples in this chapter: *t*-test, chi-square test, Spearman (rho) ranking correlation and Pearson product–moment correlation (r).

The *t*-test is a parametric test and it is appropriate for use when you want to compare the difference between the mean scores of two groups of data. The data have to be of interval type and normally distributed, and can be used, for example, to find out if there is a significant difference in the unit cost between two types of contracts.

The chi-square test is a test of association between two sets of data and can be used when the data are nominal or ordinal. It predicts how many subjects in each group fall into certain categories, for example, how many companies that are marketing oriented also have high financial performance, and how many product-oriented companies also perform poorly financially.

Spearman's ranking correlation (rho) is a non-parametric test for measuring the difference in ranking between two groups of respondents, scoring a number of issues, attitudes or factors. It can be used, for example, to find out how two groups of people, say managers and operatives, rank their priorities against a list of job satisfaction factors. The question at issue here is whether there is a significant difference in their rankings.

The Pearson product–moment correlation (r) is a test used when you have two sets of data and you want to calculate whether there is a strong relationship between them. The relationship can be either positive or negative and the strength of it is measured on a scale that varies from +1 through 0 to −1. For example, it can be used to find out whether speed of construction is related to size of project.

References

Adams, B. and Durfee, W. (2009) *Student Writing Guide – Lab Report.* Department of Mechanical Engineering, University of Minnesota, p. 15.

Green, J. and D'Oliveirs, M. (1993) *Learning to Use Statistical Tests in Psychology: A Student's Guide.* Open University Press, Buckingham.

Naoum S.G., Whitworth, T. and Fong, D. (2011) 'Is there a relationship between the lean concept and productivity rate of construction projects?', *6th International Structural Engineering and Construction Conference* (ISEC – 6), 21–26 June, Zurich. Paper ID S1–C33.

Nachmias, C. and Nachmias, D. (1996) *Research Methods in the Social Sciences.* 5th edn. Arnold, London.

Taj, S. (2008) Lean manufacturing performance in China: assessment of 65 manufacturing plants. *Journal of Manufacturing Technology Management,* 19 (2), 217–234.

Whitworth, T. (2010) *Transferring the Success of the Lean Theory: Quantifying the Relationship Between Leanness and Productivity in the UK Construction Industry,* MSc dissertation, London South Bank University.

Zikmund, W. (1997) *Exploring Marketing Research.* 6th edn. Dryden Press, New York.

Additional reading

Farrell, P., Sherratt, F. and Richardson, A. (2017) *Writing Built Environment Dissertations and Projects – Practical Guidance and Examples.* 2nd edn. Wiley Blackwell, Chichester. *Read Chapters 4 and 6.*

Laycock, E., Howarth, T. and Watson, P. (2016) *The Journey to Dissertation Success for Construction, Property and Architecture Students.* Routledge, London. *Read Chapter 8.*

Siegel, M. (1995) *Theory and Problems of Statistics (Schaum's Outline Series).* McGraw-Hill, New York.

Swinscow, T. (1987) *Statistics at Square One.* British Medical Association.

9 *Structuring and writing the dissertation*

This chapter will explain the general format for writing, organising and presenting your dissertation. These formats will provide you with a guide to structure your dissertation which should make it easier for the reader to understand what your dissertation is all about. Specific requirements for presenting the dissertation may vary from one discipline to another and from one university to another; for example, the number of copies required, format of the front cover, size of paper, typesetting and the like. However, the general formats of presentation are much the same in most disciplines, and so the main task is to make sure that you write and organise your dissertation contents correctly.

This chapter will give you guidance on how to structure and write your dissertation. It gives examples of writing an abstract, an introduction, a piece of literature review, presenting the research design and presenting the chapter of findings and conclusions. The examples given in this chapter should be treated as guidance which can serve as a model only. The contents of Chapter 9 are shown in Figure 9.1.

Typical dissertation structure

The structure of your dissertation may take the following order:

1 A page showing the title, your name, department and a copyright statement.
2 Summary of figures (if any).
3 Summary of tables (if any).
4 Acknowledgements.
5 Abstract.
6 Introduction to the research: one chapter.
7 Literature review: usually two or three chapters reviewing previous work (theory/theories and/or previous evidence).
8 Questionnaire design and method of analysis: one chapter. If the dissertation is purely based on analysing archival data, then you may name the chapter 'Procedure of data gathering'.
9 Analysis of the results: one chapter. If the dissertation is based on appraising previous work, then you may name it 'Analysis of secondary data' or 'Critical appraisal of previous work'.

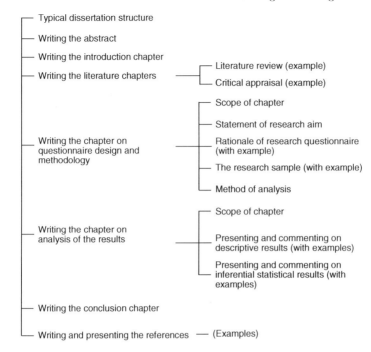

Figure 9.1   *Contents of Chapter 9.*

10 Conclusions and recommendations for further studies and practice.
11 References.
12 Appendices.

☞ See Figure 3.2 in Chapter 3, page 42 of this book – Example of designing the contextual framework which can also be used to provide an overview of chapters.
☞ Also see Figure 8.38 in Laycock et al. (2016, p. 200) – A model of the relationship of chapters, discussion and conclusion.

Writing the abstract

The abstract is a brief summary of the research, usually about 200–300 words in length. It should give information on the research problem that was studied, the method used to study the problem (including information on the type of sample), the results and major conclusions. The abstract should provide enough information to the examiners about your research as well as information to other readers so that they may decide whether to read the entire dissertation. The abstract should also make the dissertation easier to comprehend when it is read. Although the abstract appears at the beginning of your dissertation, you will probably want to wait until the body of the dissertation is complete before you write the abstract.

You may need several attempts before you achieve a sufficient brief. The following example fulfils all the requirements of an abstract, and might serve as a model. Box 9.1 is an example of writing an abstract.

Box 9.1 – Abstract (example of writing-up style)

Abstract

This dissertation is about reviewing the state-of-the-art literature in productivity research and to present the findings of a survey into factors that can impair productivity on construction sites. A critical review of the literature was conducted and a structured questionnaire was constructed under six general headings, these are: (1) factors related to pre-construction activities; (2) activities during construction; (3) managerial and leadership styles; (4) motivational factors; (5) organisational factors and (6) external factors. In total, 46 productivity determinants were extracted from these headings and were assessed by a sample of 60 contract managers and 57 site managers using the SurveyMonkey tool. The literature review revealed that while there has been advancement in developing techniques and tools to improving productivity on site, more needs to be done to invest in technology and innovation. The survey indicated that factors associated with pre-construction activities, namely, the 'experience of the selected site and project managers'; 'design errors'; 'buildability of the design'; 'project planning'; 'communication'; 'leadership style'; and 'procurement method' as the most critical factors influencing site productivity. Another highly ranked factor by both samples is 'lack of integration of project information'. Given the large number of computer systems available, this must be disheartening and reflects similar findings of recent research in the use and application of IT systems.

☞ **For more examples on how to write a dissertation abstract, visit the following links:**
  https://www.scribbr.com/dissertation/example-dissertation-abstract/
  https://www.google.com/search?q=how+to+write+a+dissertation+abstract
  &ie=utf-8&oe=utf-8&client=firefox-b

Writing the introduction chapter

This chapter of your dissertation should introduce the reader to the area being investigated. It basically includes most of your proposal contents. After reading the introduction, the reader should know why you decided to do the research and how you decided to go about it. In general, the introduction chapter may be composed of five sections:

- Rationale
- Research goals
- Outline methodology
- The research road map
- The dissertation structure

Section 1 – The research rationale

The first section of your introduction chapter starts with a description of past *key* research which is relevant to the problem. This section may be entitled 'Nature of the problem', 'Scope of the research', 'Rationale for the research', 'Background to the problem' or the like. Here, an exhaustive review of past research is not necessary; rather you want to describe only the research and/or theoretical issues that are clearly related to your study. You should state explicitly how this previous work is logically connected to your problem. This tells the reader why your research was conducted. (See Box 9.2 – Example of writing the rationale section of the introduction chapter.)

Box 9.2 Example of writing the rationale section of the introduction chapter. Dissertation title – Factors influencing labour productivity on UK construction sites – A state-of-the-art literature review and a survey

Chapter 1 – Introduction

1 Rationale

The productivity of a major industry like construction is of significant importance for the economic growth of a nation. According to the European Construction Industry Federation, the construction industry constitutes 9.7 per cent of the gross domestic product in the European Union with a total construction value of 1,186 billion in 2010, providing 6.6 per cent of Europe's total employment. This means that construction productivity must grow and should be the Holy Grail of construction research and development. The term 'productivity' is generally defined as the maximisation of output while optimising input. Borcherding et al. (1986) referred to Construction Labor Productivity (CLP) in terms of labour cost to the quantity of outputs produced. While Horner and Talhouni (1995) referred to CLP in terms of earned hours. It relies on the establishment of a set of standard outputs or 'norms' for each unit operation. Thus, a number of 'earned' hours are associated with each unit of work completed. The difficulty with this concept, however, is in establishing reliable 'norms', for setting standards. It also depends on the method used to measure productivity, and on the extent to which account is taken of all the factors which affect it.

A project-specific model is normally represented by the following equation:

$$\text{Productivity} = \frac{\text{Output}}{\text{Labor } + \text{ Equipment } + \text{ Material}}$$

Given the numerous definitions of productivity that have been published in the literature, the construction industry has reportedly demanded the development of acceptable measures to site productivity (Love and Smith, 2003; Abdel-Hamid et al., 2004; Cottrell, 2006; Liao et al., 2011). The majority of construction companies do not have formal measures in place at site level. This is evident in a survey of 77 UK contractors by Chan and Kaka (2003) which revealed that more than half of the contractors do not monitor productivity levels at project level. To address the issue, several attempts have been made to measure and benchmark the construction processes (Yeung et al., 2013). However, Lin and Huang (2009) criticised previous techniques that were developed in 1980s and 1990s as they lack objectivity. In addition, Crawford and Vogl (2006) and Bröchner and Olofsson (2012) both criticised the methods as they fail to reflect how technologies can affect the calculated productivity rate. Thus, different methodologies have been developed in the new millennium for deriving baseline productivity from a variety of estimation such as index number-based accounting methods; data envelop analysis; and econometric methods. All these methods have their strengths and weaknesses and researchers can choose the appropriate method to fit the purpose of their studies.

The UK construction industry has typically witnessed low levels of productivity and it is considered one of the most daunting problems that is facing the industry (Alinaitwi et al., 2007). According to Horner and Duff (2001), an increase of 10 per cent in the UK's Construction Labor Productivity is equivalent to a saving of £1.5 bn to the industry's clients, sufficient to procure perhaps an additional 30 hospitals or 30,000 houses per year. To meet this challenge, the UK government has called to cut both the cost of construction and the whole-life cost of built assets by 33 per cent and to deliver 50 per cent faster projects by 2025 (McMeeken, 2008). Therefore it is essential for contractors to rise to this challenge by increasing their productivity level and this requires the efficient use of labour, accurate and complete drawings, no delays in work, safe work and quality workmanship (Hughes and Thorpe, 2014).

This research has identified four main components as to the main causes of low productivity, these are: 'technical' such as ineffective planning of the resources and building design; 'social' such as the motivation of labourers on site; 'managerial' such as leadership and project control; 'contractual' such as the procurement method adopted for the project. Myers (2013) identified four other causal factors that are related to the industry itself, these are: first, the construction industry struggles to generate quality staff. Second, construction projects are short term and lessons are not adopted after each job. Third, the industry suffers from poor levels of investment and innovation and finally, technology is not embraced fully as with other sectors.

With this background in mind, the aim of this research is to critically evaluate the factors that can influence the rate of productivity on site and to provide guidance to construction project managers for the efficient utilisation of the labour force. To achieve this aim, a theoretical framework was developed to identify the relationship among the productivity factors and then to evaluate the relative importance of these factors as perceived by the UK construction industry. As labour forces are under the management and supervision of the main contractor, the survey of this research has concentrated on collecting data from construction contractors and more specifically from contract mangers and site managers. The outcomes of this dissertation can help practitioners to develop a wider and deeper perspective of the factors influencing the productivity of operatives.

The following sections of the introduction chapter provide further details about the research goals (section 2), outline methodology (section 3), the dissertation road map (section 4), structure of dissertation (section 5).

Section 2 – Research goals

The second section of the introduction chapter tells the reader what your aim is, what objectives are to be achieved and what hypothesis and/or key questions are being examined and answered. Box 9.3 is an example of stating the research goals:

Box 9.3 Example of writing the research goals in Chapter 1 of your dissertation

2 The research goals

2.1 The research aim

To develop a conceptual framework for evaluating the factors that can have the most impact on Construction Labor Productivity (CLP) on site. Guidance to construction project managers will be provided for the efficient utilisation of the labour force and areas for productivity improvement.

2.2 The research objectives

Objective 1: To review the state of the art and trends in construction productivity research.

Objective 2: To critically evaluate the group of factors that may influence productivity on construction sites, classified under (1) pre-construction activities; (2) factors during construction; (3) managerial and leadership issues; (4) organisational factors; (5) motivational factors; and (6) external factors.

Objective 3. To find out if there is a significant difference in views between contract and site managers into the factors that can impair productivity on site.

Objective 4: To construct a comparative table in the form of descriptive statistics showing the ranking of the relative importance of the labour productivity factors.

2.3 The hypothesis

There are significant differences in views between contract managers and site managers with regard to factors impairing on site.

2.4 The key research question

What are the commonalities and differences between contract managers and site managers concerning productivity factors on site?

☞ **Also see examples of research goals in Appendix 1.**

Section 3 – Outline methodology

The third section of your introduction chapter should *outline* the method you used to achieve your aim and objectives. Box 9.4 shows an example of writing an outline methodology in Chapter 1.

Box 9.4 Example of writing an *outline* methodology in Chapter 1

3 Outline methodology of the dissertation

A six-stage methodology was adopted for this research, these are:

Stage 1 (literature review) – In order to determine the major research outputs published in first-tier journals, this research adopted similar methodology to those employed by Al-Sharif and Kaka (2004), Tsai and Wen (2005), Ke et al. (2009), Hong et al. (2012) and Yi and Chan (2014). The search engines, Summon; Emerald; Business Source Premier; Science Direct; and Sage Journals were selected to identify journals that have published the most construction productivity-related articles. The search covered the period 1970–2018 and was not limited to a particular country.

After the compilation of the literature material, the author critically analysed the information with the view to identify: similarities in the findings of previous writers; common issues raised; differences or contradictions of statements made; criticisms made by previous writers.

Stage 2 (developing the theoretical framework) – After reviewing the literature, a theoretical framework was developed to show the group of factors that may influence productivity on construction sites in order to aid designing the research questionnaire (see Figure 9.2 – The theoretical framework of this research).

Stage 3 (constructing the questionnaire) – After conducting the literature review and developing the theoretical framework for the research, a questionnaire was constructed to obtain the necessary date and information to achieve the research goals.

Stage 4 (The survey) - Following on from Stages 1, 2 and 3, a survey was conducted and analysed to show the factors impairing CLP. In this survey, the structured questionnaire was distributed to 239 professions (136 contract managers and 103 site managers). 60 contract managers and 57 site managers returned usable questionnaires. Names of the companies were obtained from a population of the top 100 contractors operating in the UK, published by the *Building* magazine www.building.co.uk.

The reason for selecting these two groups of personnel is because of their direct interaction with workers on site and therefore they can be in the best position to assess the main factors influencing Construction Labor Productivity. The rationale for asking the questions is given in the methodology chapter.

Stage 5 (Analysis of the questionnaire and presentation of the findings) – See examples below.

Stage 6 (Writing up) – See examples below.

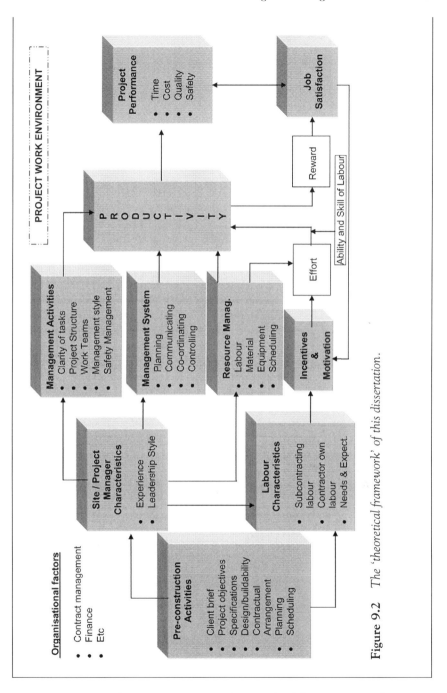

Figure 9.2 *The 'theoretical framework' of this dissertation.*

☞ See more examples on writing an outline methodology in Appendix 1.

Section 4 – The research road map

The fourth section of your introduction chapter should show a diagram that demonstrates a map of your research journey and should tie with the structure of your dissertation's chapters.

☞ **See examples of research road maps in Chapter 2 (Figure 2.3 on page 21 and Figure 2.4 on page 22).**

Section 5 – Dissertation structure

The final part of the introduction chapter should provide the reader with a short summary about the content of each chapter of your dissertation (one or two short paragraphs for each chapter). Box 9.5 shows an example of a dissertation structure in a tabulated format.

Box 9.5 Example of a dissertation structure

Chapters	Content
Chapter 1: Introduction and Background	This chapter provides background information about the research theme. It discusses the rationale for the study and also states the aim, objectives, hypothesis, outline methodology and the research road map.
Chapter 2: Literature Review (Part 1) – Previous Productive Models and Measurements	This chapter investigates the term 'productivity' and expresses the importance of the term on construction sites. Productivity indicators and previous productivity models are examined. The indicators consist of labour productivity, plant and equipment efficiency, material management and capital productivity. Productivity statistics between 1999 and 2018 are also presented in this chapter together with comparison of international construction productivity analyses.
Chapter 3: Literature Review (Part 2) – Previous Research into the Factors that Influence Labor Productivity on Construction Sites	This chapter specifically presents the site productivity factors under the following five primary groups: (1) pre-construction activities; (2) factors during construction; (3) managerial and leadership issues; (4) organisational factors; and (5) motivational factors. A critical appraisal of the literature is also inserted at the end of chapter.

Chapter 4: Research Design and Methodology	This chapter describes the *detailed* methodology used for the study and discusses the stages for conducting the research. It revises on the aim of the study and presents the 'theoretical' framework of the research. It also provides information on the questionnaire design and rationale, approach and method of analyses used for the study. The characteristic of the sample is discussed along with the measuring instrument and method of analysis. An ethical consideration of the study is also presented in this chapter.
Chapter 5: Analysis of the Results	This chapter presents and evaluates the results obtained from the survey. It discusses the results obtained from 60 contract managers and 57 site managers who participated in the study. The presentation of data is statistically analysed to quantify the existing perceptions and concerns into the factors that can influence site productivity. The statistical test (Spearman rho) has been applied to find out if there is significant difference in views between contract managers and site managers into the Construction Labor Productivity.
Chapter 6: Conclusions and Recommendations	This chapter serves as the final chapter for this study that focuses on the main problem areas. It concludes on the research aim and objectives set in the chapter. It also provides guidance to construction project managers for the efficient utilisation of the labour force and formulates areas for productivity improvement.
List of References	A complete list of all references used for the study.
Appendix	

Writing the literature chapters of your dissertation

After writing the introduction chapter for your dissertation, you should then write the literature review which is usually spread over two or three chapters. These chapters review what has been written on your topic (see Chapter 3 on how to write a literature review). Haywood and Wragg (1982, p. 1) emphasised that a critical review should show that 'the writer has studied existing work in the field with insight'. The main point is that a review should provide the reader with a picture of the state of knowledge and of the main questions in the subject area being investigated.

When writing the literature review chapters ensure that you cover the following 12 points:

1   A clear title for each chapter.
2   Division of chapter into a number of sections: it starts with 'Scope of chapter' and ends with 'Critical appraisal'.
3   Sifting of information. This means that you should include only materials which are directly related to the study.
4   Clarity in writing. Be precise and clear in presenting other people's work.
5   Clearly appraising the common issues raised by previous writers in the field, as well as the similarities and differences among them.
6   Coherence in writing: the writing of the literature and indeed the whole dissertation is coherent. The material is presented in an orderly, logical progression to facilitate understanding and good reading.
7   That the grammar, punctuation and length are correct.
8   Where relevant, the use of accurate linking phrases such as 'in contrast', 'it has been reported by', 'according to', 'there is much debate about', 'another school of thought suggests', 'all evidence points towards', 'conflict in opinion was revealed when', 'two sources, namely and … and … admitted that'.
9   The inclusion of a diagram, or other exhibits and illustrations such as tables, charts and conceptual frameworks, that were developed by previous writers is strongly recommended while writing your literature sections in order to clarify the point to be made as well as to make the reading more interesting.
10 Acknowledgement of the work of others. Most of the information provided in the literature chapters should be drawn from previous work. Therefore, almost every statement you make in the literature review should be referenced. If you use a passage drawn from an article or book, make sure that the passage is presented as a direct quotation. There is nothing wrong with quoting another author as long as you acknowledge your source (see Writing the references/bibliography on page 193).
11 A good balance of old and new references.
12 A good balance of sources. For example, include material published by refereed journals, conference proceedings, reports, secondary sources and a few websites.

Chapter 3 provided an example of writing a literature review but the example in Box 9.6 might serve as another model. It shows the style of writing a literature review and provides a critical appraisal section at the end. In this example, the material is based on the author's research and teaching material as well as an extract from his journal paper Naoum (2016). The title of the paper is 'Factors influencing labour productivity on construction sites - A state-of-the-art literature review and a survey' published by the *International Journal of Productivity and Performance Management*, vol. 65, no. 3, pp. 401–421. You may not be fully familiar with the field of study, but the review puts you in the picture as to what is expected from you.

Box 9.6 Literature review (example of writing-up style)

Chapter 3 – Literature review – Previous research into the factors that influence labour productivity on construction sites

EXAMPLE

3.1 Scope of chapter

Note to students

Start the scope of chapter by summarising what was reviewed in the previous chapter. For example, you may state:

Chapter 2 of this dissertation reviewed previous productive models and measurements. It investigated the term 'productivity' and expressed the importance of the term on construction sites. This chapter evaluates previous work on site productivity factors under the following headings:

1   Factors related to pre-construction activities;
2   Factors associated with activities during construction;
3   Factors related to managerial and leadership styles;
4   Motivational factors;
5   Organisational factors;
6   External factors;
7   Critical appraisal of Chapter 3.

3.2 Factors related to pre-construction activities

Design and procurement methods. Arguably, engineering design improvements are still regarded as areas with high potential for productivity improvement. Designers and quantity surveyors can not be expected to have sufficient understanding of the best way in which contractor's resources can be applied to improve productivity in terms of cost and speed (Hackett et al., 2007). As the design becomes more complex, the productivity rate is expected to be affected and the net result is that many designs are inefficient to build. Productivity can therefore be increased by design rationalisation, improved management, mechanisation and prefabrication.

The move away from the traditional forms of contract to new methods of procurement in the 1970s was a step towards developing a more collaborative approach, which is heralded as producing greater efficiency in project outcomes. One way of looking at collaboration is to examine the relationship among members of the building team, another is looking at the whole supply chain management concept. Loosemore (2014) investigated sub-contractors' perspectives of barriers to improving productivity within the Australian construction industry including the impact of the supply chain and the role of the sub-contractor in improving productivity. He suggested that for a sub-contractor, it is imperative that there is a strong relationship with the principal contractor, but more importantly that the sub-contractor can be seen to have an early involvement in design. It is therefore proposed by Hamouda and Abu-Shaaban (2014) that, in order to ensure that productivity is at its maximum, it must be taken into consideration at tendering and design stage. Productivity will be more difficult to improve once construction has begun.

Further information about the relationship between procurement methods, collaboration and productivity rate can be found in Stainer (1997), Cheetham and Lewis (2001), Eddie et al. (2001), Ng et al. (2002), Chan (2002), Kumaraswamy et al. (2004), Cottrell (2006), Fernie and Thorpe (2007), Hackett et al. (2007), Chartered Institute of Building (2010), Nasirzadeh and Nojedehi (2013), Fulford and Standing (2014) and Hughes and Thorpe (2014). Almost all of these studies were consistent with their conclusions in that non-traditional form of contracts, namely, design and build, management contracting and partnering would provide natural benefits such as successfully managed project, improved co-ordination, logistic, communications, closer relationship building, workplace relations and ethics. As Loosemore (2014) put it, 'productivity will be improved when information is more trustworthy, when there are fewer changes and in a more controlled way, and when there is not indiscriminate information distribution'.

Pre-construction planning. During planning and execution of construction projects, project planners and managers make various assumptions with respect to execution of construction activities, availability of resources, suitability of construction methods and status of preceding activities. However, not all of these assumptions are explicitly documented and verified before the construction activities start. Decisions made based on invalid assumptions can negatively impact the outcomes of construction projects, such as rework, activity delays and extra material cost (Gao et al., 2014). This notion supports the findings of Naoum and Hackman (1996), Dejahang (2006) and Doloi (2008) who found that ineffective project planning and design errors as the most crucial factors influencing productivity. These studies also suggested that workers' attitudes towards high productivity may not be limited to purely financial rewards, but inherently linked to many other latent factors, namely planning and programming.

According to Liu et al. (2011), the first and fundamental management action is to reduce work flow variation from the plan. Ballard et al. (2003) introduced the Last Planner System (LPS) to stabilise work flow, which has been applied in construction to improve CLP. LPS is a philosophy and a set of principles and tools designed to improve work flow reliability through better planning strategies (González et al., 2008). It has been implemented in many places in the USA, Europe, South America and Asia (Liu et al., 2011) and proved to be a successful tool. Several other planning tools were evaluated to improve the productivity of on-site operation such as the one by Pradhan and Akinci (2012) and Gong et al. (2011). In addition, Cottrell (2006) presented a regression model that relates job site productivity to Process Improvement Initiatives (PIIs) executed both before and during construction. Applied during early project stages, his model intended to help industry practitioners to predict the expected value of labour productivity based on certain inputs related to pre-construction planning and construction execution. The model demonstrates the strong relationship of project performance to a variety of PIIs including design completeness, definition of a project vision statement, testing oversight and project manager experience and dedication. The model provides project managers as front line industry practitioners with a deliberate yet practical approach to project management and productivity enhancement.

Selection of type and method of construction. Several pieces of research have been carried out to measure the productivity rate of various construction methods such as comparing the productivity rate of concreting as opposed to steel structure and the productivity rate of different types of frameworks used in construction.

For example, Jarkas (2012) explored the influence of primary buildability factors on concreting labour productivity and a sufficiently large volume of productivity data were collected and analysed by using the categorical-regression method. His findings showed that there are four significant impacts of factors that can influence the efficiency of the concreting operation. These are concrete workability; reinforcing steel congestion; volume of pours; and height relative to ground level, on labour productivity of skipped and pumped placement methods.

Off-site production of building components has become significantly more labour productive, in contrast to related on-site activities in the USA. Eastman and Sacks (2008) showed that not only do they have a higher current level of labour productivity, but their rate of productivity growth overall is greater than comparable on-site sectors. In their sample, off-site productivity grew by 2.32 per cent annually, while on-site productivity grew by 1.43 per cent. Most of these studies suggested improvement strategies in the area of mechanisation and prefabrication.

3.3 Factors related to activities during construction

Material management on site. The management of material is a worldwide problem and has been cited as a major cause of productivity loss. Extensive multiple-handling of materials, materials improperly sorted or marked, trash obstructing access and movement of materials, running out of materials and inefficient distribution methods are just a few instances of adverse material mismanagement conditions that have been reported by previous researchers Thomas et al. (1989), Abdul Kadir et al. (2005), Singh (2010) and El-Gohary and Aziz (2014). In an earlier study by Ferguson et al. (1995) in the UK, it was found that 50 per cent of the waste deposited in disposal sites is construction waste. In order to reduce waste and increase productivity, the concept of just-in-time was implemented on construction sites by the early 1990s and Pheng and Tan (1998) provided strong evidence to support the benefits of that concept. Moreover, Faniran and Caban (1998) suggested that wastage on site could be reduced if design changes were kept to a minimum during the construction work. The research also identified leftover material scraps, waste from packaging and un-reclaimable non-consumables, and design/detailing errors as being important sources of construction waste.

More recently, El-Gohary and Aziz (2014) presented an interesting summary table of factors affecting labour productivity across ten countries. The factor 'availability of the materials and their ease of handling' was discussed in most of the papers that were published. It had a weighting score of 90.34 per cent, and therefore ranked second within the management group and third among all 30 factors that were surveyed. When considering uncertainty reduction and risk management in construction planning and control, Gao et al. (2014) advocated that the stock and movement of material is the most frequently monitored information item in the last planner approach. Other factors included the movement and status of equipment, the work flow and capability of crews, the status of prior work, the availability of construction information, the safety of external conditions and the safety of the work space.

Equipment management on site. In addition to material management, construction productivity is also influenced by the management policy of the company regarding the selection of equipments and plants. In short, the policy on the type and number of equipments to use as well as getting the right balance between maintainability and replacement is a crucial decision-making process by the company. Needless to say, equipments remain idle unless they are transformed into productive use by human performance. Previous research found substantial and statistically correlated longitudinal improvements in construction craft productivity associated with equipment improvements (Goodrum and Haas, 2004; Goodrum et al., 2009) as well as the timing of ordering the plants (Odeh and Battaineh, 2002; Kazaz and Ulubeyli, 2007). Through analysis of variance and regression, Goodrum and Haas (2004) found that activities experiencing significant changes in equipment technology have witnessed substantially greater long-term improvements in labour productivity than those that have not experienced a change.

Variation orders and changes of project scope. A considerable amount of research exists on the subject of construction variation orders and how it affects site productivity (Thomas et al., 2003; Hanna et al., 1999, 2005, 2008; Ibbs, 2005; Chang et al., 2007; Liu et al., 2011; Ibbs, 2012). Disputes are common between the client and contractors when these changes. A study by Hanna et al. (1999) used data from 43 projects and a linear regression model was developed that predicted the impact of changes on labour efficiency. The model allows labour efficiency loss to be calculated in a particular project enabling both the client and the contractor to understand the impact such changes will have on labour productivity. This research provided evidence to support the assertion that disruption caused by changes in the original plan of work significantly increased the project cost through rework and decreased labour efficiency for the main contractors and sub-contractors. Although Hanna et al.'s study was limited to mechanical trade with some specific plumbing, fire protection and process piping, their study corresponded closely with earlier findings by Thomas and Napolitan (1995), Leonard (1987) and Zink (1990) who showed an average loss efficiency ranging from 10–30 per cent as a result of changing orders. Interestingly, these studies realised that changes themselves do not directly decrease productivity or efficiency but rather, it is the manpower involved in the process.

Overcrowding. Site congestion and overcrowding are usually attributed to inappropriate construction site arrangement and overcrowding of the workers in some workplaces, which can cause obstructions to the desired productivity and quality. According to Jarkas et al. (2012), the overcrowding of workers usually results from inappropriate general planning of construction site activities. This issue has been reported by Watkins et al. (2009), Dai et al. (2009), El-Gohary (2014), Cottrell (2006) and Borcherding and Alarcón (1991). Earlier, Smith (1987) provided evidence to suggest that a labour density greater than one man per 30 m^2 will lead to a decrease in productivity. As working space deceases from 30 m^2 (standard working space) to 10 m^2 per operative, it incurs about a 40 per cent productivity loss.

Skills of labour. Skill of labour has been investigated by Alinaitwi et al. (2007), Olomolaiye et al. (1998), Abdel-Wahab et al. (2008), Durdyev and Mbachu (2011), Dai et al. (2009) and Thomas and Horman (2006). According to Abdel-Wahab et al. (2008), the effective utilisation of skills rather than mere increase in the supply of skills is key to bringing about productivity improvements. Indeed future policy makers should focus on addressing other influences on productivity performance such as work organisation and management practice to support further development and progression of the UK construction industry.

3.4 Factors related to management and leadership

The construction process is a collective effort involving a team of specialists from different organisations. Welfare of workers coupled with efficient management styles to control work activities from design to construction is essential to achieve high productivity (Ailabouni et al., 2009). The success or failure of a construction project relies heavily on the effectiveness of the management of construction resources and the leadership style. Evidently, efficient management can yield substantial savings in time and cost (Shahata and Zayed, 2011). According to Rojas et al. (2003), the two areas identified as having the greatest potential for affecting productivity are management skills and manpower planning. Indeed, the managerial and leadership style can be seen as the umbrella that covers most of the factors discussed in this paper.

The leader of the team can affect the productivity of the design and construction and this also dependent upon the contractual arrangement adopted for the project. A number of studies have been conducted to investigate the relationship between leadership styles and productivity rate and found that charismatic and participative leadership behaviours primarily determine the satisfaction of the team members (Cheung et al., 2001). Moreover, leaders can have a significant role to play in fostering an innovation climate in construction firms that can lead to higher productivity. A study by Chan et al. (2014) revealed that transformational leadership is positively associated with innovation climate, whereas development exchange leadership is negatively associated with innovation climate. Here, transformational leadership refers to four core dimensions: charisma (or idealised influence), inspiration stimulation, intellectual stimulation and individualised consideration, while development exchange refers to the degree to which a leader establishes a system for followers to obtain contingent rewards for meeting an agreed-on expectation.

3.5 Job satisfaction and motivational factors

Maloney (1986) defined motivation as the worker behaviour with the objective of obtaining the means of satisfying an unfulfilled need. While Lam and Tang (2003) defined motivation as the driving force that stimulates individuals physiologically and psychologically to pursue one or more goals to fulfil their needs or expectations. Since the 1940s, there has been a tremendous amount of work done to investigate the relationship between the individual and the company (extrinsic) motivation, as well as within the individual (intrinsic) motivation. The most relevant studies to construction are the ones conducted by Hazeltine (1976), Nicholls and Langford (1987), Ruthankoon and Ogunlana (2003), Kazaz and Ulubeyli (2007) and Jarkas and Radosavljevic (2013). These articles differ with respect to the research strategy that they have adopted for their research. Most articles identified the key motivators being one or a combination of the following: salary, job security, high achievement, recognition, the nature of the work itself, responsibility and personal advancement and growth. Naturally, a key motivator for one worker compared with another worker in a certain situation may differ. The key question is whether there is a relationship between financial incentives, motivation and productivity. Critical appraisal of previous research related to construction seems to align with Herzberg's two-factor theory of motivation. The two factors are hygiene and motivators.

In short, hygiene factors such as money, supervision, status, security, working conditions, policies and interpersonal relations prevent dissatisfaction but do not motivate; they do not produce more output but prevent a decay in performance. Motivators such as work itself, recognition, advancement, possibility of responsibility and achievement can have a positive effect on job satisfaction which will lead to an increased output.

3.6 Organizational factors

Investment in technology and innovation. These factors are about applying new techniques, sciences and solutions to constructions. According to De Man (2008), innovation is 'the process of bringing new creative ideas to reality and implementing them through new work practices, processes, business models and strategic partnerships to produce new products and services which are of value to society'. It has become essential for construction organisations to innovate because of increasing pressures from clients to improve productivity, quality, reduce costs and speed up construction processes. Management effectiveness can ultimately determine profitability in most cases. According to Yi and Chan (2014), technology, including material and information technology, has had a tremendous effect on CLP over recent years. Tools, machinery and the automation and integration of information systems have increased power and modified skill requirements (Hewage et al., 2008). Therefore, investing in technology and innovation is essential to productivity, cost effectiveness and, more importantly, the sustainable development of any organisation and industry. Following rapid globalisation, technological advancement and the trend toward partnering between the public and private sectors, the importance of innovation has increased dramatically for construction firms, particularly for large-size construction firms.

An empirical research by Goodrum et al. (2009) found that those activities that experienced significant changes in material technology have also experienced substantially greater long-term improvements in both their labour and partial factor productivity. Machinery has also become more powerful and complex (Kannan, 2011). It can therefore be argued that information technology would revolutionise MISs and help management obtain accurate information that leads to faster and more accurate decisions on site. According to Baldwin (1990), rapid mechanisation within the industry has resulted in increasing productivity by the introduction of structural steel, system form work, pre-casting techniques, prefabrication and component manufacture, but the construction industry requires more innovation to remain competitive among other sectors.

3.7 Critical appraisal of Chapter 3

The subject of productivity and its relationship to project success has long been investigated and reported in academic journals. This chapter reported on past and recent literature available on productivity in the construction industry. Previous work in the field can be criticised in that, although there has been advancement in developing techniques and tools to measuring productivity, concerns can be raised for the need to invest in technology and innovation to improve the rate of productivity on construction sites. Given the large number of computer software and systems available, this must be disheartening. Moreover, there seems to be lack of research to establish the relationship between site productivity and the modern concepts of optimising performance, such as supply chain, lean construction, value engineering and BIM. These concepts are, after all, directed toward eliminating waste, minimising the transaction cost as well as the enhancement and transfer of shared knowledge and expertise among all parties.

It can also be concluded in this chapter that the majority of previous research seems to suggest that the rate of labour productivity on site can largely be affected by activities related to the pre-construction stage of the building process. This stresses and echoes the call by several articles such as El-Gohary on the importance of integrating design and construction to achieving buildability and hence increasing productivity. It can be argued that this can be accomplished by increasing the awareness of the significant impact of allowing contractors to be involved at the pre-construction stage and to encourage the use of non-traditional procurement methods such as design and build, management contracting, project management and partnering. These methods facilitate the incorporation of the construction experience at the early stage of the building process so that the desired benefits can be achieved during the construction phase.

As a final remark to critically appraise this chapter, it appears that despite its high impact on the construction industry, productivity improvement is still an area in which much research work needs to be done to explore its true potential in a practical industry context. As Ranasinghe et al. (2012)put it, 'today's construction industry seems to adopt productivity improvement initiatives to gain a competitive edge in the global market place; however, systematization of these approaches is still an area of concern'.

The next chapter of this dissertation discusses the research design and methodology for achieving the aim and objectives of the research.

References for this chapter

Note to students

For list of references of this example on writing a literature chapter, read the following research paper:

Naoum, S.G. (2016) Factors influencing labor productivity on construction sites - A state-of-the-art literature review. *International Journal of Productivity and Performance Management*, 65 (3), pp. 401–421.

☞ **Also see Chapter 3, Box 3.1, pages 44–50 for another example of writing a literature review.**

Writing the chapter on questionnaire design and methodology

This chapter needs to be inserted after the literature chapters. It may also be entitled 'Procedure of data gathering', 'Research design and methodology' or the like. In this chapter, you need to explain how the problem was investigated and describe the tool that you used to make the investigation (i.e. your questionnaire or the data collection format). You also need to state the rationale for asking the questions as well as describe the characteristics of your research sample and method of analysis. I suggest that this chapter may include the following sections:

Section 1 of the methodology chapter:
Scope of chapter

This should be a brief explanation of what the reader will expect to read in this chapter (one or two paragraphs).

Section 2 of the methodology chapter:
Statement of research aim

This should be a repeat of your stated aim to remind the reader what you intend to achieve (see examples of aims in Chapter 2 and in Appendix 1).

Section 3 of the methodology chapter:
The research methodology

In this section, you need to provide a *detailed* methodology that you adopted for conducting the research and why you selected the methodology you did (i.e. justify it). Box 9.7 shows an example of writing this section.

Box 9.7 Example of writing the methodology section

Section 3 – The detailed research methodology

A six-stage methodology was adopted for this research, these are:

Stage 1 (literature review) – In order to determine the major research outputs published in first-tier journals for the chosen topics, this research adopted similar methodology to those employed by Al-Sharif and Kaka (2004), Tsai and Wen (2005), Ke et al. (2009), Hong et al. (2012) and Yi and Chan (2014). The search engines, Summon; Emerald; Business Source Premier; Science Direct; and Sage Journals were selected to identify journals that have published the most construction productivity-related articles. The search covered the period 1999–2018 and was not limited to a particular country.

The desktop search was further refined by making reference to the journal ranking list of Chau (1997) in the area of construction engineering and management. Nine top-ranked construction journals were included in the first round of the desktop search stage: *Construction Engineering and Management (JCEM)*, *Journal of Management in Engineering (JME)*, *Construction Management and Economics (CME)*, *Engineering, Construction and Architectural Management (ECAM)*, *International Journal of Project Management (IJPM)*, *Journal of Productivity and Performance Management*, *Journal of Computing in Civil Engineering*, *Journal of Construction Innovation* and *Journal of Built Environment*. These journals were selected because they are known to have frequently published scholarly papers in the field of Construction Labor Productivity (CLP).

Moreover, they have been ranked highly by several research activists in construction management such as the list by Chau (1997). The main international conference proceedings that were reviewed are the CIB (W65) and (ARCOM). Technical reports and occasional papers were also covered as they are comprehensive and often publish up-to-date information. These are the Institute of Civil Engineering, Chartered Institute of Building and Royal Institute of Chartered Surveyors. These conference proceedings and reports were selected as they are well known to have disseminated research findings in the field of productivity and construction management.

A comprehensive desktop search was then conducted under the 'title/abstract/keyword' field to provide a content analysis of productivity papers. Search keywords included: organisational; design; planning; scheduling; procurement methods; project manager; Management Information System (MIS); construction methods; human resources; material; equipment; overcrowding; skills; variation orders; waiting time; rework; motivation; technology; innovation; and weather. These topics were chosen on the basis of previous literature in these related fields and their link with CLP. Moreover, papers with these specific terms included in the title, abstract or keyword were considered to have fulfilled the requirements of this research study. In some cases, the search was narrowed down by combining keywords such as 'equipment' and 'productivity'. As a result, a total number of 119 productivity-related articles and reports were identified and for the purpose of this dissertation, 40 references were selected for inclusion as they directly fit the purpose of this dissertation topic.

After the compilation of the literature material, the author critically analysed the information with the view to identify: similarities in the findings of previous writers; common issues raised; differences or contradictions of statements made; criticisms made by previous writers.

Stage 2 (developing the 'theoretical' framework) – See Figure 9.2 for the theoretical framework of this research. The framework contains the group of factors that might influence productivity on constructions sites. It is based on previous literature review.

Stage 3 (constructing the questionnaire) – After conducting the literature review and developed the theoretical framework for the research, a questionnaire was constructed to obtain the necessary date and information to achieve the research goals. The rationale for the questionnaire is provided in the following section and a copy of the questionnaire is inserted in the appendix of his dissertation.

Stage 4 (the survey) – After designing the questionnaire, it was distributed to 239 professions (136 contract managers and 103 site managers) with the aid of SurveyMonkey (an online survey tool). The rationale for asking the questions and the characteristics of the sample are explained in the following sections.

Stage 5 (analysis of the results and findings) – The questionnaire was divided into six sections and each section contained the relevant factors. For example, factors such as planning, scheduling, procurement method and design were grouped under 'pre-construction activities'. Factors such as variation orders, overcrowding, material and equipment management were grouped under 'activities during construction' and so on. In the questionnaire, the respondents were asked to rate each factor by using a scale from one (1) to three (3) in order of importance. The range included 'not an important determinant' (given a value of 1) to 'very important determinant' (given a value of 3).

Forty-six factors were included in the questionnaire and they were selected based on previous research on CLP, namely, the research by Ng et al. (2004); Abdul Kadir et al. (2005); Nepal et al. (2006); Alinaitwe et al. (2007); Enshassi et al. (2007); Hanna et al. (2007); Kazaz et al. (2008); Onukwube et al. (2010); Ibironke et al. (2011); Jarkas and Bitar (2012).

The questionnaire was first tested by interviewing five local contractors. The suitability of the form and areas of investigations were discussed during these interviews. Some modifications were made to the original questionnaire and the final version was sent to 239 professions (136 contract managers and 103 site managers) with the aid of SurveyMonkey (an online survey tool). 60 contract managers and 57 site managers returned usable questionnaires.

The data gathered was then analysed using the descriptive method of analysis and the ranking correlation (Spearman rho). The following section describes in detail the method used for analysing the data.

Stage 6 (writing up)

Section 4 of the methodology chapter: Rationale of the research questionnaire

In this section, you need to define and provide the rationale for asking the questions you did. How did you define the factors/variables? Why have you asked the questions you did? Remember, your questionnaire has, say, three to five section headings and each heading contains a number of questions which are related to your research objectives. Your task, therefore, is to refer back to the questionnaire, which is usually inserted in the appendix, and discuss each section individually. For instance, what did you intend to obtain from the respondent? Which objective would you achieve by asking that group of questions? Has there been a similar type of question asked by fellow researchers? If so, refer briefly to their questionnaire or to their work.

For example, in the research related to Figure 9.2, the questionnaire was used under five sections and all the sections are related to the literature review, the aim, objectives, research hypothesis and the key research questions that were identified in the introduction, Chapter 1. Box 9.8 shows an example of how to write the rationale section of the 'Research Design and Methodology' chapter.

Box 9.8 Example of writing the rationale section of the research design and methodology chapter

Section 4 – Rationale of the research questionnaire

4.1 – Questions related to pre-construction activities

4.1.1 Design and procurement methods

This factor was defined by the technical design of the project and the involvement of the contractor in the design.

The purpose of including this factor in the questionnaire is because engineering design improvements are still regarded as areas with high potential for productivity improvement. This is based on the fact that designers and quantity surveyors cannot be expected to have sufficient understanding of the best way in which contractor's resources can be applied to improve productivity in terms of cost and speed (Hackett et al., 2007). As the design becomes more complex, the productivity rate is expected to be affected and the net result is that many designs are inefficient to build. Productivity can therefore be increased by integrated procurement methods, design rationalisation, improved management, mechanisation and prefabrication.

4.1.2 Pre-construction planning

This factor was defined by the accuracy and the detailed planning of the project at the pre-construction stage by the contractor aimed at meeting a client's requirements in order to produce a functionally and financially viable project.

The purpose of including this section in the questionnaire is because previous research showed that during planning and execution of construction projects, project planners and managers make various assumptions with respect to execution of construction activities, availability of resources, suitability of construction methods and status of preceding activities. Arguably, decisions made based on invalid assumptions can negatively impact the productivity and outcomes of construction projects, such as rework, activity delays and extra material cost. This argument was supported by Naoum and Hackman (1996), Dejahang (2006), Doloi (2008) and Gao et al. (2014). Therefore it was considered necessary to include this aspect in the questionnaire.

4.1.3 Selection of type and method of construction

Several researches have been carried out to measure the productivity rate of various construction methods such as comparing the productivity rate of concreting as opposed to steel structure and the productivity rate of different types of frameworks used in construction. For example, Jarkas (2012) explored the influence of primary buildability factors on concreting labour productivity and his findings showed that the type and method of construction can influence the efficiency of the concreting operation.

4.2 – Questions related to activities during construction

4.2.1 Material management on site

This factor was defined by the capability of the contractor to plan the total material in order to assure the supply of material, optimum inventory levels and minimum deviation between planned and actual results.

The reason for including this factor in the questionnaire is because it is a worldwide problem and has been cited as a major cause of productivity loss in research such as Abdul Kadir et al. (2005), Singh (2010) and El-Gohary and Aziz (2014). For example, El-Gohary and Aziz (2014) presented an interesting summary table of factors affecting labour productivity across ten countries. The factor 'availability of the materials and their ease of handling' had a weighting score of 90.34 per cent, and therefore ranked second within the management group and third among all 30 factors that were surveyed. It is therefore crucial of asking the participant of this research on their perceptions regarding this factor.

4.2.2 Equipment management on site

This factor was defined by the efficiency of the planning system used for managing, monitoring and maintaining equipments and plants that are used during construction.

This factor was included because previous research found that effective equipment management can make a major difference to productivity and efficiency. Such research as Goodrum and Haas (2004) and Goodrum et al. (2009) as well as the timing of ordering the plants such as the work of Odeh and Battaineh (2002) and Kazaz and Ulubeyli (2007).

4.2.3 Variation orders and changes of project scope

This factor was defined by the amount of additions and deletions of work from the original scope which alters the original contract amount and/or completion date.

The relationship between construction variation orders and how it affects site productivity was evident in the work of Chang et al. (2007) and Liu et al. (2012). Therefore, the evaluation of this factor by the contract and site managers who participated in this research was thought to be crucial to include in the questionnaire.

4.2.4 Overcrowding

Defined as the condition where more people are located within a given space than is considered tolerable to control and manage.

This factor was included because site congestion and overcrowding can cause obstructions to the desired productivity and quality. This relationship was examined in the work of Jarkas (2012) into buildability factors influencing concreting labour productivity. According to Jarkas (2012), the overcrowding of workers usually results from inappropriate general planning of construction site activities.

4.2.5 Skills of labor

Defined as the required specialised training of operatives or their learned skill set to perform the work.

This factor was included for evaluation in the questionnaire following the study by Abdel-Wahab et al. (2008) who found that the effective utilisation of skills rather than mere increase in the supply of skills is key to bringing about productivity improvements.

4.3 – *Questions related to management and leadership*

4.3.1 Charisma

This is defined as the characteristic and personality of the person who is in charge of managing the project and his/her capability to influence their workers.

4.3.2 Style

Defined as whether authoritarian or democratic or in between.

This factor was included in this research because a number of studies which investigated the relationship between leadership styles and productivity rate have found that charismatic and participative leadership behaviours primarily determine the satisfaction of the team members and hence affect the rate of productivity (Naoum, 2012 and Cheung et al., 2001).

4.4 – Questions related to job satisfaction and motivational factors

4.4.1 Motivation

This factor is defined by the level of desire workers feel to perform, regardless of the level of happiness. Workers who are adequately motivated to perform will be more productive, more engaged and feel more invested in their work

The purpose of including this factor in the questionnaire is to evaluate and validate the most relevant studies to construction motivation such as the ones by Kazaz and Ulubeyli (2007) and Jarkas and Radosavljevic (2013).

4.5 – Organizational factors

4.5.1 Investment in technology and innovation

Defined by the size of investment that contractors inject into the company in order to increase the productivity and sustainability of other factors of production.

Previous studies by Hewage et al. (2008), De Man (2008), Goodrum et al. (2009), Kannan (2011) and Yi and Chan (2014) concluded that investing in technology and innovation is essential to productivity, cost effectiveness and, more importantly, the sustainable development of any organisation and industry. Therefore, it was important to include this variable in the questionnaire to assess how contract managers and site managers perceive it form their points of view.

Notes to students

If your dissertation involves collecting 'quantitative and factual / measurable variables' such as facts from case studies or project documents as shown in Table 6.2 on page 89, then you need to design a 'Theoretical Framework' and give details of the variables or factors that you are going to measure in your study. You need to give details of its components and state your argument as to how these components are interrelated. In other words, you should define the variables one by one and describe the method which you used to measure the variables (Figure 9.2 on page 153 is the initial theoretical framework of this example designed by the author of this book). Also see Figure 4.5 in Chapter 4, page 63 for another example of designing a 'theoretical framework'.

If your investigation is based purely on archival data and not a questionnaire, then you need to discuss the format that you used to gather the information. Remember, the archival information can be either statistical or descriptive.

Section 5 of the methodology chapter: The research sample

In this section of the research design and methodology chapter, you need to discuss the following:

1   The list that you drew your sample from.
2   The method that you used to select your sample and why.
3   If you used a survey questionnaire, state how many were sent out and how many were completed (i.e. response rate).
4   Describe the characteristics of your response sample. This can be discussed from the information gathered by the 'general' section of your questionnaire. Box 9.9 shows the sample related to the productivity research above that was based on a survey.

Box 9.9 Example 1 – Writing the research sample based on a large survey

Section 5 – The research sample

In order to obtain a set of data that can be statistically tested of contract managers and site managers, a survey questionnaire was compiled in SurveyMonkey (an online survey tool). The questionnaire was randomly distributed to 136 contract managers and 103 site managers in construction contractors companies. 60 contract managers and 57 site managers returned usable questionnaires. Names of the companies were obtained from a population of the top 100 contractors operating in the UK published by the *Building* magazine, www.building.co.uk. The distribution was done via email to the 'business unit' of the companies. These companies were homogenous in their characteristics in that they are all multinational and offer similar services with a large turnover and a large number of employees. The respondents were stratified in terms of age, experience on site, occupation and academic degree. The composition of the research sample is shown in Table A.

Table A – *Composition of the research sample*

Profession	No.	%	Age	No.	%	Academic degree	No.	%
Contract Managers	60	51	25–35	40	34	MS	20	18
Site Managers	57	49	35–45	35	30	BSc	80	68
	117	100	46–60	35	30	Others	17	14
			Over 60	7	6		117	100
				117	100			
Institutional Membership			**Experience on site**	No.	%			
APM	35	30	1–5 years	15	13			
CIOB	35	30	5–10	17	14			
RICS	35	30	10–15	70	60			
No membership	12	10	Over 15 years	15	13			
	117	100		117	100			

Example 2 – Writing up the research sample section based on interviews

The following example might serve as a model to show the style of presenting the research sample based on interviews. Box 9.10 shows an extract from Chapter 4 of an MSc dissertation by Zoë Elizabeth Mulholland (2010). The title of this dissertation is 'A critical examination of sustainable construction in the recession: A qualitative study among clients and professionals operating in Greater London'. Here, the researcher interviewed three clients, three architects, two cost managers and two contractors.

Box 9.10 Example 2 – Writing the research sample based on interviews

Section 5 – The research sample

The aim of the research sample was to cover as broad a range of perspectives as possible. The interviewees were selected from each stage of the project to include: client, architect, cost consultant and main contractor to attempt to capture these differing viewpoints. In addition, there was variation within each type of respondent group for small, medium or large company and mixture of public and private work, as well as refurbishment and new build. It is worth noting that none of the respondents were solely involved in specialist fields of work and all had a range of projects. The characteristics of the interviewees' organizations is set out in Table B below.

Table B – *Characteristics of the interviewees' organisations*

Respondent	Turnover (£)	No. of staff	Sectors	Types of project	Value of projects (£)	Location
Client A	N/A (portfolio value £?? million)	240	Retail park; regional shopping centres; commercial offices	Refurb; conversion; new-build	<1m, 20%; 1–10m, 20%; 10–50m, 25%; >50m, 35%	UK nationwide; France
Client B	N/A	35	Education; science research; offices; residential	Refurb; fit-out; new-build	<1m, 35%; 1–10m, 35%; 10–50m, 25%; >50m, 5%	London; South
Client C	N/A	17	Residential; 'build to let'; commercial office	Refurb; new-build	<1m, 20%; 1–10m, 70%; 10–50m, 10%; >50m, 0	London and SE England
Architect A	N/A	34	HEI; commercial; conservation; residential – top end and social	Fit-out; refurb; new-build specialist in historical contexts	<1m, 20%; 1–10m, 60%; 10–50m, 15%; >50m, 5%	London
Architect B	N/A	250	Science labs; health care; education – schools, HE, FE; commercial office; urban design; regeneration; interior design	Refurb; conversion; new-build	<1m, 10%; 1–10m, 20%; 10–50m, 60%; >50m, 10%	London; Midland North

Architect C	N/A	70	Education – school, FE, HE; health care; research; social housing	Refurb; conversion; new–build	<1m, 20%; 1–10m, 20%; 10–50m, 25%; >50m, 35%	London; Midland; Northern Ireland
Cost Manager A	N/A	2000	All	All	<1m, 10%; 1–10m, 30%; 10–50m, 30%; >50m, 30%	
Cost Manager B		100	HE; retail; commercial; health	Refurb; conversion; new–build	<1m, 30%; 1–10m, 35%; 10–50m, 35%; >50m, 0%	
Contractor A	N/A	45	Commercial fit–out; high-end residential; data centres; heritage/churches; not for profit	Refurb; fit out	<1m, 55%; 1–10m, 40%; 10–50m, 5%; >50m, 0%	London
Contractor B	N/A	100	Education; commercial	Fit out; refurb	<1m, 65%; 1–10m, 30%; 10–50m, 5%; >50m, 0%	London

After showing the overall characteristics of the interview sample, it is necessary to provide a short summary of all the organisations that you interviewed.

Box 9.11 shows a summary of the ten organisations that Zoe included in her dissertation.

Box 9.11 The characteristics of the interview sample that was conducted by Zoe Mulholland (2010)

Section 5 – The research sample (continued from Zoe's dissertation)

Characteristics of interviewees' organisations

Client A

Client A is one of the top five commercial developers. It might have been expected that this client would only be interested in the façade of being green. However, the company had a sustainability ethos engrained throughout the organisation from the top management down. Client A was one of the most enthusiastically positive respondents who saw the potential rather than the barriers to sustainable construction. The firm has an in-house sustainability department with specialist expertise but ensures that all sectors within the company have a thorough grounding in sustainable development principles so that the whole culture of the organisation embraces sustainability. As a result, Client A took the continuation of sustainable construction through the recession.

Client B

Client B is a large public sector client with an extensive estate made up of education, scientific research, office and residential accommodation. With 60 per cent of its buildings constructed in the 1960s, inefficient and energy hungry buildings are a major issue. Client B classed itself as an intelligent client with a large in-house projects department which produced comprehensive technical policy guidelines and procedures for construction on its estate. Sustainability had become a significant management issue of the past two years. Client B had appointed a senior manager to lead on sustainability issues as well as producing a policy statement and developing a strategy for greening the organisation. Sustainable construction was firmly on the organisation's management's agenda with major projects aiming for BREEAM ratings and minor ones looking at energy efficiency measures. However the major challenge identified by this respondent was convincing the end users, both academic and support staff that sustainability is a significant issue which they had to take into account.

Client C

Client C is a small developer who is driven by return on its investments. However, unlike many other major developers which build properties to sell on or lease over a long-term period, this client has a 'build to let' model where they act as the developer, estate agent and landlord. The company retains ownership of the services and maintenance costs for all its buildings. It self-rated its level of sustainability at nine out of ten and pointed to the time it has taken to educate itself on sustainable practices and the benefits it sees in customer demand, planning and legislative compliance as evidence. For Client C the most significant benefit of sustainable construction is how it can reduce long term running costs which have a direct impact on the profitability of a building. Client C was clear that its motivation for sustainable construction was purely about business: in their eyes it makes business sense to be green.

Architect A

As a relatively young firm with a main office in Oxford and a smaller satellite in London, Architect A considers itself well-informed in the area of sustainability. Its loose hierarchy mean all members of the company feel able to contribute to its direction and information is shared throughout. One of the founders of the company wrote a key publication on sustainable construction so the ethos of sustainability is ingrained in the company. The respondent said that they had been involved in sustainable construction before the term had been coined, looking at ways to minimise the impact of building on the environment through ethically sourced materials, energy efficiency and designing better buildings for improved social well-being. The sectors which the practice worked in were also more likely to include clients who were sympathetic to sustainable construction.

Architect B

Architect B is one of the largest practices in the country and works across all sectors of the industry. As such a large organisation they have a very broad range of experience of sustainable construction and have been involved in BREEAM projects from when the accreditation method was first established. The firm considers itself an industry leader which strives to improve construction practices through innovation and research. An internal sustainability group was set up to tackle sustainable construction challenges. Architect B considers part of its role is to produce excellence in design, as well as educating and advising clients in this field. It was acknowledged that the uptake of this expertise was still varied across the different sectors their clients represented.

Architect C

Architect C is a medium sized firm with offices across the United Kingdom. Although long established, it does not strive to continuously expand and asserts that it focuses more on quality than profit. It believes that for these reasons it has a very low turnover of staff and a large amount of repeat business. Architect C felt that the sustainability concept was not new at all and was in fact in line with very old fashioned notions of not creating waste, whether materials, energy or space. This respondent felt sustainable construction would be a matter of regressing back to these values out of necessity because of the recession. This practice is well versed in sustainable construction with all buildings BREEAM rated and one of the Firm's Partners listed on the Green Register of Architects.

Cost Manager A

Cost Manager A is a large international firm with over 2000 employees worldwide. It is a multi-disciplinary company, including a well establish sustainability consultancy but with cost management its primary line of work. The firm has an extremely sophisticated research ethos with its own library and dedicated researchers. Cost manager A describes the firm as 'thought leaders' on matters throughout the industry. However, even with such resources at their disposal, they commented that the attitude of clients was paramount to the success of sustainable construction in the industry. Although government legislation will be driving the sustainability agenda hard, the client organisations across public and private sectors still needed to be convinced.

Cost Manager B

Cost Manager B is a medium sized firm which belongs to a group of consultancy disciplines from architects to CDM Coordinators. This firm has offices nationwide and works across higher education, retail, commercial and healthcare giving it a broad exposure to a host of clients. The majority of their work is under £10 million in total project value and they felt that many of these jobs did not attract the same attention in terms of sustainability as some of the larger new build projects. The respondent admitted they were cynical about client attitudes to sustainability and felt that it was significantly hindered by focus on short term costs. The firm had 'moved with the times' to employ a dedicated sustainability consultant but with the onset of the recession the position did not represent value for money and it was abolished.

Contractor A

Contractor A is a recently founded company which had grown out of a much larger firm. They strive to be open, forward-thinking and to shed the negative image of construction contractors. They therefore feel that their appeal is to clients who want to feel that their builder is a partner rather than an adversary. Their ethos is to listen to what their clients want and deliver quality projects. This has included sustainable construction practices from standard green roofs and PV panels through to innovative recycled glass bottle cladding. They were very happy to engage in seminars and training in sustainability but did not feel it was their place to influence the client.

Contractor B

Contractor B focuses on fit out and refurbishment in the education and commercial sectors with project values below £7 million. The majority of their work is demanding fast track projects. The respondent had a good awareness of the issues surrounding sustainable construction but admitted there was not a significant demand within their client base. Many lighter sustainability features were considered: energy efficient services such as displacement ventilation, sustainably sourced materials and the use of recycled products. But they had never worked on a project which had included renewable energy technology. The respondent said that they would be open to the challenge of new construction practices and technologies but they were waiting for their client's instruction.

Section 6 of the methodology chapter: Method of analysis

This section of the research design chapter should explain how the data was analysed. If you selected the interview technique, have you used the trend approach in analysing the information or percentages? If you selected the postal survey or the SurveyMonkey tool, have you used the descriptive method of analysis or the statistical test(s)?

The following sections demonstrate various approaches.

Writing the chapter on analysis of the results

This chapter is the core part of your dissertation and will consist of the research findings expressed by texts, figures, tables, charts, graphs and the like. It is absolutely essential to present your results clearly. I suggest the following structure for this chapter.

Section 1 of the result chapter: Scope of chapter

This section should be a brief description of what is included in the chapter.

Note to students

Chapter 8 in this book described the methods for analysing the results. If you decided to apply the descriptive method follow Section 2, part 1; if you decided to apply the statistical test, then follow Section 2, part 2; if you decided to apply both methods, then follow parts 1 and 2.

Section 2: Analysis of the results, part 1 (the descriptive method)

This part of the dissertation will consist of questions, answers, tables, figures or charts and comments. When writing the results section, it is best to refer back to your questionnaire. The order in which your results are presented should correspond to the order of your questionnaire. In general, the analysis of the results for the descriptive method can be presented following this format:

1   *The question.* Here, you state the question as asked in the questionnaire.
2   *The results/finding.* Here, you present the analysis of the results in the form of a table, bar chart, pie chart or a graph.
3   *Comments/interpretation.* After analysing the question and presenting the results in a table, chart or other form, you need to go beyond this step and interpret the results of your study. For instance, what do they mean to you? Are your results similar or dissimilar to the results of previous studies? If your results were different, why were they different? Did you use different subjects or use different techniques?

Next are three examples showing typical presentations of descriptive types of results. The first example is adapted from a dissertation on quality management by Cooper (1995) updated and edited by Naoum (2013). It displays results of an investigation based purely on a postal survey (see Box 9.12). The second example is adapted from a dissertation by Green (1996) updated and edited by Naoum (2013) on health and safety (see Box 9.13 page 179). It shows a postal survey supplemented by interviews. The third example is adapted from a piece of research on procurement methods by Naoum (2016) (see Box 9.14 page 180).

Box 9.12 Presenting the results of a postal survey (example of writing-up style)

Question:

This question is related to the adequacy of the 'current' Quality Assurance (QA) procedures to satisfy clients' requirements and expectations. Here, the respondents were given a number of factors which can contribute to the quality of service to satisfy clients' requirements. They were asked to mark each factor with a mark 3, 2 or 1. Mark 1 means that the 'current' QA meets the client satisfaction to this particular factor. Mark 2 means that it moderately meets client satisfaction and mark 3 means it does not meet the client satisfaction at all. Table A below shows results on the average rate of response to this question.

Table A   *Adequacy of QA procedures to satisfy clients' requirements and expectations*

	Key factors adequacy ratings (%)		
	1	2	3
Overall response			
1 Performance	84	7	9
2 Features	53	20	27
3 Reliability	59	26	15
4 Responsiveness	9	36	55
5 Competence	21	44	34
6 Conformance	43	33	24
7 Access	7	14	79
8 Currency	18	36	46
9 Courtesy	7	14	79
10 Communication	12	38	50
11 Perceived quality	0	39	61
12 Security	17	39	64
13 Understanding	17	51	32
14 Tangibles	26	35	39
15 Cost	30	45	25
Average ratings	27	32	41

Comments

From the table of results shown in Box 9.12, the following picture emerges:

1   Taking an average of the ratings over all 15 'key factors' of quality, it appears that an average of only 27 per cent of responses ranked the 'current' QA procedures as completely adequate to ensure that the clients' requirements and expectations are fully satisfied. Thirty-two per cent of the responses thought 'moderately' and 41 per cent thought that 'current' QA procedures do not cover the particular 'key factors' that were listed.

2   However, these somewhat negative results (relative to what might have been expected within a firm operating an accredited QA system) may be at least partially explained by reference to the hypothesis put forward earlier in this dissertation: 'a standard accredited QA system such as ISO 9001 may not sufficiently address all the pertinent aspects of quality'.

3   Going back to the table, 84 per cent of respondents ranked 'performance' (that is, ensuring that the required basic service is actually performed) as fully satisfying the clients' requirements with the 'current' QA procedures.

4   Reliability was expected to be well within the remit of QA. Here, the results are a little lower: an average of 59 per cent of respondents ranked this item as fully satisfying clients' requirements, 26 per cent ranked it as moderately and 15 per cent as not at all. Further analysis of the results, into categories of responses, discloses that the majority of the low ranking came from the construction professionals which, presumably, are either genuinely critical to QA

procedures or otherwise may lack knowledge as to the purposes and scope of the procedures in operation.

5   In a similar vein, the remainder of the overall 'top six' quality components appear to illustrate aspects of quality which are, indeed, less well covered by standard QA systems, such as ISO 9001. The extreme example of this is 'perceived quality', which refers to the trustworthiness of the firm or contact personnel to the client.

6   Though proposed by the majority of respondents as an important aspect of quality in the selection, retention and recommendation of the professional firm's services, not one respondent suggested that 'current' QA procedures would ensure that clients' reasonable requirements and expectations are fully satisfied in this respect. Indeed, 61 per cent indicated that they believed that 'current' QA procedures did not cover this factor. However, this finding should be treated with caution. The answers are the respondents' own perceptions and not necessarily the organisation's. A larger sample needs to be surveyed in order to confirm this finding.

7   Similar results apply to 'communication' and 'responsiveness', where 50 per cent and 55 per cent of respondents, respectively, indicated that QA procedures did not cover these key factors.

8   The respondents were also asked to rank the 'five most important' factors of quality and the 'five least important' factors that the QA procedure should take into consideration. Table B shows the results:

Table B   *Ranking the 'five most important' factors of quality and the 'five least important' factors that the QA procedure should take into consideration*

Most important factors	Least important factors
1 Reliability	1 Tangibles
2 Understanding	2 Features
3 Perceived Quality	3 Security
4 Performance	4 Currency
5 Communication	5 Conformance

Presenting postal survey supplemented by interviews (example of writing-up style)

This example is related to health and safety in construction. Postal and interview questionnaires were designed. The postal questionnaires were sent to four companies: three contractors and one construction consultancy. The recipients were mainly quantity surveyors and project managers. A total of 130 questionnaires were distributed, of which 77 completed forms were returned (60 per cent response). The returned responses were from 25 managers, 25 supervisors, 21 operatives and 6 consultants. All the returned questionnaires were usable. This high response to the survey was because the author had a good contact base which was formed during the professional placement. To support the findings, the student also decided to undertake interviews with the companies that responded to the survey. Box 9.13 is an extract from the analysis of the results.

Box 9.13 Example of presenting a postal survey supplemented by interviews

Question

This question was related to health and safety as opposed to programme time. The respondents were, therefore, asked the following question:

Do programme times imposed through contract clauses directly affect safety? Table A presents the results.

Table A *Results into programme time and safety performance*

	Managers		Supervisors		Operatives	
Question	Agree	Disagree	Agree	Disagree	Agree	Disagree
Do programme times imposed through contract clauses directly affect safety?	6 (65%)	9 (35%)	7 (28%)	18 (72%)	17 (80%)	4 (20%)

Comments

From the table of results shown on safety culture and programme time, an interesting finding emerged. It shows that, although senior managers and operatives agreed with the question, supervisors expressed a different view. Analysis of the results indicates that 65 per cent of senior site managers agreed that programme time imposed through contract clauses directly affect safety. It was commented that penalty clauses are too high and programme times are too tight, imposing a false induced money consciousness in the industry. One manger stated during the interview:

> There is a lot of pressure brought about at the present time, clients want the shortest programme, the highest quality and lowest price. Therefore, there is an awful amount of pressure on everyone involved with the contract at site level, particularly the site managers. I agree programme times do have an effect on safety, it's not a perfect world as we also put pressure on sub-contractors to get the work done, forcing them to carry out work in a dangerous manner.

When supervisors were asked the same question, 72 per cent disagreed with the question. During an interview with a supervisor, he stated:

> You can still produce to the required level and effectively if you plan safely into your production process. People tend to work better in a safer environment. Today we think more consciously about safety, so whilst there is a lot of pressure on the main contractor, the emphasis is on building it on time, with quality, within budget and in the safest manner

Another interviewee commented:

> Under current regulations and working practices, safety is a fatal element in any construction sequence, along with staffing, materials and plant. It cannot be

> differentiated or taken aside from. On that basis you cannot regulate it, in many ways it should be in the forefront.

A third interviewee put the view that:

> You have to do it the right way, even though it will cost more or take longer. This industry is very dangerous, a serious accident will cost the contractor more than it would have cost to do it safely in the first place. The trouble is that people do not see risks until it's too late.

From this analysis one can conclude that present contractual arrangements allow the pursuit of safety to come into conflict with the demand for the cheapest and speediest completion of a contract. The widespread use of contract penalty clauses and unrealistic productivity targets can result in a poor safety culture as it can place supervisors under considerable pressure to take the quickest and cheapest option. However, the health and safety issue should be part of the contractual package and, as one interviewee stated, it should be in the forefront.

Presenting results based purely on interviews (example of writing-up style)

This example compares the views of ten experienced clients on various aspects on the use of management contracting and the traditional method. Structured interviews were adopted to supplement data collected by questionnaire. The questionnaire was divided into seven section headings to correspond with the research objectives. The questionnaire was sent to the ten client organisations prior to the interview. The organisations were coded as client A, B, C, D, E, F, G, H, I, J. Interviews were carried out by running through the questionnaire to comment on the answers of each section heading and were documented using a mini tape-recorder. Box 9.14 shows an extract from the analysis of the results.

Box 9.14 Example of presenting a postal survey supplemented by interviews

Questions

The following questions were investigated:

1   Who are the clients that used MC?
2   How do client organisations view MC?
3   Why have clients used MC?
4   What are the clients' criteria of satisfaction?
5   What is the level of client satisfaction with MC?
6   Is MC favourable to traditional contracting?
7   What is the clients' attitude towards the use of MC in the future?

Table A provides the results followed by a sample of discussion that was made on the results. This should give you some idea of how to write and discuss the interview results.

Table A   *Responses to questions on MC versus traditional method*

Question	Response out of 10		
	Yes	Same	No
1 Is MC riskier to clients?	6	2	2
2 Is MC more profitable to the contractor?	10	–	–
3 Does MC involve fewer claims?	3	4	3
4 Is MC more flexible to variations?	10	–	–
5 Does MC allow an earlier start on site?	10	–	–
6 Is MC quicker to design and build the project?	10	–	–
7 Is MC more reliable in predicting the build time?	9	1	–
8 Is MC more reliable in estimating the project cost?	6	3	1
9 Is MC cheaper?	2	4	4
10 Does MC provide more control for sub-contractors?	9	1	0
11 Does MC exercise more control over construction operations?	9	1	–
12 Does MC provide a better building design?	1	1	8

Comments on the results

1   As can be seen from Table A, there is a conflict of opinion concerning the risk to be absorbed by clients when dealing with a management contractor. Clients A, B and D saw the principal risk arising from the absence of a tendered lump sum price from the main contractor prior to construction. Client F claimed that:

Clients are subject to a greater risk in respect to costs because of the staggering and phasing of orders for specific work over a longer period. While in the traditional method it was the main contractor who was taking that risk by putting a lump sum bid out at the outset. With MC the contractor is likely to settle for a smaller guaranteed profit and abandon a higher potential profit through the management of implicit risks. This balance between profit and risk has implications for clients. Larger clients may be better placed to take risks and consequently have a cheaper project.

2   All the clients that were interviewed agreed that MC is flexible in that it enables variations to the original design and specifications throughout the course of construction; they added that cost can be controlled by changes in the design without affecting project performance. Client H stated: 'with the amount of changes our organisation made for the last management contract, it would have been a disaster if we had used the traditional form of contract'.

3   However, not all clients reacted positively regarding the assertion that fewer claims arose with MC. Client D, although generally satisfied with MC, was

unconvinced that MCs were less claims-conscious than traditional contracts. Clients A, B, F, H and J did not experience any differences in claims between traditional contracting and MC. This was unexpected because many articles that were published by management contractors stressed that the system involves fewer claims. In an article published by the *Building* magazine, a management contractor stated that: 'you could run a MC without a form of contract. It is a philosophy, an attitude and a contract of trust'.

4   Frequently, the time factor was seen as one of the major advantages of MC: none of the client's that were sampled commented unfavourably about MC's time performance. All clients agreed that MC reduced the pre-contract period by overlapping the design and construction process. This enabled the project to be completed in a shorter time than for a traditional method. However, clients A, B and D expressed the view that their experience with past MCs counted for a good deal in considering the company's other needs.

5   Conflicting attitudes about the cost factor were noted. On interviewing a large public client (A), a mismatch between its expectations and the procedures of MC with its uncertain final costs, could be observed. The client stated:

Due to the way the public sector is organised, it is naturally biased towards caution in committing tax payers' money and ensuring that their accounting officer (i.e. Chief Executive) has answers to critical questions which might be put to him by the Public Accounts Committee.

However, a second public organisation did not feel constrained in using management contracting due to public accountability because they had to change their building procedures. According to McKinney (1983), the public sector has experienced cost reimbursement contracts for many years. This particular form of contract would certainly seem to be far more in conflict with the concept of public accountability than would a 'pure' MC, simply because the contractor carries out some of the work himself with little provision for realistic and comprehensive competition. Traditionally, the public sector has taken a narrow view and awarded contracts by means of open competition on the basis of drawings and a bill of quantities. A private banker (B) stated that:

there is a tendency for greater involvement of the professional consultants: the architect and quantity surveyor get involved more than they should in some work which is the MC's job. This overlapping responsibility was reflected in higher fees being paid.

Four private clients had a fairly positive attitude toward the cost performance of MC. Clients C, E, F and G had a fairly positive attitude toward the cost performance of MC. One distinguishing characteristic amongst this group was that low costs were not considered as essential for client satisfaction.

6   None of the clients interviewed felt that MC produced a better building design than the traditional method, but most clients stated that they did not choose a MC for that reason in the first place.

7   Finally, the management contractors and clients who participated in the study criticised many contracting organisations for entering MC without the right personnel. Client C noted that:

> although from the client's point of view, the intention is to integrate them with the professional team of architect, structural engineers and quantity surveyors at an early stage in the proceedings to gain the advantage of their know-how within the building industry, many have not yet understood or chosen to understand this change in status and merely regard themselves as administrative middle-men in between the sub-contractors and client and the professional team and thus do not inject any creative ideas, which is one of the objects of the exercise and is indeed the reason why certainly in our case, after a careful selection process, we bring them into the proceedings at the earliest possible stage.

Note to students

Also see Appendix 6 for another example of presenting interview results in a tabulated format.

Section 2: Analysis of the results, part 2 (test of correlation and/or association)

If you applied inferential statistical tests such as the *t*-test, chi-square test, correlation coefficient and ranking correlation (Spearman rho), then the second part of your dissertation results chapter should consist of hypothesis testing, tables of correlation or association and interpretation of the results.

Table A in Box 9.15 shows an example of a survey by the author that investigated whether there are significant differences in opinions between contract managers and site managers on factors that influence construction productivity. This example is related to the research shown in Boxes 9.1, 9.2, 9.3, 9.4, 9.5, 9.6, 9.7 and 9.8. In short, several productivity factors were extracted from the literature review and were assessed by 60 contract managers and 57 site managers. The findings were presented as follows.

Box 9.15 Example 1 – Presenting results using inferential method of analysis (manual calculation)

The research question

Do contract managers and site managers perceive productivity factors differently?

The research hypothesis

It is hypothesised that there are significant differences in perceptions between contract managers and site managers with regard to factors impairing productivity on site. These differences are related to (1) pre-construction activities; (2) activities during construction; (3) managerial; (4) motivational; (5) organisational; (6) external factors.

The null hypothesis

There is no difference in ranking to productivity factors between contract managers and site managers.

Statement of hypothesis testing

Table A shows that there seems to be an overall agreement by both samples with regard to productivity factors (rho = 0.91). This indicates that high ranking by contract managers of the productivity factors correspond to high ranking by site managers of the same factors, and vice versa.

Comments on the results

Based on the rankings in Table A, the following interpretations can be made:

1   At pre-construction level, both respondents identified 'ineffective project planning (F1)' as the most crucial factor that can affect the rate of productivity on site; 'design and buildability related issues (F2)' as well as 'procurement method (F3)' and 'specification (F4)' were also ranked highly by both samples. This finding supports the earlier study of Borcherding et al. (1981) who stated that:

> [T]he planning/design level is probably the key communication link in the hierarchy model between the 'realities' of the site construction level and the 'abstract' of the policy and programme management levels. The planning/design level becomes the controlling element in the industry's effort to translate productivity information from above into a common language with a terminology meaningful to the desired audience.

2   The difference in perception between the two samples was registered in the area of 'poor selection of project personnel (F9)'; 'lack of consultation in the decision-making process (F21)'; and 'attitude of site personnel (F22)'. It was identified that contract managers assigned a high score to these factors while site managers gave it a low scoring. On the other hand, site managers expressed more regard to 'delegation of responsibilities (F31)'; 'opportunities to exercise skill (F39)' and 'mismatch of beliefs among personnel on site (F40)'.
3   The factors that seem to be of importance to both samples in questions related to activities during construction are that of 'system of communication'; 'control system'; 'lack of integration of the management information system for the project'; 'mismanagement of material', 'ineffective site planning leading to program disruption' as well as 'group co-ordination and overcrowding'.

This emphasises the importance of focusing on the management of information as well as the technical information for design-related issues. As far as mismanagement of material is concerned, comments from site managers indicated that most acute problems, caused by material mismanagement, are with material supply and storage, which can have a great impact on the sequence of work, and rework due to disruptions (see F15). This highly ranked factor corresponds closely with the work of El-Gohary and Aziz (2014) who emphasised that timely delivery of material rather than the selection of the material is thought to be of importance. This finding can also be linked with 'project planning' (before and during construction) which was ranked highly by both samples. With regard to 'disruption of site program', this factor can cause delay in executing the work and prevent optimising utilisation of available resources. Timely input from all levels of management can reduce the risk of overlooking activities necessary to complete the project. Therefore, delays contributing to lowering a worker productivity can be reduced by planning the work to efficiently utilise manpower.

4   Other highly perceived factors by both samples were registered for 'management/leadership style'; 'project structure / authority and influence' and 'team/ group integration'. These three factors cut across the managerial and the social aspects throughout the building process. The level of productivity attained by a firm is determined by a variety of organisational, technical and human factors, many of them directly controlled or influenced by management decisions. It could therefore be argued that a better site management can be associated with increased decentralisation of decision-making authority within the project, and with greater level of site manager influence over operations and decisions on site. The fairly high ranking of these factors can be linked with 'system of communication' and 'lack of integration of the management information system for the project' that were discussed earlier.

5   Previous researchers regarded the Management Information System (MIS) as the linking mechanism of the aforementioned factors, i.e. decision-making, site supervision and communication. The productivity of a project depends on the management's access to accurate information to aid in timely decision-making. Information which does not flow promptly from one group to another will cause rework and delays, hence, decreases productivity (as shown in a relatively high ranked factor of F15). Under the issue of decision-making and authority, Sanvido and Paulson (1992) have empirically tested the possible utilisation of practical tools (from a productivity improvement view-point) that can support various theoretical decision-making phases. They demonstrated that jobs where the planning and control functions were performed at the right level in the site hierarchy, were more profitable, finished sooner and were better constructed than those where the functions were performed at the wrong level of the hierarchy.

6   At organisational level, 'experience of the selected personnel and training' was ranked the highest by both samples. Obviously, each task requires specific skills and knowledge of how to use these skills. Formal education and training programmes have been considered by previous researchers as a substitute for leadership, by developing individuals to work independently or with minimal

Table A Ranking of contract managers and site managers of factors influencing site productivity

Factors	Contract managers actual scores (%)	Contract managers ranking (A)	Site managers actual scores (%)	Site managers ranking (B)	di (A−B)	di^2
A. Pre-construction activities						
F1. Ineffective project planning	82	1.0	85	1.0	0	0
F2. Design and buildability related issues	80	3.0	83	3.0	0	0
F3. Procurement method	80	3.0	81	5.0	2	4
F4. Specification	78	5.0	78	8.0	3	9
F5. Clarity of client brief and project objectives	76	7.0	72	12.0	5	25
F6. Site managers involvement at contract stage	75	9.0	73	11.0	2	4
F7. Poor scheduling of project activities	75	9.0	70	14.5	5.5	30.25
F8. Subcontractor involvement	71	13.0	72	12.0	1	1
F9. Poor selection of project personnel	75	9	64	20	11	121
B. Activities during construction						
F10. Delay caused by design error and variation orders	81	2.0	84	2.0	0	0
F11. Communication system	81	2.0	84	2.0	0	0
F12. Supervision of subordinates	79	4.0	76	10.0	6	36
F13. Lack of integration of the management information system for the project	78	5.0	83	3.0	2	4
F14. Management of material	78	5.0	83	3.0	2	4
F15. Ineffective site planning leading to program disruption	78	5.0	78	8.0	3	9
F16. Delay/rework	77	6.0	77	9.0	3	9
F17. Site safety	77	6.0	77	9.0	3	9
F18. Clarity of tasks	77	6.0	72	12.0	6	36
F19. Control system	76	7.0	83	3.0	4	16
F20. Group co-ordination / overcrowding	76	7.0	83	3.0	4	16
F21. Lack of consultation in the decision-making process	75	9.0	64	20.0	11	121
F22. Attitude of site personnel	75	9.0	64	20.0	11	121
F23. Co-ordination of subcontractors	74	10.0	69	15.0	5	25
F24. Direct V subcontract labour	73	11.0	69	15.0	4	16
F25. Accuracy of tech. information	67	14.5	80	6.0	8	64

(continued)

F26. Interference on workmanship	67	14.5	73	11.0	3.5	12.25
F27. Management of equipment / use of inappropriate tools/equipment for operations	67	14.5	70	14.5	0	0
F28. Inefficient site layout	63	21.0	62	24.5	3.5	12.25
C. Managerial						
F29. Management / leadership style	81	2.0	81	5.0	3	9
F30. Project structure / authority and influence	77	6.0	82	4.0	2	4
F31. Delegation of responsibilities	58	24.0	70	14.5	10	100
D. Motivational and social						
F32. Work environment	81	2.0	83	3.0	1	1
F33. Team/group integration	81	2.0	79	7.0	5	25
F34. Job security	72	12.0	70	14.5	2.5	6.25
F35. Salary and incentives	55	26.0	62	24.5	2	4
F36. Resentment of company policy	65	18.0	64	20.0	2	4
F37. Response to employee grievances	58	24.0	62	24.5	0.5	0.25
F38. Reappraisal of site managers and promotion	53	27.0	64	20.0	7	49
F39. Opportunities to exercise skill	39	29.0	68	17.0	12	144
F40. Mismatch of beliefs among personnel on site	60	22.0	78	8.0	14	196
F41. Constraints on a worker's performance	81	2.0	83	3	1	1
E. Organisational						
F42. Experience and training	80	3.0	80	6.0	3	9
F43. Construction technology and methods	67	14.5	80	6.0	8.5	72.25
F44. Availability of skilled workers	65	18.0	77	9.0	9	81
F45. Contract administration skill	65	18.0	64	20.0	2	4
F46. Knowledge of techniques	64	20.0	62	24.5	4.5	20.25
F. External factors						
F47. Weather	60	22.0	63	23.00	1	1
Total						1237.75

$$r(\text{rho}) = 1 - \frac{6 \times \Sigma di^2}{n(n^2 - 1)}$$
$$= 1 - \frac{6 \times 1237.75}{47(47^2 - 1)}$$

$$r(\text{rho}) = 0.91$$

supervision. Workers today are comparatively well educated, so training or teaching job skills are a necessity. Horner (1989) suggested that management must bear the burden of controlling the rapidly changing technological and social conditions, and that training programmes and methods of assessment must be relevant and appropriate to the needs of the organisation. They must be designed and implemented in joint ventures between academia and industry. In addition, site managers assigned a higher value to 'construction technology and methods' (F43). They noted that waiting time can significantly be reduced by adopting the appropriate method of construction to the operation and this perception is in line with the finding of Jarkas (2012) discussed earlier.

7   In reviewing the results described by previous researchers, there would appear to be difference in views as to whether work force motivation can affect construction productivity. Several behavioural and psychological researches indicated that the expenditure of effort by a worker is the physical manifestation of motivation; the greater a worker's motivation, the greater his/her expenditure of effort. Ranking on questions related to motivation shows that there was little support to most of the questions that fall under this category. However, a substantial proportion of both samples were in agreement that 'work environment' and 'constraints on worker's performance' arising from ineffective management will affect their performance at work and consequently influence worker's productivity. It can be argued that both these factors fall under Herzberg's hygiene theory of motivation. In short, hygiene factors such as money, supervision, status, security, working conditions, policies and interpersonal relations prevent dissatisfaction but do not motivate; they do not produce output but prevent a decay in performance. This finding is also congruent with the very earlier conclusions (of Borcherding and Ogglesby, 1974; Borcherding and Garner, 1981) in that the major sources of dissatisfaction commonly expressed by both tradespeople and supervisors, are problems related to delay and reworking. According to Thomas et al. (1989), frequently cited problems included the lack of tools, materials, delayed decisions, late information and changes in orders. The link between satisfaction and improved productivity is based upon the impact that such conditions are assumed to have on workers' and supervisors' motivation. It can therefore be concluded that individual needs for opportunities for advancement as well as the satisfaction from the work itself can be frustrating and, consequently, the potential for significant productivity gains as being thwarted by inappropriate or inadequate managerial actions.

Example 2 – Presenting results using inferential method of analysis (using the SPSS software package) (also see Example 2 in Chapter 8, page 135)

This example is based on a study that was conducted at London South Bank University by Brian Hemmings in 2009, and the result was later published in 2011 (Naoum et al., 2011). See details in Box 9.16.

Box 9.16 Results of curvilinear regression analysis

Title of research

Is there a correlation between contractors' health and safety (H&S) performance and their profit margin?

Aim

To demonstrate in a graphical format, the relationship between the performance of H&S on site and the profit margin of the contractor.

Brief research methodology

To achieve this aim, data from 22 construction projects was collected, in particular: (1) data project information; (2) procurement method; (3) start and end date; (4) actual completion date; (5) contract value; (6) final account value; (7) H&S audits and scores; (8) percentage of profit.

For each of the projects, the percentage increase or decrease of its final cost against its final value was calculated so that the percentage of profit could be analysed. Health and safety audits were carried out on all projects every month by either the project manager or the surveyor of the individual project. In order to conduct the audit, each site was issued with an H&S register and within the register there were 39 different sections covering a wide range of site-specific tasks, requirements and statutory duties. Pertinent to the specific site, each site was audited once a month to check whether the tasks and duties, as set out in the register, had been carried out.

The information garnered from the audit was then transferred to a spreadsheet which monitored whether the site agent had been compliant or non-compliant with each section of the register.

Measurement of health and safety score

The H&S score is, perhaps, one of the most important headings. It gives the average score throughout the duration of the project. The score is calculated out of 100 per cent, with 100 per cent being the highest score possible. If a project scored 100 per cent it could be concluded that it had performed brilliantly, throughout its duration. The H&S score was calculated by analysing the monthly audits of the H&S register; this is explained in greater detail in the following paragraphs.

The H&S register comprises 39 different sections which place a duty on the site agents to either check certain tasks have been completed or to ensure statutory guidelines have been adhered to. Once a month, either the project manager or project surveyor will audit the register to check that the site agent has complied with the relevant sections pertinent to the project. The sections within the register include: (1) Site commencement; (2) Accident reporting; (3) Asbestos; (4) Cartridge tools; (5) Control of noise; (6) COSHH; (7) Demolition; (8) Electricity on site; (9) Excavation/groundwork; (10) False work; (11) Fire prevention; (12) General H&S (13) HFL & LPG; (14) Site visits; (15) Lifting operations; (16) Manual handling; (17) Permits to work; (18) PPE; (19) Piling; (20) Construction phase plan; (21) Risk assessment; (22) Road works; (23) Scaffold/work platforms; (24) Site induction; (25) Site instructions; (26) Site security; (27) Statutory records; (28) Steel fabrication; (29) Subcontractor safety; (30) Traffic management; (31) Training/toolbox talks; (32) Under/over ground services; (33)

Waste management; (34) Welfare; (35) Work equipment; (36) Working at high level; (37) Working in confined spaces; (38) Young persons; (39) Environment.

The project manager or surveyor fills out a report that highlights which sections have or have not been complied with. This information was transferred to a monthly audit summary which plots each of the sections that the project had been non-compliant with.

This summary data was then extracted to a table which scheduled out the complete duration of the project month by month. For every month an H&S score was calculated by plotting the number of non-compliant sections out of 39. The amount of compliant sections were then divided by 39 and multiplied by 100 to get a percentage out of 100.

Measurement of profit percentage

The percentage of profit made is the second most important heading as it gives the actual amount of profit the project made. This was done by calculating the difference in the actual cost against the final out-turn value (final account sum), dividing it into the cost and multiplying by 100 to get a percentage.

Presentation of results

Table A gives a breakdown of each project's final account, its out-turn cost, its H&S score and the percentage of profit. The results show that out of the 22 projects, 16 made a profit and they each had H&S scores higher than 70 per cent, with the average score being 95 per cent and the average profit margin 20 per cent. Fourteen had an H&S score of higher than 95 per cent; all but one made a loss. The average profit was 20 per cent.

Table A   *Project values with health & safety score and profit margin*

Proj	Final Account (£)	Out turn Cost (£)	H&S Score (%)	Profit (%)
1	346,039	295,176	90	17
2	403,450	420,000	100	−4
3	554,950	423,863	99	31
4	1,250,000	1,098,166	100	14
5	628,000	628,000	100	0
6	3,250,000	3,050,000	96	7
7	4,152,000	2,875,000	98	44
8	1,148,864	1,062,446	99	8
9	260,212	243,716	99	7
10	1,675,428	1,675,428	89	0
11	190,018	152,515	99	25
12	6,885,812	5,900,000	79	17
13	2,375,012	2,300,000	96	3
14	6,000,000	3,500,000	99	71
15	2,945,431	2,471,812	96	19
16	765,057	837,842	52	−9
17	1,655,476	1,701,419	70	−3
18	449,054	445,000	81	1
19	1,675,428	1,650,428	88	2

(continued)

20	2,951,619	3,179,997	91	−7
21	2,350,000	1,735,799	95	35
22	221,534	191,849	98	15

Source: Reproduced from Naoum et al. (2011).

Comment on Table A: Amongst the 16 projects that had an H&S score of 90 per cent or higher, all but two projects made a profit. The average profit margin was 18 per cent. For the six non-profit making projects, their average health and safety score was 84 per cent. Amongst them, four projects made a loss with an average H&S score of 78 per cent. Overall, the average score was 92 per cent with the average amount of profit at 13 per cent.

Calculating the strength of the relationship using the SPSS package

In order to calculate the significance of the correlation, the following steps were taken:

1   Formulate the research hypothesis: 'Projects that score high in health and safety performance will result in a higher rate of profit margin'.
2   By implication, the null hypothesis is: 'There is no significant relationship between health and safety performance and the profit margin of the contractor'.

The calculation of the correlation coefficient was performed using the SPSS package as shown in Appendix 5.

Box 9.16 demonstrates the scatter plot of profit on project (*y*) against H&S score (*x*). Regression analysis of profit margin on H&S score suggested that there is no significant linear relationship ($R^2 = 0.1677$, $p > 0.05$). Instead, curvilinear regression analysis in SPSS revealed that profit best correlates with H&S score with $R^2 = 0.4556$ at $P < 0.001$ in an exponential growth curve model with a plausible equation (1) of:

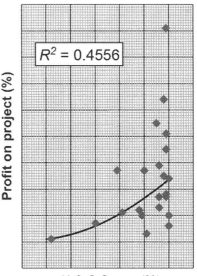

$R^2 = 0.4556$

Profit on project (%)

H & S Score (%)

Comments on Box 9.16

Although projects with a full H&S score did not all yield an overall profit, which suggests profitability depends on factors other than H&S management, projects that had an H&S sore of above 95 per cent had an average profit margin of 20 per cent. As the H&S score got lower, so did the average corresponding amount of profit. It can therefore be concluded that the better the H&S score of a project, the more profit that project is likely to make. It can also be said that the worse performing sites, in terms of score, actually make less profit. The results show that there is a link that can be drawn between H&S performance and profit.

The results also back up previous research and literature by the Health and Safety Executive that suggested investing in health and safety management can be a major contributor to business success.

Writing the conclusion chapter

The conclusion chapter is the end product of your investigation and should not be confused with the results chapter or a summary. It should be tied very closely with your introduction chapter. Before writing the conclusion chapter, you need to read your research aim, objectives and hypothesis (or key questions), and start to conclude what you investigated within the broader context of your proposal. Start reading the whole dissertation thoroughly and make a note of key issues or findings. The contents of the conclusion chapter should include the following:

1   Scope of chapter (one or two paragraphs).
2   Comments on the research objectives. Here, take each objective in turn and conclude what you have achieved in each objective. Are your conclusions similar or dissimilar to those of previous writers in the subject area?
3   Comments on the research hypothesis or the research questions (whichever is applicable). Here state whether your investigation proved or disproved your research hypothesis.
4   Achievement of the research aim. Remember that in your proposal as well as in the introduction chapter, you provided a statement of aim which was phrased as if you were to deliver some kind of a product such as to provide professional guidelines, to develop a conceptual framework, to construct a comparative table, to design a management system, to develop a chart or to derive a mathematical formula. In this section of the conclusion chapter, you need to demonstrate the achievement of that stated aim. Appendix 7 shows an example of an achieved aim which is related to Proposal 2 in Appendix 1 and also to the methodology road map in Figure 2.4 on page 22. The aim of this research was 'To provide a guideline to clients on the selection of the appropriate procurement method for their projects'.
5   Personal recommendations (practical) as to what should and should not be done: perhaps a modification of your conceptual model or a development of a new framework.

6   Limitations of your research. Here, state what difficulties you were faced with throughout the research process that hindered you from achieving part of your objectives.
7   Further research.

Writing the references/bibliography

There are several different ways of citing references in your dissertation and describing the sources of your references, such as the Harvard (author–date) system and the Vancouver (numerical) system. Guides can be found in most libraries. It has to be stressed that it is essential that you use references in accordance with the guidance issued by your course, which may be included in unit guides or as a separate school publication.

Before describing how to compile your references, general information on using the Harvard system in your dissertation is provided in Table 9.1. It covers the basic information that is needed for different types of sources.

Note to students

Table 9.1 is constructed with the aid of guides from LSBU and UWL on how to reference in the Harvard Style. For more information on referencing sources, visit the following link:

☞ **https://my.lsbu.ac.uk/my/wcm/connect/7f0a7e1d-efd6-49b1-9c6d-3566d3f97094/Harvard_updated+Jan+2018.pdf?MOD=AJPERES**

Or simply type into Google 'Referencing LSBU guide 2017'.

☞ **https://www.uwl.ac.uk/library/finding-and-using-information/referencing**

Or simply type into Google 'UWL – Cite them right on line'.

What does 'referencing' mean?

References to the particular source are required if you draw upon another writer's ideas in your dissertation, or if you make a direct quote. Important reasons for referencing are:

1   to acknowledge other people's ideas;
2   to show that you are not just giving your own opinions but are also including those of other people;
3   to illustrate a point or to offer support for an argument you want to make;
4   to enable readers of your work to find the source material.

A well-used quotation can make a point clearly and concisely, but try not to overuse quotations. It is important that you demonstrate your understanding of what you have read and are able to develop your own ideas by putting points or arguments into your own words.

Table 9.1 *A general guide for writing references*

Type of Referencing	Format	Example	In Text Citation If END Paragraph	In Text Citation If BEGINNING of Paragraph
Book	Author's surname, Initials. (Year of publication) Title of book. Edition if later than the first e.g. 2nd edn. Place of publication: Publisher.	Naoum, S.G. (2011) People and Organizational Management in Construction. ISBN 978-0-7277-4151-6, 2nd edn. London: ICI Publishers.	(Naoum, 2011)	According to Naoum (2011) …
Book by two authors	Authors' surnames, Initials. (Year of publication) *Title of book.* Edition if later than the first e.g. 2nd edn. Place of publication: Publisher.	Burns T. and Sinfield, S. (2006) *Essential Study Skills – The Complete Guide to Success at University.* Sage, London.	(Burns and Sinfield, 2006)	According to Burns and Sinfield (2006) …
Book by more than two authors	Authors' surnames, Initials. (Year of publication) *Title of book.* Edition if later than the first e.g. 2nd edn. Place of publication: Publisher.	Laycock, E., Howarth, T. and Watson, P. (2016) *The Journey to Dissertation Success for Construction, Property and Architecture Students.* Oxford: Routledge.	(Laycock et al., 2016)	Laycock et al. (2016) argue …
Chapter in a book	Author's surname, Initials. (Year of publication) Title of the chapter, in: Editor's surname, Initials. (ed.) or (eds.) *Title of the book.* Edition if later than the first e.g. 2nd edn. Place of publication: Publisher, page range of chapter.	Naoum, S.G. (2015) Productivity in Construction Projects, in: Robinson, H. et al. (eds.) *Design Economics for the Built Environment.* Wiley-Blackwell Publishers, Chichester. pp. 128–141.	… although other authors have denied this (Naoum, 2015).	Naoum (2015) refuted the premise that …
Print journal article	Author's surname, Initials. (Year of publication) Title of the article, *Title of the Journal,* volume number (issue number), page range of the article.	Naoum, S.G. and Hackman, J. (1996) Do site managers and the head office perceive productivity factors differently? *Journal of Engineering, Construction and Architectural Management,* 3 (1), pp. 147–160.	The term 'productivity' is generally defined as the maximisation of output while optimising input (Borcherding et al. 1986).	This notion supports the findings of Naoum and Hackman (1996) who found that ineffective project planning and design errors as the most crucial factors influencing productivity.

Online journal article	Author's surname, Initials. (Year of publication) Title of the article, *Title of the Journal*, volume number (issue number), page range of the article. DOI: DOI number.	Dainty, A. and Edwards, D. (2003) The UK building education recruitment crisis: a call for action. *Construction Management and Economics*, 21 (7), pp. 767–775. [Online]. Available from: Taylor & Francis Online. http://0-www.tandfonline.com.lispac.lsbu.ac.uk/doi/pdf/10.1080/0144619032000072146 [Accessed 25 February 2018].	This crisis prompted industry leaders to implement new initiatives aimed at easing the skills shortage; one of which was an effort to diversify the workforce, with measures being taken to recruit more women into the construction industry (Dainty and Edwards, 2003).	Chandra and Loosemore (2004) surveyed the self-perception of women in construction, legal and nursing professions in Australian in an effort to find out how the attitudes and self-confidence of women working in male-dominated fields differ from those in female-dominated industries and industries. They found …
Multiple references with the same author and publication year	Documents with the same author and publication year can be distinguished from each other by putting a letter after the year in both the in-text citations and reference list.	Leung, M. Y., Chan, Y. S. and Olomolaiye, P. (2008a) Impact of stress on the performance of construction project managers. *Journal of Construction Engineering and Management*, 134, pp. 644–652.	(Leung et al., 2008a), (Leung et al., 2008b) etc. …	as Leung et al. (2008a) confirm …
Multiple references for the same idea or concept	When you use multiple references to back up an idea, the in-text citations should be written in chronological order.	Brown (1998), Chandra, (2001), Smith (2009), Yates (2015) confirmed that …	… as multiple authors confirm (Brown, 1998; Chandra, 2001; Smith, 2009; Yates, 2015) …	
Citing a direct quote	If you quote the exact words directly from a text you must use quotation marks to indicate this. The author(s) and date must be stated, and if available the page number.	Naoum, S.G. (2015) Critical review of procurement method research in construction journals. *Procedia Economics and Finance*, 21, pp. 6–13.	A procurement method can be defined as a: 'mechanism for linking and coordinating members of the building team together throughout the building process in a unique systematic structure, both functionally and contractually. Functionally, via roles, authority and power; contractually, via responsibilities and risks. The main aim is to deliver a project that meets its objectives and fulfil the client criteria needs and expectations.' (Naoum, 2015, p. 6).	Naoum (2015, p. 16) defined a procurement method as a: '……………………………………; ……………………………………'.

(continued)

Table 9.1 (Continued)

Type of Referencing	Format	Example	In Text Citation If END Paragraph	In Text Citation If BEGINNING of Paragraph
Secondary referencing	If you want to cite a work which is referenced in another work, you should try and track down the original. However, if this isn't possible, make it clear in your text where you found the information and only include a reference to the document you've read.	Your reference list will include a reference to Creswell and Creswell's work, but not to Kerlinger's. Creswell, J. and Creswell, D. (2018) *Research Design: Qualitative, Quantitative Approach and Mixed Methods Approach*. 5th edn. Sage, London.	(Kerlinger 1979, cited in Croswell and Croswell, 2018, p. 73). Kerlinger (1979) revealed that . . . (cited in Croswell and Croswell, 2018, p.73).	Kerlinger (1979), cited by Croswell and Croswell (2018, p. 73), defined a theory as: 'a set of interrelated constructs (variables or questions), that presents a systematic view of phenomena by specifying relationships among variables, with the purpose of explaining natural phenomena. Here, the systematic view might be an argument, a discussion, or a rationale that helps explain (or predict) phenomena that occur in the world'.
Print conference paper	Author's surname, Initials. (Year of publication) Title of conference paper, in: *Title of conference*, Location, date of conference. Place of publication: Publisher, page range of paper.	Khalfan, M., McDermott, P. and Cooper, R. (2004) Integrating the supply chain within construction industry, in: *20th Annual ARCOM Conference*, Heriot Watt University, September 1–3, 2, pp. 897–904.	(Khalfan et al., 2004)	. . . While Khalfan et al. (2004) stated that, 'Supply chain management is directed toward the minimisation of transaction cost and the enhancement and transfer of expertise between all parties'.
Online conference paper	Surname, Initials. (Year of publication) Title of conference paper, in: *Title of conference*, Location, date of conference, page range of paper. Available from: Name of database. URL [Accessed day month year].	Galea, N. and Loosemore, M. (2006) Men and conflict in the construction industry, in: *22nd Annual ARCOM Conference*, 4–6 September 2006, Birmingham, UK. [Online]. Available from: ARCOM http://www.arcom.ac.uk/-docs/proceedings/ar2006-0843-0850 [Accessed 17 March 2013].		

Source type	Format	Reference list example	In-text citation example	Running text example
Dissertations and theses	Author's surname, Initials. (Year submitted) *Title of dissertation/thesis.* Level of award, Location of awarding institution if not clear from name: Name of awarding institution.	Dreschler, M. (2009) *Fair competition: how to apply the economically most advantageous tender (EMAT) award mechanism in the Dutch construction industry.* MSc dissertation, Delft University of Technology, Delft.	Based on this principle, the Most Economically Advantageous Tender (MEAT) evaluation methods need to be elaborated to clarify the winning chance of the bid with the most optimal value-price ratio (Dreschler, 2009).	Dreschler (2009) asserted that the MEAT method differs from the tender that focuses only on price minimisation (i.e. lowest price bid for fixed-requirements) or the tender that focuses only on value maximisation (i.e. fixed-price design contest). MEAT's aim is optimisation of the value-price tender.
Standards	Name of organisation (Year of publication) *Standard number: Title of standard.* Place of publication: Publisher.	British Standards Institution (2005) BS 7000-6: 2005: *Guide to managing inclusive design.* London: BSI.	(British Standards Institution, 2005)	According to the British Standards Institution (2005)
Legal cases (option 1 – if the case was heard *before* 2001)	*Names of parties* (year) volume number abbreviation for name of report and first page of report	*R v Eduard (John)* (1991) 1 WLR 2017		The case of *R v Eduard (John)* (1991)
Legal cases (option 1 – if the case was heard on or after 2001)	*Name of parties* [year] abbreviation of court case number, (year) volume number abbreviation for name of report and first page of report	*Joseph v Spiller* [2010] UKSC 53, (2011) 1 AC 852		The case of *Joseph v Spiller* [2010]

How many references do I need to make?

There is no hard and fast rule as to how many references are required in a dissertation and much may depend upon the topic. Generally it would be impossible and unwieldy if you referenced every point you made but general guidance is that the main points or arguments you present, and especially direct quotes or ideas drawn directly from other people's work, should be acknowledged and referenced. Failure to give credit to other people's work appropriately could be considered plagiarism.

What is plagiarism?

Plagiarism is to 'use the thoughts, writings, inventions, etc. of another person as one's own' (Soanes and Stevenson, 2004). Usually we are all formulating our own ideas from different information heard and read, but plagiarism involves a deliberate attempt to pass off someone else's ideas as your own, or to copy sections or chunks of texts from another's work without attempting to put these ideas into your own words or to acknowledge the sources. It is a form of theft and is certainly regarded as a serious offence in educational settings.

☞ **To find out more about 'avoiding the charge of plagiarism', see section 3.12 in Farrell et al. (2017, pp. 62–64)**

How do I incorporate references and quotations into my dissertation?

Using the Harvard system, you must always give the author(s) and year of publication of your source. References can be incorporated into the text in a variety of ways, such as in the following examples:

- In the following example, you are making a statement in your own words and giving a reference for the source of your ideas or support for your argument:

  According to Naoum (2018), there are variations in the way productivity can be defined. Further examples: A recent television programme discussed … (BBC, 2018).
  Research undertaken by Naoum (2016) indicated that … Statistics show that … (HSE, 2018).

- In the following example, you are making a direct quote (note that you must include the page number also): Kerlinger (1994) states that:

  a theory is a set of interrelated constructs (variables or questions), that presents a systematic view of phenomena by specifying relationships among variables, with the purpose of explaining natural phenomena. Here, the systematic view might be an argument, a discussion, or a rationale that helps explain (or predict) phenomena that occur in the world. (Kerlinger, 1994, p. 73).

How do I refer to a work which I have not seen myself but which is referred to in something that I have read?

These are known as secondary or second-hand references. Ideally they should be avoided as you should have read the original items yourself but, if it is unavoidable, it is important to make clear that this is a secondary reference, as follows:

> Example: Dunn (2018), as cited by Naoum and Egbu (2016), believed ... or Dunn (2018) revealed that ... (cited in Naoum and Egbu, 2016) or ... (Dunn, 2018, cited in Naoum and Egbu, 2016). Your reference list will include a reference to Naoum and Egbu's work, but not to Dunn's.

The 'cited by' statement makes it clear that you have not seen the item by Dunn, only what Naoum and Egbu say about it. Details of the item by Naoum and Egbu will then appear in the reference list at the end of your dissertation as this is the source of your information, that is:

> Naoum, S.G. and Egbu, C. (2016) Modern selection criteria for procurement methods in construction: A state-of-the-art literature review and a survey. *International Journal of Managing Projects in Business.* Issue 3/4, 2016, p. 310.

Compiling the reference list and bibliography

What is the difference between a reference list and a bibliography?

A reference list contains details of any item you have referred to or quoted from in your dissertation. A bibliography is a list of items you have made use of in preparing your dissertation, but not referred to in your text.

How do I set out my reference list and bibliography?

Both lists are placed at the end of your dissertation and usually the reference list appears first. Both lists will be arranged in alphabetical order of author (following the Harvard system), and details given should be presented in a consistent format. Usually it is not necessary to include in your bibliography any item already listed in your reference list.

What details are required and where do I find these details?

Details required for a book can be found on the front and reverse of the title page, which is usually the first or second unnumbered page inside the book.

Details for a book should be set out in the following order: Author, Initials (year) *Title*. Edition (if later than first). Place of publication (Town): Name of publisher. Example:

> Naoum, S.G. (2013) *Dissertation Research & Writing for Construction Students*. London: Routledge.

Details required for a journal article can usually be found on the contents list, the front cover or the article itself. Details for a journal article should be set out in the following order:

Author, Initials (year) Title of article. *Name of journal*. Volume number (Issue number), Date of issue, First and last pages. Example:

> Naoum, S.G. (2016) Factors influencing labour productivity on construction sites: A state-of-the-art literature review and a survey. *International Journal of Productivity and Performance Management*, 65 (3), pp. 401–421.

It is not necessary to put authors' names in capitals but it can help to make them stand out. Equally it can help readers if you underline titles or use a different typeface.

How do I give details from an edited book when the chapters are by different authors?

It is important to give details for each of the chapters you have referred to or used. The details of the chapter come first and then details of the book as a whole. Example:

> Brewster, C. (1992) Managing industrial relation in Towers, B. (ed.) *A Handbook of Industrial Relations Practice: Practice and law in the employment relationship*. 3rd edn. London: Kogan Page. Ch. 8.

Points to note:

1   *Authors*: If there are more than two authors it is acceptable to put the first author listed followed by *et al.* (which means 'and others') in the text. If you need to refer to two or more items written by the same author in the same year use letters to differentiate the items, for example Naoum (2016a), Naoum (2016b).

2   *Dates*: Occasionally items do not give a date of publication, in which case you put the abbreviation 'n.d.' in brackets (this stands for 'no date'). This shows that you have checked for the date and not just forgotten to include it.

3   *Edition*: Include edition statements only if later than the first edition. No edition statement indicates that it is a first edition. Make sure that you match the edition statement with the correct year of publication. This should be indicated clearly on the reverse of the title page.

4   *Page numbers*: You should always put a page number for a quote. In some cases the point you make might be referred to on a specific page or between specific pages (e.g. pp. 172–175). Sometimes it may be difficult to give specific page numbers as an argument may be supported by the item as a whole.

How do I describe a government report or an Act of Parliament?

Most reports will have a government department, body or committee as an author, or may be well known by the name of the chairperson of the group or committee. With Acts of Parliament it is acceptable, and often easier, to cite the title of the Act in your text and then to include it in the reference list in alphabetical order of the first main word of the Act. Examples:

Secretary of state for health (1992) Health of the nation: a strategy for health in England. London: HMSO.
Education ACT 1988. London: HMSO.

NB: HMSO is frequently the publisher of government reports and of all Acts. This abbreviation is acceptable. However, it is incorrect to describe HMSO as the author of a report, even if there is no clear author.

What about describing other types of material such as videos, leaflets and internet-based resources?

These are important sources of information but sometimes can be harder to describe. The golden rule always is to describe items as fully and clearly as possible, and in a consistent format. In the case of television/radio programmes, make sure you note the date and channel of transmission. Unless self-evident it may be useful to indicate that an item is an audio or video-cassette.

In the case of leaflets, the author is often the organisation publishing the leaflet. Example:

London South Bank University (n.d.) *Referencing using the Harvard System: Frequently asked questions*. London.

Finally, remember to:

*   Keep a careful note of all your sources as you prepare your dissertation.
*   Make a note of book details before you return the book to the library.

- Make sure you have the details you require on any photocopies you make.
- Make sure you are referencing according to any guidelines set by your course.

This may seem like hard work but it is a vital part of your dissertation and you may lose marks for incorrect referencing.

Summary

This chapter provided the guidelines that simplify the writing and organising of the dissertation material. It illustrated the logic of structuring the dissertation. In general, a dissertation is composed of three main parts. Part I covers the introduction chapter as well as two or three chapters of literature review. Part II covers the research design. Part III covers analysis of the results and conclusions. The main points to remember are:

1   The abstract should be brief, stating what you are investigating, how and the main finding(s).
2   The introduction chapter should state the problem, purpose of study, aim, objectives, hypothesis and contents of the dissertation.
3   The literature chapters should be divided into sections with specific themes. All quotations must be acknowledged. At the end of each chapter, you need to appraise (critically or otherwise) the material that you included.
4   The research design chapter should give the technique that you used to gather the information, the rationale to the questionnaire, the source of data, characteristics of the sample, the method of analysis and/or the format for presenting the findings.
5   The results chapter should clearly state the issues under investigation, the findings and comments on or interpretation of the results.
6   The conclusion chapter should comment on the objectives and hypothesis/es that are stated in the introduction chapter.
7   The references/bibliography should follow a uniform system.
8   Other mechanics of presenting a dissertation, such as length and page formatting, should be followed in accordance with the rules and regulations set by your institution.

References

American Psychological Association (1974) Publication manual. *Journal of Personality and Social Psychology*, 29, 80–85.
Bell, J. (2005) *Doing Your Research Project: A Guide for First-Time Researchers in Education and Social Science*. 4th edn. McGraw-Hill International, New York.
Cooper, H. (1995) *Quality assurance in practice*, BSc dissertation, School of Construction, London South Bank University.
Green, S. (1996) *An investigation into the effect of safety culture and site operatives behaviour on construction site safety in the UK*, BSc dissertation, School of Construction, London South Bank University.

Hackman, J. (1993) *An investigation into the factors that impair the productivity of site managers*, MSc dissertation, School of Construction Economics and Management, London South Bank University.

Haywood, P. and Wragg, W. (1982) *Evaluating the Literature, Rediguide 2*. University of Nottingham, School of Education, Nottingham.

Hemmings, B. (2009) *A study into the correlation between contractor's Health and Safety performance and contractors profit: Can effective safety management improve a contractor's profit margin?*, MSc dissertation, Department of the Built Environment, London South Bank University.

Howard, M. (1995) *Marketing and the quantity surveyor: Understanding clients*, MSc dissertation, School of Construction, London South Bank University.

Mulholland, Z.E. (2010) *An examination of sustainable construction in the recession*, MSc dissertation, Department of the Built Environment, London South Bank University.

Naoum, S.G. (1989) *An investigation into the performance of management contracts and the traditional methods of building procurement*, PhD thesis, Brunel University, Middlesex.

Naoum, S.G. (1991) Procurement and project performance: A comparison of management and traditional contracting. Occasional Paper No. 45, Chartered Institute of Building, Ascot.

Naoum, S.G. and Hackman, J. (1996) Do site managers and the head office perceive productivity factors differently? *Journal of Engineering, Construction and Architectural Management*, 3, March/June, 147–159.

Naoum, S.G. and Langford, D. (1987) Management contracting: The clients' view. *Journal of Construction Engineering and Management*, 111 (3), Sept, 369–384.

Naoum, S.G., Hemmings, B. and D. Fong (2011) Is there a correlation between contractor's health and safety performance and their profit margins? *6th International Structural Engineering and Construction Conference (ISEC – 6)*, 21–26 June, Zurich. Paper ID S1–C32.

Soanes, C. and Stevenson, A. (2004) *Concise Oxford English Dictionary*. Oxford University Press, Oxford.

South Bank University (n.d.) *Referencing Using the Harvard System: Frequently Asked Questions*. London South Bank University, London.

Additional reading

Farrell, P., Sherratt, F. and Richardson, A. (2017) *Writing Built Environment Dissertations and Projects – Practical Guidance and Examples*. 2nd edn. Wiley Blackwell, Chichester. *Read Chapter 3 (Review of theory and the literature)*.

Laycock, E., Howarth, T. and Watson, P. (2016) *The Journey to Dissertation Success for Construction, Property and Architecture Students*. Routledge, London. *Read Chapter 5 (Evaluating the existing literature)*.

10 Dissertation supervision and assessment

Once you have decided on the topic of your study and your proposal gets approved, your department should then appoint a personal supervisor for you. It is therefore important to know the role of your supervisor and what is expected from him/her.

This chapter will discuss the basics of what you should expect from your supervisor. It first explains what the role of the supervisor is and what it is not. Second, it illustrates how you may plan your dissertation and finally how would you expect to be assessed in the end.

It has to be stressed, however, that the information provided in this chapter is what is known as the standard, and different institutions might have other requirements and regulations.

Getting started

Most universities run dissertation workshops that cover a range of issues such as identification of research questions, assessing whether the topic is researchable, planning and undertaking a literature review, research strategies, research techniques, data analysis, writing and structuring the dissertation.

Following these workshops, each student will then submit a dissertation proposal (similar to the ones shown in Appendix 1). This proposal usually gets approved by the dissertation tutor (a person who is responsible for the dissertation module in your department).

After that, the dissertation tutor will allocate you a supervisor to look after your work. This allocation takes place during your study term and usually in the middle of the last term.

Once you are allocated a supervisor, it is your responsibility to arrange meetings with him/her. It is advisable to arrange a meeting with your supervisor as early as possible. Your supervisor should have a copy of the approved proposal, which forms the basis of discussion in these initial meetings.

It is strongly recommended that students and supervisors should meet at least twice following their initial meetings (proposal stage): once in the middle of the process to discuss progress, and once in the final stages to discuss the final draft. Additional meetings may be required for some students to discuss progress and drafts of individual chapters as they are written (see Dissertation supervision log section on page 206). These additional contacts may take place electronically, for example, by e-mail.

Note to students

It is unlikely that you can change your allocated supervisor. On rare occasions, students may find it difficult to work with the allocated supervisor. In such cases, the dissertation tutor should act as a mediator to resolve the differences through some agreed action plan. If this fails, then a different allocation should be arranged. It must be stressed, however, that, if this unlikely situation occurs, it should be acknowledged and sorted as soon as possible before it is too late. Your supervisor is a resource, so use him/her to your advantage. He/she has normally been allocated time by the department to supervise you, so make sure you take advantage of this, but bear in mind that your supervisor is there to help you, not to do your work for you.

The role of the supervisor

The role of supervisor is to guide students towards the production of their dissertation by discussing each part of the process. The role of your supervisor can be summarised as follows:

1 To help you to develop your idea/topic further.
2 To help you to focus on your aim and objectives.
3 To help you sharpen your research questions and/or hypotheses.
4 To provide you with initial sources of literature such as up-to-date journal papers to help kick start your investigation.
5 To provide you with guidance about the appropriate research approach.
6 To approve your questionnaire before you distribute it to respondents.
7 To assist you in structuring your dissertation.
8 To discuss and monitor your progress.
9 To provide you with feedback on your chapters. This may be in the form of criticisms of your work.
10 To help you to present the final dissertation.

☞ **Also see 'list of supervisors' role' in Laycock et al. (2016, pp. 40–51).**

What is not the role of the supervisor?

From the previous section, it is clear that your supervisor's duty is to guide you so that you can produce your best work. However, there are certain limitations on what is expected from your supervisor. These can be summarised as follows:

- Supervisors are not obliged to act as proofreaders of your work.
- Students should not expect their supervisor to provide detailed feedback on more than one draft of each chapter (writing a dissertation is not an iterative process), or to correct spelling, grammar, punctuation and so on.
- It is recommended that supervisors read the whole of the final draft before submission. However, if they do so, it is on the understanding that the result of the final examination is not in any way pre-judged.

- Supervisors are not to assist with continual revision until the dissertation has acquired a certain grade that you may have as a target. Therefore, the supervisor's approval of your progress cannot be taken to imply any particular grade or classification. It is not expected that you request this from your supervisor at any stage of the dissertation module.

Planning your dissertation

In order not to let things drift, it is absolutely crucial to plan and time-manage your dissertation process. Figure 10.1 is an example of a work schedule for a typical dissertation.

Notes to students

- Many of the aforementioned activities may overlap or take place before or after the suggested activities within the work schedule. For example, writing your literature chapters may take place while you analyse your questionnaire.
- There might be other activities involved in your research. For example, your dissertation might include a separate chapter on 'Discussion'. Alternatively, you might wish to include a separate chapter titled 'Critical appraisal of literature' and insert it after Chapter 3 in the suggested work schedule shown in Figure 10.1. Your dissertation topic may necessitate a further chapter of literature review, so you should allow time for it.

Therefore, you need to design your work schedule to fit your own needs (Figure 10.1).

Dissertation supervision log

As mentioned, you should arrange 'formal' meetings with your supervisor at least three times throughout the whole process. I call them 'formal' because, at each of these meetings, it is recommended that you fill out a 'log' form like the one shown in Figure 10.2. Some institutions even require these logs to be signed by the supervisor.

The purpose of these log forms is to keep a record of your progress and to act as milestones. You can arrange as many meetings as you and your supervisor think necessary, but the three essential meetings are:

Meeting 1: Proposal stage
Meeting 2: Progress
Meeting 3: Final draft

Notes to students

- You may need more than one progress meeting.
- After you complete the log form, it is strongly recommended that you send a copy to your supervisor for information and filing. You can do this by electronic means.

Activity	Planned starting date	Tick when completed	Comments
1. Identify a topic			
2. Undertake background reading			
3. Identify working title			
4. Prepare dissertation proposal			
5. Proposal approved by dissertation tutor			
6. First meeting with your supervisor after proposal approved			
7. Undertake literature review			
8. Building up your literature file			
9. Designing a questionnaire (if applicable)			
10. Designing a data collection format for secondary data (if applicable)			
11. Questionnaire or data collection format approved by your supervisor			
12. Building up a list of respondents for postal survey or interviews			
13. Sending out questionnaire			
14. Conducting interviews (if applicable)			
15. Collating secondary data for analysis (if applicable)			
16. Analysing the questionnaire, interviews or secondary data			
17. Write Chapter 1–Introduction			
18. Write Chapter 2–Literature			
19. Write Chapter 3–Literature			
20. Write Chapter 4–Research design and methodology			
21. Write Chapter 5–Findings			
22. Write Chapter 6–Conclusions			
23. Write list of references			
24. Write abstract			
25. Give final draft to a critical reader to proof read			
26. Give final draft to your supervisor for final comments and feedback			
27. Write acknowledgement			
28. Insert appendices			
29. Insert list of tables and figures			
30. Send to binding			
31. Submit			

Figure 10.1 *Example of typical dissertation work schedule.*

Dissertation Supervision Log

Student's Name _____   **Supervisor's Name** _____

Meeting Number _____   **Date:** _____

Issues Discussed/Comments:

1.

2.

3.

4.

5.

Figure 10.2   *Example of a typical log form.*

Dissertation assessment: Qualities in assessing at MSc level

In the following notes, an overview is given about the qualities expected in the three marking bands (distinction, pass and fail) at London South Bank University (Buckley and Naoum, 2011). I cannot stress enough that this is only an example of assessing the quality of dissertations at MSc level and it may not be considered the norm. Other universities or courses, such as BSc, may apply different qualities of assessment.

There are three aspects to consider when assessing the qualities of a Masters dissertation:

1 Descriptions of qualities.
2 Judgement of the degree of difficulty.
3 Key words. They are designed as prompts for the marking teams and the qualities should be considered in combination and should not be interpreted mechanically.

Descriptions of qualities

Distinction (70 marks or over)

The dissertation will contain some originality in the research subject chosen or in the research questions that have been developed. The study will demonstrate a sustained and rigorous use of theoretical/conceptual or empirical evidence to support the argument or discussion. Definitions and assumptions will be clear throughout the work. There will be strong evidence of critical analysis, judgement, originality or interpretation.

There will be discussion of methods and sources that link the research design or research approach to appropriate literature about research methods. There will be reflection about the research process or the questions for further research, which are suggested by the findings of the study. There must be an argument put forward to support the methods adopted.

The study will be well structured and written in good English. A coherent and well-considered argument will be developed. Accurate referencing of sources will be shown in an appropriate way throughout the study.

Pass (50–69 marks)

The study will include a systematic review of relevant literature or other sources of information or data. There may be some evidence of originality in the research question(s) or in the approach taken to the subject. The research will contain a synthesis of appropriate ideas, evidence or data. Good use will be made of data and information to highlight new knowledge, to support argument, or to criticise current ideas, approaches, research methods or practices.

The discussion of methods and sources will include arguments in support of the methods or approach taken, or a description of the project design. There will be some references to the research methods literature or similar appropriate material. An attempt will be made to reflect on the research method used.

The dissertation will be well structured and written in good English. Accurate referencing of sources will be shown in the appropriate way.

Fail (49 marks or under)

The research question(s) will not be well developed. There will be a limited review of appropriate literature or sources of information or data. The dissertation will contain an incomplete or sketchy treatment of theoretical or empirical material. The development of the data or information collected will be descriptive and may not be used in the right way. Argument is less likely to be developed or sustained.

Discussion of research methods will not be developed and is likely to contain important errors. There will be a lack of judgement about the research method used.

The dissertation will be poorly written. Referencing will be generally inaccurate or inadequate.

An example of a final dissertation marking scheme (grid) is shown in Table 10.1.

☞ **See another example of a 'marking grid for dissertation' in Laycock et al. (2016, p. 227).**

Degree of difficulty

The degree of difficulty of the research that the student has attempted needs to be distinguished. This can be done by judgement of *one or more* of the following four criteria:

1   The degree of difficulty contained within the research question(s).
2   The degree of difficulty contained in the methodology; findings.
3   The degree of difficulty in the evidence collected or arguments presented.
4   The degree of difficulty in synthesis and the organisation of the research.

The quality standard of the dissertation (distinction, pass or fail) may be judged by assessing the key words in the three categories shown in Box 10.1.

Box 10.1 Key words

Distinction	Pass	Fail
accuracy	analysis	brief
ambition	application	description
appraisal	calculation	error
balance	demonstration	incomplete
critical	experiment	irrelevant
evaluation	ideas	narrow
evidence	knowledge	omission
imagination	organisation	superficiality
interpretation	reflection	vagueness
judgement	review	
originality	sources	
rigorous	structure	
scope	synthesis	
style		
testing		
theory		

Note to students

Distinction level should also include criteria of the Pass category.

Table 10.1 *University of West London – Assessment grid*

ORGANISATION AND COHERENCE	20	0–8	9–14	15–20	Grade Awarded
• The study must be clearly structured and presented. • The introduction must state an aim and explicitly identify the relevant arguments and areas to be addressed. • These areas, once identified must be followed up logically in the main body of the study. • There must be a firm conclusion of the areas discussed.		Poor organisation and structure. Limited discussion.	Some attention paid to the structure and organisation/coherence. Evidence of discussion.	Good structure, presentation and coherently expressed. Widely discussed.	

CONTENT	35	0–13	14–24	25–35	
• The contents must clearly relate to the area of study, and the learning outcomes being tested, and demonstrate originality and creativity. • Knowledge and understanding must be applied to practice.		Limited relevance to the area of study and practice. Does not meet the theoretical learning outcomes.	Addressed the aims of the area of study with some originality and creativity. Applied to practice. Just meets all the theoretical learning outcomes.	Clearly relevant. Original and creative. Application and integration of knowledge to practice. Clearly meets all the theoretical learning outcomes.	

CLARITY OF EXPRESSION	15	0–4	5–10	11–15	
• Areas must be clearly expressed, articulate and fluent, whether written or graphical, using appropriate technical terminology. • Accurate spelling and grammar. • Accurate calculations and logic.		Vague, over simplistic, unclear. Poor spelling and grammar. Poor calculations and logic.	Communication clear. Spelling and/or grammar needs some improvement. Calculations and logic need some improvement.	Articulate and fluent. Good spelling and grammar. Good calculations and logic.	

(continued)

Table 10.1 (Continued)

		0–4	5–7	8–10
LEVEL OF ANALYSIS AND SYNTHESIS • There should be a clear critical analysis and synthesis of issues, which are well integrated and evaluated, as appropriate.	10	Wholly or mainly descriptive.	Shows some critical thinking and the beginnings of synthesis and evaluation.	Well integrated study with clear evidence of critical analysis/synthesis, and evaluation relevant to the area of study.
USE OF LITERATURE SHOWING KNOWLEDGE AND UNDERSTANDING • The study must demonstrate an appropriate use of academic literature/ research, which is appropriate to the study.	10	Limited use of academic literature/research evidence.	Moderate range but depth and complexity appropriate to area of study.	Extensive range, depth and complexity, which is appropriate to the area of study.
QUALITY OF REFERENCING • All key sources must be cited, and a consistent and accurate use of Harvard referencing system must be maintained.	10	Main key sources not cited. Limited or no use of an accepted referencing system.	Most sources cited using an accepted referencing system.	All key sources cited. Consistent and accurate use of an accepted referencing system.
				TOTAL

Note to students: This is only an example of assessing the quality of a dissertation and it may not be considered the norm. Other universities or courses may apply different qualities of assessment.

Examples of supervisors' feedback (see Boxes 10.2, 10.3 and 10.4)

Example 1 – Supervisor's feedback on an outstanding dissertation (Box 10.2)

Box 10.2 Example of a supervisor's feedback on an outstanding dissertation

1 **Formulation of research question (and/or hypothesis), aims and objectives**
(10%)___9___

Clarity of formulation
Appropriateness in terms of level and breadth
Clarity in articulation of background to and rationale for the research

Comments

Well considered questions based on detailed literature and personal knowledge. Also please see overall comments below.

2 **Literature review** (30%) ___28___

Relevance to the research question
Range of reading
Effectiveness in synthesis and evaluation

Comments

Excellent and effectively brings the literature related to error, health, safety and integration up-to-date at a standard more of a doctorate than a Masters dissertation.

3 **Selection and use of research methods** (20%)___16___

Appreciation of relevant methodological issues
Articulation of the rationale for selection of research approach
Competence in relation to information gathering and analysis
Awareness of strengths and weaknesses of approach taken

Comments

Appropriate, given the nature of the study. The expected limitations of statistical study were well recognised, but their use was also adequately justified. Qualitative interviews provided an appropriate second method and introduced the possibility of triangulation of findings.

---

4   **Coherence and quality of argument in response to the research question**
(30%) ___25___

Internal consistency of the whole work
Use of information to support argument throughout the whole work
Validity of conclusions
Awareness of strength and limitations of the work

Comments

This aspect was particularly strong, with a very detailed critique of methods, both pre and post study. There exists a very strong thread of reasoning from initial aim to recommendations in this work.

5   **Presentation**   (10%) ___8___

Use of Harvard referencing; style and comprehensiveness
Appropriateness of structure and presentation of text, figures and tables
Appropriateness of writing style and use of English

Comments

With very minor exceptions this was of good standard.

Overall general comments

This is an excellent dissertation, reporting research examining the link between levels of project integration and safety on construction sites in the United Kingdom. Considerable anecdotal and qualitative evidence has suggested that modern integrated forms of procurement and the use of 'partnered' projects have benefits in terms of business performance, health and safety. However, little empirical work has been attempted to provide an underpinning evidence base for this in relation to safety. Using data from 55 construction projects, within a single major UK based construction firm, the research involved firstly a statistical study to see if there was a significant difference between levels of integration on safety performance. A second study involved interviews with three senior project managers to both provide further evidence and establish cause. Significant differences were found ($P < 0.05$) for one measure of safety performance between traditional (or near traditional) projects and integrated projects (design and build or partnered), but generally the statistical study did not produce significant results. In contrast, the interviews revealed strong links between levels of integration (particularly between designers and constructors) and safety.

All aspects of the study and dissertation report were well executed, with only minor criticisms of detail. The literature review consisted of two parts, related to error/safety in construction and integration/partnering respectively. It was detailed, appropriate and thorough. The methods were appropriate, well justified and discussed and honestly critiqued post-study. The handling and discussion of intervening variables was particularly thorough. The selection of statistical tests was good and examination of their validity detailed and correct. Follow up interviews were well reported and both interview and statistical studies were rigorously linked back to the study aim, objectives and hypotheses. Conclusions followed through from findings and recommendations were appropriate and constructive. A minor criticism is that some of the methodology and findings sections contained unnecessary detail.

Overall, an outstanding dissertation. There is potential for a publishable paper based on its findings.

Total Mark   86 / 100

Example 2 – Supervisor's feedback on an average quality dissertation (Box 10.3)

Box 10.3 Example of a supervisor's feedback on an average quality dissertation

1   **Formulation of research question (and/or hypothesis), aims and objectives**
(10%) ___6___

Clarity of formulation
Appropriateness in terms of level and breadth
Clarity in articulation of background to and rationale for the research

Comments

Clearly set out in pages 13–15 and supported by a rationale that is more fully explored in the literature review. The development of the dissertation does not meet fully the overarching aim as stated.

2   **Literature review (30%)**   ___18___

Relevance to the research question
Range of reading
Effectiveness in synthesis and evaluation

Comments

Sources selected are relevant to the research and provide a generally sound theoretical underpinning to the dissertation. Some further incorporation of current initiatives and practice with particular reference to post-development impact assessment, e.g. CEEQUAL (referred to later in the work) would have been useful here and may have served to encourage a greater range of more specifically focused survey questions.

3   **Selection and use of research methods (20%)**   ___12___

Appreciation of relevant methodological issues
Articulation of the rationale for selection of research approach
Competence in relation to information gathering and analysis
Awareness of strengths and weaknesses of approach taken

Comments

The methodology chapter is reasonably robust in terms of its justification of survey-based research, its strengths and weaknesses. The consideration of other research methods is more limited and the decision to rely only on a survey is questionable. This is acknowledged by the author in the critical analysis of the chosen methodology in Chapter 5.

4   **Coherence and quality of argument in response to the research question** (30%) ___18___

Internal consistency of the whole work
Use of information to support argument throughout the whole work
Validity of conclusions
Awareness of strength and limitations of the work

Comments

Reasonable, although focus and consistency are intermittent in terms of developing and retaining a narrative that focuses on the overall aim, i.e. to critically evaluate the extent to which the EIA process is effective in the UK at the post-development stage. This is unfortunate, not least because this is a key issue that merits investigation. The analysis of the results from the survey questions was systematic and carefully considered but the author's own research could have been set up to focus more extensively on the main aim of the dissertation. Some subsequent statements, e.g. on pages 65 and 71, were not supported by evidence. Nevertheless some useful, if limited conclusions were drawn and the reflection on the strengths and weaknesses of the approach taken and suggestions for further research indicate a degree of academic maturity.

5   **Presentation (10%) ___6___**

Use of Harvard referencing; style and comprehensiveness
Appropriateness of structure and presentation of text, figures and tables
Appropriateness of writing style and use of English

Comments

Good overall, clearly written and set out, with very few editorial errors. Use of appendices is appropriate, although there should be reference to them in the main text.

Overall general comments

The author has demonstrated clearly a sound understanding of the nature and process of producing a dissertation. The main weakness of the submission is that it fails to address fully the dissertation's main aim, although it is addressed in part and the research provides a useful snapshot of the current state of practice in terms of attitudes of key stakeholders and their engagement with the EIA process. The diligence of the author to the task is evident and while the research results are limited, a considerable amount of care has been taken in the analysis and presentation of her findings.

An average dissertation.

Total Mark   60 / 100

Example 3 – Supervisor's feedback on a poor dissertation (Box 10.4)

Box 10.4 Example of a supervisor's feedback on a poor dissertation

1 **Formulation of research question (and/or hypothesis), aims and objectives**
(10%) ___3___

Clarity of formulation
Appropriateness in terms of level and breadth
Clarity in articulation of background to and rationale for the research

Comments

No clear or meaningful statement of aims and objectives. This is a fundamental flaw in the work. Aims and objectives are set out on page 2 but nevertheless could benefit from some further refinement so as to provide a clearer, more meaningful and deliverable research question. No clear rationale emerges and this is another fundamental flaw in the work.

2 **Literature review** (30%)___9___

Relevance to the research question
Range of reading
Effectiveness in synthesis and evaluation

Comments

Limited. References are sometimes incomplete and not fully up-to-date. There is little in the work that contributes to any sort of constructive analysis and evaluation of relevant literature, and although some useful research reports are referred to, due to the work's overall lack of focus and coherence, the helpfulness of such references is inevitably limited.

There is a cursory literature review on pages 3–5. This short section contains a number of editorial mistakes. No indication is given in the review as to whether the 'one case in 6 years' issue is considered to be a positive or negative development. The usefulness of this question has been commented upon in section 2 above. While there are references to some relevant literature elsewhere in the work, references are sometimes incomplete and not fully up-to-date. There is little in the work that contributes to any sort of constructive analysis and evaluation of relevant literature.

3 **Selection and use of research methods** (20%)___6___

Appreciation of relevant methodological issues
Articulation of the rationale for selection of research approach
Competence in relation to information gathering and analysis
Awareness of strengths and weaknesses of approach taken

Comments

This is provided on pages 6 and 7 but is limited in scope and in detail and fails to convince the reader that the author has an appropriate level of understanding of its general significance and application within the work itself. Sequencing of points and themes in this section could be improved. Further reflection on the usefulness of some proposed avenues of research (e.g. why only one case had come to the magistrates' court in 6 years) is needed. More explanation needed, e.g. as to the rationale for sending a questionnaire to local authorities; the response rate to the questionnaire was not clarified – see e.g. pages 47 and 65; and there should be some very careful reflection on the usefulness of asking a question on which there is no data, in the context of the work. Overall a weak aspect to the dissertation.

4   **Coherence and quality of argument in response to the research question**
(30 %) ___9___

Internal consistency of the whole work
Use of information to support argument throughout the whole work
Validity of conclusions
Awareness of strength and limitations of the work

Comments

There is no coherent debate, hence such debate as exists also lacks quality. It endeavours to embrace some sort of account of the contaminated land regime introduced by the Environment Act 1995, at the same time as considering the suitability of magistrates' courts as a forum for environmental enforcement which is a much wider issue. Much of what is written is descriptive, yet often lacking in context and at times is poorly sequenced.

As an introduction, Chapter 1 is much too diffuse and lacking in direction. It bears little relation to the environmental debates and issues relating to contaminated land. Pages 50–60 of Chapter 3 fail to focus on contaminated land and overall the relevance of Chapter 4 to the preceding chapters is unclear. Only Chapter 2 deals with contaminated land and the account is often jumbled, with limited and often outdated referencing, see e.g. pages 26 and 34. Within Chapter 2, sequencing is often poor, e.g. pages 27, 33 and 38, with no clear and logical development of themes and no attempt to link what is basically a descriptive account of the legal regime for contaminated land with preceding or succeeding chapters. This chapter would benefit additionally from more extensive legal referencing. Candidate needs to consider carefully where certain sections in Chapter 2 could be more appropriately located within the work, e.g. sections on pages 31, 42 and 46.

The candidate has produced what are essentially four separate and unrelated chapters, and has failed not only to identify a key research question / hypothesis but also to provide a clear structure and rationale for the work. Despite the title, Chapters 1, 3 and 4 have as their main focus such diverse subjects as world and UK 'environmental atlas', general accounts of historical and contemporary legislation, magistrates' courts, their constitution and general role, access to justice and information, social inequality. Chapter 3 does contain an account of a contaminated land case but this not fully integrated into the work.

Little or no critical evaluation or analysis – much more careful thought needs to be given to content and sequencing. There is a lack of robust discussion / investigation in respect of the stated aims and objectives. No clear discussion of objective 2 – why, for example was no reference made to Lewis on this issue? As regards objectives 3 and 4, the premise / rationale for these objectives is not fully explored and as regards contaminated land appears to be based on a faulty / misconceived hypothesis, i.e. only 1 case in the magistrates' court to discuss and confusion over why there is only 1 case to discuss. It is not clear if the writer regards the existence of only one case dealt with by the magistrates' courts in 6 years as good or a bad thing: he fails to explore the implications of this state of affairs or make clear links to relevant literature. He is therefore unwise to draw the firm conclusions he attempts to do.

There is a failure to set up and deliver a clear and logical development of themes due to some extent to poor sequencing, repetition and a failure to develop points fully. Inaccuracy of expression / confusion over the law in places, see e.g. pages 35 and 46 compounds the problem.

As a result, the conclusion is unhelpful.

5   **Presentation**   (10%)___3___

Use of Harvard referencing; style and comprehensiveness
Appropriateness of structure and presentation of text, figures and tables
Appropriateness of writing style and use of English

Comments

Poor structure and often inaccurate or incomplete referencing. A number of editorial errors. Incomplete bibliography – e.g. title of text often omitted.

Overall general comments

A most unfortunate outcome for a candidate who has evident enthusiasm for a wide range of environmental issues relating to law, policy and practice as well as wider environmental concerns. He needs to make a firm decision to focus on one of the four issues he endeavoured to deal with in the work.

A very poor dissertation.

Total mark   30 / 100

Summary

This chapter explained the role of the supervisor and the importance of planning your research to achieve the desired outcome. In short, your supervisor will provide you with the appropriate direction towards the production of your dissertation. He/she can advise you on the research strategy, methodology and structure of your dissertation. Your supervisor is not obliged to proofread or correct spelling and grammar.

It is essential that you time-manage your work. Therefore, drawing up a realistic work schedule is highly recommended.

It is also important to keep in close contact with your supervisor. You should arrange a formal meeting with him/her at least three times throughout the whole process.

It is also recommended to keep the log form up to date in order to record your progress.

Finally, it is essential that you have a vision into your university's dissertation marking scheme so that you work towards achieving the grade you are aiming at.

Reference

Buckley, M. and Naoum, S.G. (2011) *Dissertation Guide: Instructions for Preparation, Control and Presentation of the Dissertation.* Department of Property, Surveying and Construction, London South Bank University.

Additional reading

Laycock, E., Howarth, T. and Watson, P. (2016) *The Journey to Dissertation Success for Construction, Property and Architecture Students.* Routledge, London. *Read Chapter 4 (The role of the supervisor) and Chapter 9 (Writing up and assessment).*

Appendix 1
Examples of dissertation proposals

Proposal 1: Proposal for a descriptive type of research

Working title

Marketing and the private house-building companies in the UK: which marketing philosophy do successful companies have?

Rationale

The subject of this proposal developed from a personal interest in the dichotomy between technical excellence and customer orientation. In their book *In Search of Excellence*, Peters and Waterman (1982) point out that the most successful US firms were characterised by a common dedication to marketing. More specifically, the key to success lies in 'keeping close to the customer'.

The size of the private housing market in relation to total construction output is rather significant. It accounts for 14 per cent of construction output for an all work total and 24 per cent of construction output for total new work (National Economic Development Office, 2017). Hence, the proposed study is an important one and the author will be focusing on the marketing philosophy of the private house-building companies.

Literature provides numerous alternative definitions of marketing; most have certain basic features in common, especially the notion of looking at the firm from the point of view of the customer or striving to ensure mutual profitability from the marketing exchange. Other definitions place the emphasis on the essential managerial nature of marketing. Marketing, however, should be distinguished from selling (Foster, 1984). Selling is only one of several marketing functions and may not be the most important (Kotler and Armstrong, 2013). In addition, selling may require a different set of skills from those needed for marketing (Fisher, 1986).

Another important aspect of marketing which deserves close attention is 'Relational Marketing'. The marketing-led enterprise change management initiated by a major UK contractor was explored by Smyth and Fitch (2009) in their paper titled 'Application of relationship marketing and management: a large contractor case study'. Their premise was that procurement-led initiatives try to induce changes to behaviour through market governance. In their abstract, they stated:

Relationship marketing and management proactively change organizational behaviour, the enterprise taking responsibility for its own destiny. Investment and resource allocation, and organizational behaviour have posed constraints, particularly concerning service continuity in construction. Relationship marketing is the conceptual starting point, application developing into relationship management in line with theory. In the case explored, key account management (KAM) principles are adopted as the conceptual point of departure for introducing relationship marketing processes. Adoption resulted in some minor restructuring and provided the basis for a series of process changes. Application is producing early results in terms of increased client satisfaction, consequential repeat business, inducing greater cross-functional communication and collaboration within the firm resulting in cross-selling opportunities between market segments. Some repeat business is producing higher margins in response to meeting demands of the clients.

The principal theme of this research is to use Stanton and Futrell's (1987) marketing profiles and place each of the companies to be studied in a particular category and then link it to its financial performance. Stanton and Futrell established three marketing profile categories, namely, production orientation, sales orientation and marketing orientation.

The following sections of this proposal give further details about the principal objectives for this research.

Research goals

Aim

To construct a reference table that demonstrates those marketing philosophies of private house-building that led to a high financial performance.

Objectives

1 To survey large private house-building companies and investigate the following:
   a their business philosophy;
   b organisational structure;
   c marketing information system;
   d marketing planning and policy.
2 To explore companies' views concerning the philosophy of relational marketing.
3 To test the relationship between the companies' marketing philosophy and their financial performance.

Key questions

1 How do private house-building companies differ in marketing their businesses?

2 How do different private house-building companies view relational marketing?
3 Which marketing philosophy leads to higher financial performance?

Hypothesis

1 Most private house-building companies adopt the 'sales oriented' philosophy.
2 Relational marketing can increase client satisfaction.
3 Private house-building companies that adopt a 'high relational marketing' perform better financially.

Note to students

Notice that in this proposal, the student formulated three objectives, three key questions and three hypotheses. They are all interlinked in such a way that objective 1 is related to key question 1 and to hypothesis 1. Objective 2 is related to key question 2 and to hypothesis 2, and so on.

Initial literature review

In this part of the proposal, the student provided a two-page initial literature review about the subject of 'marketing'. This part of the proposal is basically an extension of the Rationale section given earlier. Do not forget to supplement your initial literature with supporting empirical facts that are fully referenced.

Methodology

Note to students

In this section of the proposal, you need to draw the methodology road map related to your research as shown in the example in Figure 2.3 on page 21 and Figure 2.4 on page 22.

Below is an outline of the stages involved

Stage 1: Literature review

This study will be confined to the private house-building sector, where there is a more direct link between the company and the end user. The initial survey of the literature reveals no specific study of marketing in the private house-building industry. However, the desk work for this study will concentrate on research which has looked at the construction industry in general, such as the earlier research of O'Callaghan (1986) and Stilgoe (1985). This should provide a useful point of reference.

Stage 2: Pilot study

Data collection will take the form of a structured postal questionnaire. However, an initial pilot study will be conducted to test the validity of the questionnaire through in-depth interviews with marketing managers.

Stage 3: Main survey questionnaire

The feedback from the pilot study should assist in finalising the questionnaire and preparing the ground for the main survey. The questions will centre around the areas mentioned in the aforementioned objectives. In order to obtain a high level of response, a multi-option format will be designed and limited to about 30 questions. Open questions are considered to be inappropriate as they would require the respondents to formulate an answer which needs lengthier input and will therefore be more difficult to analyse.

Stage 4: Analysing the postal questionnaire

The analysis of the questionnaire will take two forms. First, to determine the level of agreement or disagreement of the respondents to each question within the questionnaire by counting the number of respondents who answered favourably or unfavourably. Judging by the response, each company will be placed in one of the three marketing profile categories, that is production orientation, sales orientation or marketing orientation. Second, to correlate each of the marketing philosophy questions to the financial performance of each company. Financial information will be obtained from the business ratio report and from companies' annual reports. The level of financial performance will be gauged by establishing a marketing rating system applicable to private house-building companies.

Stage 5: Writing the research report

This stage involves writing up the content of the dissertation and should cover the chapters proposed in the following section.

Proposed structure of the dissertation

Chapter 1: Introduction
Chapter 2: Marketing theory and principles
Chapter 3: Marketing and the construction industry
Chapter 4: Research design and methodology
Chapter 5: Analysis of the results and discussion
Chapter 6: Conclusions and suggestions for further research
Chapter 7: References

Initial references

Fisher, N. (1986) *Marketing for the Construction Industry*. London: Longman.
Foster, D. (1984) *Mastering Marketing*. Hong Kong: Macmillan.
Kotler, P. and Armstrong, G. (2013) *Principles of Marketing*. 7th edn. New Jersey: Prentice Hall, Inc.

National Economic Development Office (2017) *Construction Forecast 2010–2011–2012*. London: HMSO.

O'Callaghan, J. (1986) '*Managerial Characteristics and Financial Performance of Construction Companies*'. MSc thesis, Brunel University.

Peters, T.Z. and Waterman, R.H. (1982) *In Search of Excellence: Lessons from America's Best Run Companies*. New York: Harper and Row.

Smyth, H. and Fitch, T. (2009) Application of relationship marketing and management: a large contractor case study. *Construction Management and Economics*, 27 (4), 399–410.

Stanton, W. and Futrell, C. (1987) *Fundamentals of Marketing*. International edition. New York: New McGraw-Hill.

Stilgoe, G. (1985) *Marketing Policy and Construction Firms*. MSc dissertation, Brunel University.

Programme of work

In this section of the proposal, a bar chart or a breakdown of activities, like the one shown in Figure 10.1 on page 207, should be attached showing the programme of work for the dissertation. It should also indicate the target dates for the completion of each of the stages shown in the methodology section.

Proposal 2: Proposal for the analytical approach/theoretical framework

Working title

The influence of procurement method on project performance: a comparative study between management contracting and the traditional form of contracts.

Rationale

It is axiomatic of construction management that a project may be regarded as successful if the building is completed as scheduled, within budget and quality standards as well as achieving a high level of client satisfaction. Increasingly, the fulfillment of these criteria has been associated with the problem of procurement method for construction. In short, the selection of the appropriate method can shape the success of the project.

Broadly speaking, the problems that are facing the building process are considered in relation to: separation of design from construction; lack of integration; lack of effective communication; uncertainty; changing environment; changing clients' priorities and expectations; and increasing project complexity. These, problems together with economic changes (e.g. inflation and recession), have led construction professionals and the industry to offer alternative methods of building procurement such as design and build, management contracting and construction project management. There are other mechanisms in procuring a project such as partnering, Public Finance Initiative (PFI), PPP, alliancing and ProCure 21 which may also be considered to fall under the term 'procurement method'. However, according to Clamp et al. (2007), they might be more accurately described as an approach to procurement. Naoum (2003) described it as a 'philosophy and a contract of trust'. For example, most partnering arrangements are an over-arching agreement, which encompass one or several contracts let under one of the three key procurement routes, namely, the fragmented route such as the traditional method, fully integrated such as design and build, partially integrated such as management contracting.

The large amount of research has given rise to a similarly large number of definitions of procurement method. Two of the many definitions are:

> [...] a procurement system is an organizational system that assigns specific responsibilities and authorities to people and organizations, and defines the relationships of the various elements in the construction of a project
>
> (Love et al., 2012)

> [...] a mechanism for linking and coordinating members of the building team together throughout the building process in a unique systematic structure, both functionally and contractually. Functionally, via roles, authority and power; contractually, via responsibilities and risks. The main aim is to deliver a project that meets the objectives and fulfil the client criteria needs and expectations
>
> (Naoum and Egbu, 2016)

The literature shows that construction procurement has been subject to considerable transformation from lowest cost to best value procurement with a revised agenda (Okunlola, 2012). However, although the design and build has increased by contract value since 1985, the traditional form is still the dominating procurement route (Adekunle et al., 2009). In a case study carried out by Shehu et al. (2014), traditional procurement was the most popular with 291 projects; design and build with 58 projects; then project management with nine projects.

With the increase in use of alternative procurement methods, a number of researchers have developed decision-making charts in order to investigate the criteria for their selection and their rate of success in terms of time, cost and quality. Among the most popular ones are by National Economic Development Office (NEDO, 1985), Skitmore and Marsden (1988), Brandon et al. (1988), Franks (1990), Singh (1990), Bennett and Grice (1990), Naoum (1991), Griffith and Headley (1997), Love et al. (2012), Alhazmi and McCaffer (2000), Chan (1995), Cheung et al. (2001), Chang and Ive (2002), Luu et al. (2005), Seo and Hyan (2004), Li et al. (2005) and Heravi and Ilbeigi (2012).

As far as is known, apart from the work of Love et al. (2012), all other procurement decision-making charts were developed over a decade ago. With construction changing so rapidly in recent years, the question rises if these charts are still valid and whether they are reliable to predict the most suitable procurement method for clients. Over the years, the selection process has become increasingly complex, mainly as a result of the continuing proliferation of different methods of procuring building projects, the projects' ever-increasing technical complexity and the clients' need for more-value-for-money projects. Hence, it is imperative to say that the classic criteria of time, cost and quality alone are now too simplistic in the context of today's complex construction project environment. Therefore, the decision charts need updating to include modern concepts and new industrial principles such as supply chain, lean construction, sustainability, innovation, value engineering, e-procurement and Building Information Modeling (BIM).

This dissertation builds on the work of Naoum and Egbu (2016) that seeks to address these modern concepts and principles worldwide when selecting various procurement routes. A literature review was conducted from 1980 to 2016 with the aim of developing an up-to-date multi-attribute decision-making chart for selecting the appropriate procurement method for the project. The chart is intended to offer decision makers an opportunity to broaden their horizon on the different alternative procurement routes that could lead to different consequences.

The case study approach has been used previously to illustrate the performance of management contracting, but either the results were based on small samples or the number of management contracts studied were very limited. Moreover, there have been relatively few investigations which have analysed the characteristics of the client, the designer and project within the scope of one study.

Research goals

Aim

To develop a decision-making chart in the form of a scoring matrix showing the level of performance between management and traditional form of contracts.

Objectives

1 To establish the background, apparent advantages and disadvantages to the client in adopting management and traditional contracting.
2 To evaluate the client criteria and priority when selecting management contracting.
3 To find out whether the characteristics of the client have a significant effect on project performance.
4 To find out whether the characteristics of the project have a significant effect on project performance.
5 To compare the performance of time and cost of commercial projects completed under management and traditional contracts.

Key research questions

1 How would the client benefit from selecting the procurement route of management contracting and what are its shortfalls?

2 What would be the main criteria used by clients to choose management contracting for their future commercial projects?
3 To what extent does the experience of the client with the building process have an effect on project success?
4 To what extent does the characteristic of the project have an effect on project success?
5 How did commercial projects perform, in terms of time and cost, under management contracting compared with similar projects built using the traditional form contract?

Theoretical argument

The theory that I will use will be the contingency theory. It was developed by Kast and Rosenzweig (1973) and it was used to study the management of organisation, including organisation design, leadership, behavioural change and operations. The contingency theory indicates that there is no one way to design, manage or to organise a business enterprise; it is contingent or dependent upon the problem or situation in hand (independent variables). As applied to my study, this theory will hold that I would expect my independent variables (client and project characteristics) to influence the intervening variable (procurement method) and in turn influence the dependent variable (project performance). This proposition is thought to apply to my research because the contingency approach recognises the complexity involved in managing modern organisations, but uses the pattern of relationships and/or configurations of subsystems in order to facilitate improved practice.

The research hypotheses

Based on the above theoretical argument and the literature review, the following hypotheses are formulated:

Main hypothesis

'In order to achieve a high level of project performance, the procurement method should be selected in accordance to the characteristics of the client and the project'. This main hypothesis can be broken down into the following sub-hypotheses:

1 Management contracting has certain advantages to offer but also has some shortfalls.
2 Management contracting can be best used when time is of the essence.
3 Management contracting can be best used for inexperienced clients.
4 Management contracting can be best used for highly complex projects.
5 Traditional contacts are more likely to deliver projects within budget when compared with similar projects delivered under management contracting.

Note to students

Notice that in this proposal, the author formulated five objects, five key questions, five sub-hypotheses. They are all interlinked in such a way that objective 1 is related to key question 1 and to hypothesis 1. Objective 2 is related to key question 2 and to hypothesis 2, and so on.

Initial literature review

Note to students

In this part of the proposal, the author provided a two-page initial literature review about the subject of 'procurement methods'. This part of the proposal is basically an extension of the Rationale section given earlier. Do not forget to supplement your initial literature with supporting empirical facts that are fully referenced. (See Box 3.1 on pages 44–45 for a summary of literature review related to this research.)

Outline methodology

The methodology road map related to this research is shown in Figure 2.4 on page 22 and next is an outline of the stages involved.

Stage 1: Literature review

This study will first review the relevant literature on the subject of procurement methods, in particular, looking at previous building process models which studied the performance of the procurement method. For example, the work of Sidwell (1990) is particularly relevant.

The main sources of information will be the following: ARCOM Abstract (www.arcom.ac.uk/abstracts.html), ASCE, CME, ECAM, IPM Journals and previous dissertations and PhD theses.

Stage 2: Designing the research framework/model

It is the author's intention to modify and update the theoretical framework shown in Figure 4.5 on page 63. This will be used to test relationships and associations among the variables using case studies.

Stage 3: Constructing the questionnaire

The literature review and the design of the theoretical framework will be followed by constructing a data collection questionnaire which will be used to compare the performance of management and traditional contracts.

It is intended to adopt the quantitative data collection approach, which means obtaining facts and figures from previously completed projects in addition to obtaining opinions and views of those involved in the project. It is also intended to obtain a large sample of cases, approximately 60 projects, all of which will be analysed statistically. (Table 6.2 on page 89 is an extract from Naoum's questionnaire.)

Stage 4: The pilot study

As recommended by previous writers, this research will conduct a pilot study before collecting the final data from the whole sample. This should provide a trial run for the questionnaire of Stage 3 just mentioned, which involves testing the wording of the questions, identifying ambiguous questions, testing the technique that I will use to collect the data, measuring the effectiveness of my standard invitation to respondents and so on.

The author's pilot study will take the form of structured interviews with two clients and two contractors who have commissioned and experienced 'pure' management projects. An interview questionnaire will be used for this pilot study in order to validate the appropriateness of the main study questionnaire.

Stage 5: The main study

The pilot study should prepare the ground for modifying the main study questionnaire which will be used to compare the performance of management and traditional contracts.

The inferential statistical tests will be applied. It will consist of hypotheses testing, tables of correlation and association, and interpretation of the results. The tables will show whether there are significant differences in time, cost, quality and safety performance between management contracting and the traditional form of contracts.

Stage 6: Writing up

This stage involves writing up the content of the dissertation and should cover the chapters proposed in the following section.

Proposed structure of dissertation

Chapter 1: Introduction and background to the problem
Chapter 2: Review of the traditional and management contracting
Chapter 3: Review of previous models of the building process
Chapter 4: Research design and method of analysis
Chapter 5: Analysis of the results
Chapter 6: Conclusions
Chapter 7: References

Initial references

Adekunle, O., Dickinson, M., Khalfan, M., McDermott, P. and Rowlinson, S. (2009) Construction project procurement routes: an in-depth critique. *International Journal of Managing Projects in Business*, 2 (3), pp. 338–354.

Alhazmi, T. and McCaffer, R. (2000), Project procurement system selection model. *Construction, Engineering and Management*, 126 (3), pp. 176–184.

Bennett, J. and Grice, A. (1990), *Procurement Systems for Building, Quantity Surveying Techniques – New Directions*, BSP Professional Books, Oxford.

Brandon, E., Basden, A. and Hamilton, I.W. (1988) *Expert System: The Strategic Planning of Construction Projects*, Royal Institution of Chartered Surveyors and University of Salford, London.

Chan, A. (1995) Towards an expert system on project procurement. *Journal of Construction Procurement*, 1 (2), pp. 111–123.

Chang, C. and Ive, G. (2002) Rethinking the multi-attribute utility approach based procurement route selection technique. *Construction Management & Economics*, 20 (3), pp. 275–284.

Cheung, S., Lam, T., Leung, M. and Wan, Y. (2001) An analytical hierarchy process based procurement selection method. *Journal of Construction Management and Economics*, 19 (3), pp. 427–437.

Clamp, H., Cox, S. and Lupton, S. (2007) *Which Contract? Choosing the Appropriate Building Contract*, RIBA Publishing, London.

Franks, J. (1990). *Building procurement systems: A guide to building project management*. Chartered Institute of Building (CIOB), Ascot.

Griffith, A. and Headley, J. (1997) Using a weighted score model as an aid to selecting procurement methods for small building works. *Construction Management and Economics*, 15 (4), pp. 341–348.

Heravi, G. and Ilbeigi, M. (2012) Development of a comprehensive model for construction project success evaluation by contractors. *Engineering, Construction and Architectural Management*, 19 (5), pp. 526–542.

Kast, F. and Rosenzweig, J. (1973) *Organization and Management*. 5th edn. McGraw- Hill, New York.

Li, B., Akintoye, A., Edwards, P.J. and Hardcastle, C. (2005) PFI procurement for construction projects in the UK: findings from a questionnaire survey. *Engineering, Construction and Architectural Management*, 12 (2), pp. 125–148.

Love, P., Edwards, D., Irani, Z. and Sharif, A. (2012) Participatory action research approach to public sector procurement selection. *Journal of Construction Engineering and Management*, 138 (3), pp. 311–322.

Luu, D., Ng, T. and Chen, S. (2005) Formulating procurement selection criteria through case-based reasoning approach. *Journal of Computing in Civil Engineering*, 19 (3), pp. 269–276.

Naoum, S.G. (1991) Procurement and project performance: A comparison of management and traditional contracting. *Occasional Paper No. 45*, Chartered Institute of Building. Ascot.

Naoum, S.G. (2003) An overview into the concept of partnering. *International Journal of Project Management*, 21 (1), pp. 71–76.

Naoum, S.G. and Egbu, C. (2016) Modern selection criteria for procurement methods in construction: A state-of-the-art literature review and a survey. *International Journal of Managing Projects in Business*, Issue 3/4, April 2016.

National Economic Development Office (NEDO) (1985). *Thinking About Building*, HMSO, London.

Okunlola, S. (2012) PROMA – a decision support system to determine appropriate procurement method research. *Journal of Applied Sciences, Engineering and Technology*, 4 (4), pp. 316–321.

Seo, Y.C. and Hyan, C.T. (2004) Procurement system selection model reflecting past performance. *Journal of Construction Procurement*, 10 (2), pp. 89–95.

Shehu, Z., Endut, I.R., Akintoye, A. and Holt, G.D. (2014) Cost overrun in the Malaysian construction industry projects: a deeper insight original research article. *International Journal of Project Management*, 32 (8), pp. 1471–1480.

Skitmore, R. and Marsden, D. (1988) Which procurement system? Towards a universal procurement selection technique. *Construction Management and Economics*, 6, pp. 71–89.

Sidwell, A C (1990) Project management: dynamics and performance. *Construction Management and Economics*, 8 (2), 159–79.

Singh, S. (1990) Selection of appropriate project delivery system for building construction projects, Proceedings: CIB-90 Building Economics and Construction Management, University of Technology Sydney, pp. 469–480.

Research programme

In this section of the proposal, a bar chart or a breakdown of activities, like the one shown in Figure 10.1 on page 207, should be attached showing the programme of work for the dissertation. It should also indicate the target dates for the completion of each of the stages shown in the methodology section.

Proposal 3: Proposal for the problem-solving approach

Working title

An evaluation of the total quality management system: a case study.

Rationale

The problem of quality and its associated costs has been of great concern to most industries since the early 1960s. As a result, some large construction contractors have pursued and implemented innovative quality management techniques such as Quality Assurance (QA) and Total Quality Management (TQM). Oakland (2004) defined TQM as a way of managing to improve the effectiveness, flexibility and competitiveness of a business as a whole. It applies just as much to service industries as it does to manufacturing. It involves whole companies getting organised in every department, every activity and every person at every level.

Once management acknowledges that there is a problem, it can take the second step to develop a clear understanding of underlying principles and elements of TQM such as training (Imai and Kaisen, 2015), team work (Aubrey and Felkins, 1988), supplier involvement, customer services and its implementation, which is considered by Juran (2016) as the primary quality management tool.

According to Boardman and Croxson (1994), several senior TQM representatives from various client and contracting organisations forming the European

Construction Institute TQM Task Force were discussing this very topic of measuring, where their companies were on the TQM journey, and it became manifestly obvious that there were various methods for the measurement of TQM. The preliminary literature review revealed that Boardman's measurement chart is simple but comprehensive and can be used to give a visual representation of the organisation's current position in a TQM programme.

Based on such a background, this research will be using the matrix model developed by the Trafalgar House Quality Management Services organisation as the tool to identify the specific problems within the author's organisation and to make recommendations, if appropriate, for improving the quality system.

Aim

To propose a guideline for implementing a total quality management system for large contracting organisations.

Objectives

1   To review the concept and principle of TQM.
2   To assess the advantages of the TQM systems.
3   To measure the efficiency of the current quality management system in the author's organisation and to identify any present problems within the system.
4   To design and recommend a new TQM system for the organisation.
5   To evaluate the proposed TQM.

Hypothesis

Note to students

With the problem-solving approach, formulating a hypothesis is not usually applicable. It is applicable only when the proposed solution is to be put to the test, which is not practical at undergraduate level. Instead, a number of key questions can be formed.

Key questions

1   What are the reasons that drive the construction industry towards accreditation of standard QA?
2   Does accreditation of QA assure the customer of an optimum standard of services?
3   What are the differences between QA and total TQM?

Methodology

Note to students

Here you need to draw the methodology road map related to your research as shown in the example in Figure 2.3 on page 21 and Figure 2.4 on page 22.

Here is an outline of the stages involved

Stage 1: Literature research

A comprehensive review of the relevant literature including a computer-assisted search will be undertaken in order to develop an understanding of previous work in the field of TQM.

Stage 2: Exploratory interviews

This stage will explore the matrix designed by the Trafalgar House Quality Management Services House. The exploration will be achieved through unstructured interviews with five companies that are known to have implemented a TQM system.

Stage 3: Case study

The author will then use his or her own organisation as a case to study the possible implementation of a systematic TQM. Interviews with employees will take place to score the level of quality effectiveness.

Stage 4: Evaluation of the organisation's present TQM system

This stage will bring together and review the information collected in the previous stages in which the present TQM system has to be studied.

Stage 5: Writing up

This stage involves writing up the content of the dissertation and should cover the chapters proposed in the following section.

Proposed contents of dissertation

Chapter 1: Introduction
Chapter 2: Total quality management – the concept
Chapter 3: Implementation of TQM
Chapter 4: Designing the case study and research methodology
Chapter 5: Analysing and evaluating the case study evidence
Chapter 6: Conclusions and further studies
Chapter 7: References

Initial references

Aubrey, C. and Felkins, P. (1988) *Teamwork: Involving People in Quality and Productivity Improvement*. Milwaukee: American Society of Quality Control.
Boardman, R. and Croxson, J. (1994) *Trafalgar Quality Management Services*. Unpublished report by the Trafalgar House Company, UK, 25 pages.

Imai, M. and Kaisen, L. (2015) *The Key to Japan's Competitive Success.* New York: Random House.
Juran, J. (2016) *Juran on Planning for Quality.* New York: The Free Press.
Oakland, J. (2004) *Total Quality Management.* Oxford: Butterworth-Heinemann.

Programme of work

In this section of the proposal, a bar chart or a breakdown of activities, like the one shown in Figure 10.1 on page 207, should be attached showing the programme of work for the dissertation. It should also indicate the target dates for the completion of each of the stages shown in the Methodology section.

Proposal 4: Proposal for the desk study approach – analysis of secondary source of data

Working title

Safety and the construction industry: a statistical analysis of facts and figures of the safety record during boom and bust of the construction industry.

Rationale

In the construction industry, the risk of a fatality is five times more likely than in a manufacturing-based industry, and the risk of a major injury is two-and-a-half times higher. A Health and Safety Executive study (HSE, 2017) reveals that construction has one of the highest ratios of non-injury to injury accidents of all UK industries. Apart from the human cost of suffering an accident, the economic effect can be devastating. Direct costs of accidents such as injury, illness or damage can be insured against, although this is the tip of a very large iceberg. Every £1 of the accident costs that an insurance company has to pay out could cost the contractor between £5 and £50 in indirect costs. These indirect costs will range from product and material damage to legal costs (Travers Morgan Ltd, 1995).

Therefore, the Health and Safety Executive has, for many years, sought to promote a business case for health and safety management, including highlighting the downside costs of poor management such as lost time, lost productivity and fines as well as the business benefits, such as increased profits (Antonelli et al., 2006).

A better Health and Safety (H&S) management would help reduce accidents, which would eliminate damage to equipment, machinery and raw materials. This in turn leads to an increase of output to firms and thereby to higher output in the economy. Naoum et al. (2011) suggest that safer work conditions and healthier workers may increase the productivity of labour hours and thereby contribute to higher productivity and output.

Wright et al. (2005) state that 'evidence that good health and safety improves productivity' is the top ranked incentive for improving health and safety. It is further reported by Shearn (2004) that 10 per cent of UK businesses will be prepared to increase their effort in H&S management, if they are provided with evidence that it would result in 'business benefits'. These benefits include a mix of both tangible and intangible benefits, such as maintenance of reputation, client requirements, controlling insurance premium costs and reduction in absence rates as well as general improvements in health and safety (Antonelli et al., 2006). To compound this point, research by McCon (1997) has suggested that in firms that have demonstrated good, sustained safety performance, you will usually find the added benefits of good housekeeping, good product quality and high morale.

Despite the many ethical and moral reasons to invest in H&S, organisations seem motivated to improve aspects of H&S because of the potential risk to the business if H&S is not addressed. Research by Antonelli et al. (2006) concluded that although some organisations are convinced of carrying out H&S initiatives, this tends to be driven by the need to manage costs (mainly insurance premiums) or by demands made by customers (to ensure they are eligible to participate in tendering processes, and also to maintain existing business), or by the risk of being non-compliant and the adverse effects this may have on the prospect of winning new business.

Unfortunately, to date, evaluations of H&S activities have tended to focus on H&S-based performance metrics such as injury rates. Little attention has been given to the economic contributions and impacts that H&S may bring. There appears to have been few coordinated attempts to identify and assess the full spectrum of potential economic benefits and impacts, both to individual organisations and to the UK economy.

According to Smallman (2001), almost no scientific base was found for supporting the assertion that there is a business case for investment in H&S, in other words, that such investment produces returns to stakeholders. The little evidence that exists is based largely around anecdotes, which claim that excellence in H&S does produce returns, and mainly from reduced insurance premiums. Notwithstanding this, whereas the economic and moral cases for investment in H&S are indisputable, the argument that 'safety pays', frequently used by government, is spurious.

Research goals

Aim

To analyse historical HSE statistics and find out whether there is a link between the economic climate and the rate of accidents in the construction industry.

Objectives

1   To provide a general overview of the history of accidents in the construction industry before and after the introduction of the CDM 2015 (Construction, Design and Management) regulations.

2   To analyse the ratio of accidents to employees in order to find out the trades with the highest accident rate.
3   To analyse the cost and benefits of implementing safety policies by the contractors.
4   To find out whether there is a correlation between the state of the general economy and the rate of accidents.

Key questions

1   How did different contractors respond to the CDM regulation?
2   What is the ratio of accidents to number of employees in the UK construction industry compared with the manufacturing industry?
3   How much would companies benefit from having a H&S policy?
4   To what extent would safety in construction be affected by the state of the economy and vice versa?

Assumptions

1   CDM regulations are applied in the construction industry as a force rather than a belief.
2   Accident rates in construction are twice as high as in the manufacturing industry.
3   The benefits of investing in safety outweigh the cost by more than eight times.
4   Productivity rate can be an accurate indicator for measuring the link between safety and the economic climate.

Note to students

Notice that in this proposal, the student formulated four objects, four key questions, four assumptions. They are all interlinked in such a way that objective 1 is related to key question 1 and to assumption 1. Objective 2 is related to key question 2 and to assumption 2, and so on.

Methodology

Note to students

Here you need to draw the methodology road map related to your research as shown in the example in Figure 2.3 on page 21 and Figure 2.4 on page 22.

Here is an outline of the stages involved

Stage 1: Literature review

The basic concern throughout the review stage is to identify some of the broader parameters likely to be relevant in studying the construction industry's safety statistics. In order to achieve the first objective, a systematic literature review is to be conducted which will cover textbooks, institutional and statutory publications, periodicals and trade/academic journals, seminar and conference papers. In particular, the following sources will be cited:

- The Loughborough University Research;
- HSE report No. CRR229/1999;
- HSE report No. CD 207.

Stage 2: Analysing the facts and figures

The second objective of the study can be achieved by analysing published and unpublished accident statistical data, which will be acquired from the Health and Safety Statistical Services Department in Liverpool.

The third objective will be achieved by gathering information from the Health and Safety Executive report entitled *Cost Benefits of Implementing the CDM Regulations 2015*. This objective will show how the distribution of accident costs affect the industry and society.

To achieve the fourth objective, information about the economic climate during the last decade will be gathered from the HMSO construction output and then correlated with the accident record, in an attempt to find out whether the rate of accidents is related to recession. The statistical package SPSS will be utilised to assist in evaluating this relationship.

Stage 3: Producing tables and graphs to present the results

Note to students

This is part of the writing-up stage in which all the results will be presented in graphical format to allow discussion and interpretation to be made on the research findings.

Proposed structure of dissertation

Chapter 1: Introduction to the safety problem.
Chapter 2: Health and safety and the employment trend.
Chapter 3: Safety culture in the construction industry.
Chapter 4: Previous empirical research on construction safety.
Chapter 5: Analysis of the secondary data.
Chapter 6: Discussion and critical appraisal.
Chapter 7: Conclusion and recommendation for further research.
Chapter 8: References.

Initial references

Antonelli, A., Baker, M., McMahon, A. and Wright, M. (2006) *Six SME Case Studies that Demonstrate the Business Benefit of Effective Health and Safety Management: Contract Research Report 504, Prepared by Green Street Berman for HSE*, HMSO, London.

HSE (Health and Safety Executive) (2017) *The Costs of Accidents at Work*. Health and Safety Commission, HMSO, London.

McCon, P. (1997) Housekeeping & injury rate: A correlation study. *Professional Safety*, pp.29–32.

Naoum, S.G., Hemmings, B. and Fong, D. (2011) Is there a correlation between contractor's health and safety performance and their profit margins?, *6th International Structural Engineering and Construction Conference (ISEC – 6)*, 21–26 June, Zurich. Paper ID S1–C32.

Shearn, P. (2004). *Workforce Participation in the Management of Occupational Health & Safety*. Health & Safety Executive Report No. ERG/04/01, London.

Smallman, C. (2001) The Reality of 'Revitalizing Health and Safety'. *Journal of Safety Research*, 32, 391–439.

Travers Morgan Ltd (1995) The Economics of Safety Management. A paper given by Mr Mike Crocker of Travers Morgan Ltd at Walfords, London.

Wright, M., Antonelli, A., Doyle, J.N., Bendig, M. and Genna, R. (2005) An evidence based evaluation of how best to secure compliance with health and safety law, *Health and Safety Executive Research Report 334*. HSE Books, Suffolk.

Proposed programme of work

In this section of the proposal, a bar chart or a breakdown of activities, like the one shown in Figure 10.1 on page 207, should be attached showing the programme of work for the dissertation. It should also indicate the target dates for the completion of each of the stages shown in the Methodology section.

Appendix 2
London South Bank University: Example of a questionnaire

MARKETING QUESTIONNAIRE

Please respond to the following questions by either ticking the appropriate box or writing your answer in the space provided.

Please note: All information provided will be treated in the strictest of confidence.

Section 1 – Questions related to company details

1.1 Please indicate the approximate turnover of your practice.

Less than £2m	£2.1–6m	£6.1–10m	More than £10m
			(Please state)
☐	☐	☐	_____

1.2 What percentage of this is attributed specifically to marketing (approximately)?

Less than 1%	1–2%	3–5%	More than 5%
			(Please state)
☐	☐	☐	_____

1.3 Does the practice have a separate marketing department? YES ☐ NO ☐
IF YES

A. How many people are employed in this department? Please tick appropriate box.

1–2	3–5	6–8	More than 8
			(Please state)
☐	☐	☐	_____

B. How long has this marketing department been established? Please tick.

0–2 years	3–4 years	5–6 years	More than 6 years
			(Please state)
☐	☐	☐	_____

If No
Please tick one box to indicate for what reasons.

– A marketing department is not considered necessary ☐
– The practice is too small to employ individuals for this ☐
– Marketing tends to be a management role ☐
– Other (please specify) ☐

_____

_____

_____

1.4 What does the practice perceive as its future marketing trend over the next 5 years?

– To decrease ☐
– To remain stable ☐
– To increase ☐

1.5 Which statement best describes your organisational philosophy? Please tick one box.

– To achieve modest growth ☐
– To achieve a greater share of the market place ☐
– To achieve service and quality ☐

Section 2 – Questions related to marketing strategy and policy

2.1 What level of priority is given to marketing within your business strategy? Please tick one box.

– High priority ☐
– Moderate priority ☐
– Low priority ☐

2.2 Which statement best describes the role of marketing within your practice? Please tick one box.

    – It is perceived to be the role of upper management   ☐
    – Marketing plays a role with all our staff   ☐
    – It is left to the marketing department/key individuals   ☐

2.3 Which statement best describes the way in which your practice is driven? Please tick one box.

    – Technology driven   ☐
    – Customer driven   ☐
    – Market driven   ☐

2.4 Are planning and operations within departments orientated towards customer satisfaction? Please tick one box.

    – Yes, very much so   ☐
    – Yes, in some departments   ☐
    – No, other factors dominate   ☐

2.5 Which statement best describes the way your practice allocates its resources to a project? Please tick one box.

    – Resources are governed by the fee and required profit   ☐
    – Governed by the client's actual requirements   ☐
    – Governed by the type of client (i.e. new client, etc.)   ☐

2.6 Is training given to your staff on the basics of marketing? Please tick one or more box(es).

    – Yes, we undertake regular training sessions   ☐
    – We have in the past given staff training   ☐
    – No, we have never given any formal training   ☐

2.7 Does your marketing department seek advice from outside PR agencies?
    YES ☐   NO ☐
    If Yes, for how long? _____Yrs
    If No, for what reasons? (Please specify)_____

    _____
    _____

Section 3 – Questions related to the marketing techniques

3.1 From the following marketing and promotional techniques, please indicate which techniques your firm practises by stating Yes/No. If Yes, how important do you consider them in making clients aware of your firm?

Marketing/promotional techniques	Do you use? Yes/No	← Not important/Very important →				
		1	2	3	4	5
Company brochure	___	___	___	___	___	___
Company newsletter	___	___	___	___	___	___
Seminars	___	___	___	___	___	___
Presentations	___	___	___	___	___	___
Videos	___	___	___	___	___	___
Entertaining	___	___	___	___	___	___
Advertising through media	___	___	___	___	___	___
Other forms of advertising (i.e. site boards, etc.)	___	___	___	___	___	___
Introduction letter	___	___	___	___	___	___
Company logo	___	___	___	___	___	___

3.2 If your practice was presenting itself to a client, which statement would best describe the initial approach it would use to sell itself? Please tick the relevant box(es).

 – We would concentrate on past projects, with emphasis on experience and reputation ☐
 – We would focus on the particular client's needs, relative to the project ☐
 – We would promote the technical facilities and capabilities of the practice ☐
 – We would promote value for money and cost ☐

3.3 How often does your practice thoroughly research a new client and the services they require? Please tick the relevant box(es).

 – We attempt to do this for all clients ☐
 – We do research, but not as much as we should ☐
 – We tend to offer our own range of services first ☐

3.4 Which statement best describes the primary objectives of your marketing strategy?

 – To achieve increased market share and new clients ☐
 – Service excellence is our primary objective ☐
 – Technical excellence and expertise should be exploited ☐

Section 4 – Questions related to the selection process

4.1 In making initial contact with a client, how influential are the following? Please tick the appropriate box.

Forms of initial contact	← Least influential / Most influential →				
	1	2	3	4	5
Advertisements	____	____	____	____	____
Recommendations	____	____	____	____	____
Introduction letters/portfolios	____	____	____	____	____
Industry reputation	____	____	____	____	____
Previous working relationships	____	____	____	____	____
Contacts	____	____	____	____	____
Following leads	____	____	____	____	____
Others (please state and rank):	____	____	____	____	____
_____	____	____	____	____	____
_____	____	____	____	____	____

4.2 How important do you consider the following criteria when being selected by a client for your services? Please tick the appropriate box.

CRITERION	Little importance	Some importance	Quite important	Important	Very important
Turnover/size of practice					
Status/market share					
Financial standing/stability					
Technical capability/ excellence					
Quality of personnel and expertise					
Obtaining/having QA					
Being chartered					
Experience					
Professional reputation/ track record					
Prior business relationships/clients					
Lowest price/fees					
Presentation					
Previous projects (type)					
Range of services offered					
Geographical location					
Attention to detail					
Company offices and general image					
Negotiating skill					
Informal contacts					
Responsiveness					

Section 5 – General questions

5.1 What are the main hurdles/problems in reaching a client? Please give brief details.

_____

_____

_____

5.2 Do you feel there is any way QS practices can improve the services they offer (if necessary)?

_____

_____

_____

_____

Thank you for your participation, please send the completed questionnaires in the pre-addressed envelope provided.

Appendix 3
Statistical tables

Table A *Distribution of t*

df	\multicolumn{6}{c}{Probability}
	0.5	0.1	0.05	0.02	0.01	0.001
1	1.000	6.314	12.706	31.821	63.657	636.619
2	0.816	2.920	4.303	6.965	9.925	31.598
3	0.765	2.353	3.182	4.541	5.841	12.941
4	0.741	2.132	2.776	3.747	4.604	8.610
5	0.727	2.015	2.571	3.365	4.032	6.859
6	0.718	1.943	2.447	3.143	3.707	5.959
7	0.711	1.895	2.365	2.998	3.499	5.405
8	0.706	1.860	2.306	2.896	3.355	5.041
9	0.703	1.833	2.262	2.821	3.250	4.781
10	0.700	1.812	2.228	2.764	3.169	4.587
11	0.697	1.796	2.201	2.718	3.106	4.437
12	0.695	1.782	2.179	2.681	3.055	4.318
13	0.694	1.771	2.160	2.650	3.012	4.221
14	0.692	1.761	2.145	2.624	2.977	4.140
15	0.691	1.753	2.131	2.602	2.947	4.073
16	0.690	1.746	2.120	2.583	2.921	4.015
17	0.689	1.740	2.110	2.567	2.898	3.965
18	0.688	1.734	2.101	2.552	2.878	3.922
19	0.688	1.729	2.093	2.539	2.861	3.883
20	0.687	1.725	2.086	2.528	2.845	3.850
21	0.686	1.721	2.080	2.518	2.831	3.819
22	0.686	1.717	2.074	2.508	2.819	3.792
23	0.685	1.714	2.069	2.500	2.807	3.767
24	0.685	1.711	2.064	2.492	2.797	3.745
25	0.684	1.708	2.060	2.485	2.787	3.725
26	0.684	1.706	2.056	2.479	2.779	3.707
27	0.684	1.703	2.052	2.473	2.771	3.690
28	0.683	1.701	2.048	2.467	2.763	3.674
29	0.683	1.699	2.045	2.462	2.756	3.659
30	0.683	1.697	2.042	2.457	2.750	3.646
40	0.681	1.684	2.021	2.423	2.704	3.551
60	0.679	1.671	2.000	2.390	2.660	3.460
120	0.677	1.658	1.980	2.358	2.617	3.373
∞	0.674	1.645	1.960	2.326	2.576	3.291

Source: Adapted by permission of the authors and publishers from Table III (Fisher and Yates, 1974).

Table B   *Distribution of χ^2*

df	Probability					
	0.5	0.1	0.05	0.02	0.01	0.001
1	0.455	2.706	3.841	5.412	6.635	10.827
2	1.386	4.605	5.991	7.824	9.210	13.815
3	2.366	6.251	7.815	9.837	11.345	16.268
4	3.357	7.779	9.488	11.668	13.277	18.465
5	4.351	9.236	11.070	13.388	15.086	20.517
6	5.348	10.645	12.592	15.033	16.812	22.457
7	6.346	12.017	14.067	16.622	18.475	24.322
8	7.344	13.362	15.507	18.168	20.090	26.125
9	8.343	14.684	16.919	19.679	21.666	28.877
10	9.342	15.987	18.307	21.161	23.209	29.588
11	10.341	17.275	19.675	22.618	24.725	31.264
12	11.340	18.549	21.026	24.054	26.217	32.909
13	12.340	19.812	22.362	25.472	27.688	34.528
14	13.339	21.064	23.685	26.873	29.141	36.123
15	14.339	22.307	24.996	28.259	30.578	37.697
16	15.338	23.542	26.296	29.633	32.000	39.252
17	16.338	24.769	27.587	30.995	33.409	40.790
18	17.338	25.989	28.869	32.346	34.805	42.321
19	18.338	27.204	30.144	33.867	36.191	43.820
20	19.337	28.412	31.410	35.020	37.566	45.315
21	20.337	29.615	32.671	36.343	38.932	46.797
22	21.337	30.813	33.924	37.659	40.289	42.268
23	22.337	32.007	35.172	38.968	41.638	49.728
24	23.337	33.196	36.415	40.270	42.980	51.179
25	24.337	34.382	37.652	41.566	44.314	56.620
26	25.336	35.563	38.885	42.856	45.642	54.052
27	26.336	36.741	40.113	44.140	46.963	55.476
28	27.336	37.916	41.337	15.419	48.278	56.893
29	28.336	39.087	42.557	46.693	49.588	58.302
30	29.336	40.256	43.773	47.962	50.892	59.703

Source: Adapted by permission of the authors and publishers
from Table IV (Fisher and Yates, 1974).

Table C   *Critical values of ρ (rho) at various levels of probability (Spearman rank correlation coefficient)*

For any *N*, the observed value of ρ is significant at a given level of significance if it is *equal* to or *larger* than the critical values shown in the table.

N (number of subjects)	Level of significance for one-tailed test			
	0.05	0.025	0.01	0.005
	Level of significance for two-tailed test			
	0.10	0.05	0.02	0.01
5	0.900	1.000	1.000	–
6	0.829	0.886	0.943	1.000
7	0.714	0.786	0.893	0.929
8	0.643	0.738	0.833	0.881
9	0.600	0.683	0.783	0.833
10	0.564	0.648	0.746	0.794
12	0.506	0.591	0.712	0.777
14	0.456	0.544	0.645	0.715
16	0.425	0.506	0.601	0.665
18	0.399	0.475	0.564	0.625
20	0.377	0.450	0.534	0.591
22	0.359	0.428	0.508	0.562
24	0.343	0.409	0.485	0.537
26	0.329	0.392	0.465	0.515
28	0.317	0.377	0.448	0.496
30	0.306	0.364	0.432	0.478

Note: When there is no exact number of subjects, use the next lowest number.

Table D *Critical values of r at various levels of probability (Pearson product movement correlation)*

For any particular N, the observed value of ρ is significant at a given level of significance if it is equal to or larger than the critical values shown in the table.

	Level of significance for one-tailed test				
	0.05	0.025	0.01	0.005	0.005
	Level of significance for two-tailed test				
df = N − 2	0.10	0.05	0.02	0.01	0.001
1	0.9877	0.9969	0.9995	0.9999	1.0000
2	0.9000	0.9500	0.9800	0.9900	0.9990
3	0.8054	0.8783	0.9343	0.9587	0.9912
4	0.7293	0.8114	0.8822	0.9172	0.9741
5	0.6694	0.7545	0.8329	0.8745	0.9507
6	0.6215	0.7067	0.7887	0.8343	0.9249
7	0.5822	0.6664	0.7498	0.7977	0.8982
8	0.5494	0.6319	0.7155	0.7646	0.8721
9	0.5214	0.6021	0.6851	0.7348	0.8471
10	0.4793	0.5760	0.6581	0.7079	0.8233
11	0.4762	0.5529	0.6339	0.6835	0.8010
12	0.4575	0.5324	0.6120	0.6614	0.7800
13	0.4409	0.5139	0.5923	0.6411	0.7603
14	0.4259	0.4973	0.5742	0.6226	0.7420
15	0.4124	0.4821	0.5577	0.6055	0.7246
16	0.4000	0.4683	0.5425	0.5897	0.7084
17	0.3887	0.4555	0.5285	0.5751	0.6932
18	0.3783	0.4438	0.5155	0.5614	0.6787
19	0.3687	0.4329	0.5034	0.5487	0.6652
20	0.3598	0.4227	0.4921	0.5368	0.6524
25	0.3233	0.3809	0.4451	0.4869	0.5974
30	0.2960	0.3494	0.4093	0.4487	0.5541
35	0.2746	0.3246	0.3810	0.4182	0.5189
40	0.2573	0.3044	0.3578	0.3932	0.4896
45	0.2428	0.2875	0.3384	0.3721	0.4648
50	0.2306	0.2732	0.3218	0.3541	0.4433
60	0.2108	0.2500	0.2948	0.3248	0.4078
70	0.1954	0.2319	0.2737	0.3017	0.3799
80	0.1829	0.2172	0.2565	0.2830	0.3568
90	0.1726	0.2050	0.2422	0.2673	0.3375
100	0.1638	0.1946	0.2301	0.2540	0.3211

Note: When there is no exact df, use the next lowest number.

Reference

Fisher, R. and Yates, F. (1974) *Statistical Tables for Biological, Agricultural and Medical Research*. 6th edn. Longman Group Ltd., London.

Appendix 4
Construction industry employee injury statistics

A typical example of injuries to employees in the construction industry, as reported to the Health and Safety Executive's Field Operations Division.

Occupation	Fatal	Major	Over 3 days	Total
Bricklayer	2	72	550	624
Carpenter/joiner	2	136	1127	1265
Demolition worker	–	16	37	53
Electrician	–	108	330	438
Glazier	1	12	96	109
Ground worker	4	58	139	201
Painter, decorator	–	61	233	294
Pavior, roadman	3	39	443	485
Pilling hand	1	6	33	40
Plasterer	–	22	158	180
Plumber, pipe fitter	–	71	543	614
Scaffolder	2	62	222	286
Slater, roof worker	7	64	195	266
Steel erector	–	24	36	60
Steel fixer, bar bend	–	10	30	40
Steeplejack	–	6	2	8
Welder	–	20	72	92
Other const. trade	5	109	378	492
Drivers	4	120	539	663
Electrical linesman	–	8	23	31
Electrical fitter	–	10	50	60
Electrical jointer	–	4	14	18
Communications engineer	–	1	8	9
Labourer	9	316	1659	1984
Maintenance personnel	5	60	294	359
All managerial	2	120	473	595
Manual production	2	104	548	654
Other occupations	–	78	623	701
Not known	–	81	520	601
Total	49	1798	9375	11222

Appendix 5
Using SPSS

From Daniel Fong, handout notes to MSc Surveying and Construction Project Management, London South Bank University.

Introduction

SPSS is one of the most widely used statistics analysis packages in providing detailed and comprehensive statistics analysis on various types of data. The spreadsheet-like interface allows users to enter data easily and to conduct in-depth data analysis.

SPSS is often used in research as a tool to analyse survey/questionnaire feedback. Although the graphics output may not have the level of customisation offered by Excel, it is often used in conjunction with Excel to provide full statistical analyses and professional presentation of data in research reports and dissertations.

1   Starting SPSS

Click on **Start** button at bottom left of the screen, then click
All Programs, SPSS Inc, PASW Statistics 18, PASW Statistics 18

The dialog box below will appear:

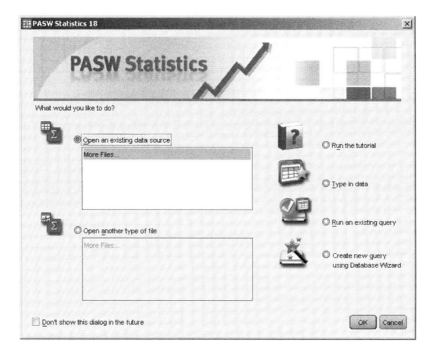

Check **Type in data**. The dialog box will disappear and the SPSS Data Editor will surface.

2   Data types

Measurement of data		Examples of data

Non metric data

Nominal	Labels with no mathematical properties such as categories.	Profession (Architect, Building Surveyor, Construction Manager). Answer (Yes or No).
Ordinal	Ranked or ordered categories. Difference not in equal proportion.	Rank order (1st, 2nd, 3rd, etc.). Academic Qualification (PhD, Masters, Degree, Higher National, A-level equivalent).

Use non-parametric statistical techniques

Metric data

Interval	Ordered in equal interval, with arbitrary zero point.	Temperature (0°C ≠ no temp!). IQ score.
Ratio	Ordered in equal interval, with a real zero.	Cost, weight, height.

Use parametric statistical techniques

Discussion: What type of measurement do Likert items conform to:

(Hint: the Likert scale of 1–5 typically consists of the following Likert items:)

- Strongly disagree
- Disagree
- Neither agree nor disagree
- Agree
- Strongly agree

3   Data entry

Suppose we send out the following questionnaire to project managers and received 22 responses:

Questionnaire

For the most recent project you have completed, please answer the following questions:

Q1.   The original target cost of the project   £. . . . .
Q2.   The actual cost of the project   £. . . . .
Q3.   The Health & Safety assessment score (0–100)   . . . .

The data should be entered in the following way in SPSS with 22 rows, each represents the answers of one responding case:

Question 1   **Question 2**   **Question 3**

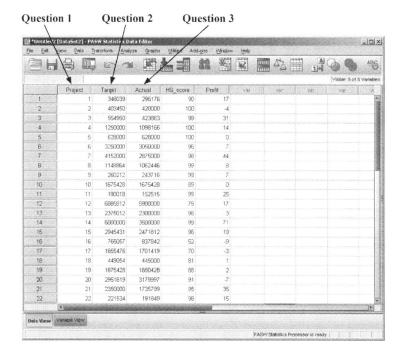

Step 1

The first step is to define the type of data for each column. Switching to **Variable View** allows us to create a structure for the data.

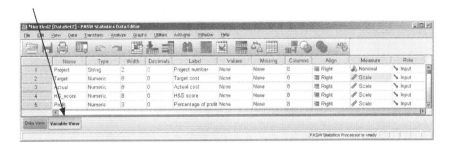

The first data column is Project which is used to label the case.

The second data column refers to the Target cost of the project.

The third data column records the Actual cost of a particular project.

The fourth data column elicits the respective Health & Safety score for the project.

The fifth data column is not from the questionnaire: we define the variable!

* **The Name of a data column must consist of only letters and numbers without any space.** Full text can be entered under **Label**.

Step 2

For this questionnaire, suppose we need to establish an additional fifth column of data which evaluates the profit margin. Click on **Transform, Compute Variable** from the menu:

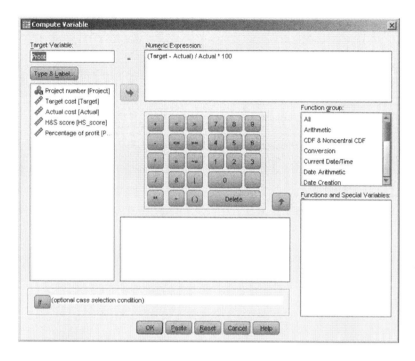

Step 3

Once the structure of all data columns is defined, return to **Data View** to enter the cases.

4   Data analysis

The application of statistics techniques depends on the type of measurement, and what we intend to investigate.

Correlation analysis

Correlation analysis is used to test the hypothesis H_0: **No correlation between variables**

Pearson Coefficient of Correlation is often used to measure if two interval or ratio variables are linearly related. Normality of variables not required. The coefficient r lies between -1 and 1.

- r close to 1 Significant positive relationship between variables;
- r close to -1 Significant negative relationship between variables;
- r close to 0 Little of no significant relationship.

* *Note:* If the variables are related in a non-linear way, r may have a value close to 0. However, the curvilinear relationship could be uncovered with other statistical techniques. It is therefore recommended to always plot the two variables against each other (scatterplot) and examine any possible relationship visually prior to drawing any conclusion.

To examine if there is any association between H&S Score and Profit, click on **Analyze, Correlate, Bivariate** …

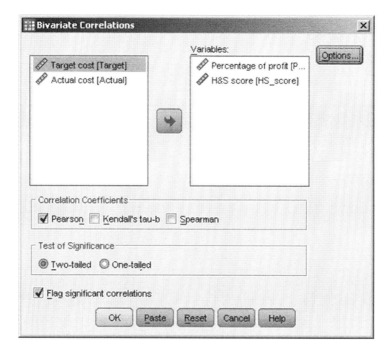

Select and move the two variables to this column.

Check **Pearson** correlation coefficient and click OK.

The following results should appear on the **Statistics Viewer**:

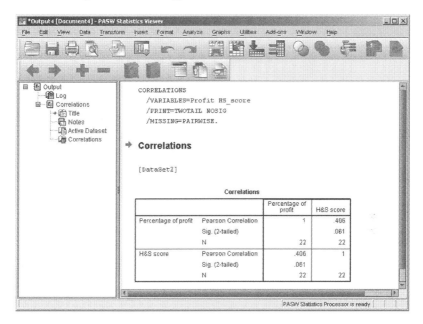

A Pearson correlation coefficient *r* of 0.406 is computed, with a significance of 0.061 (or written as *p* = 0.061).

Normally, a significance of less than 0.05 ($p < 0.05$) is needed to conclude a relationship.

Scatterplot

Go to **Graphs, Legacy Dialogs, Scatter/Dots ..., Simple Scatter**

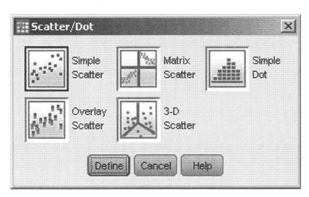

Click **Define**.

Move the two variables under Y and X axes accordingly and click **OK**.

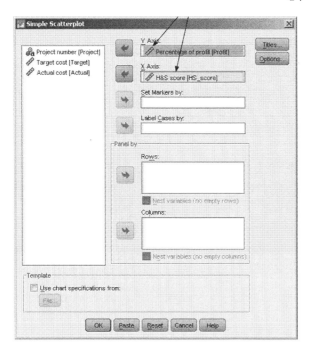

The following chart output will appear.

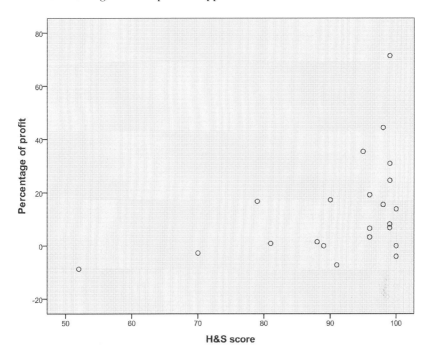

Although there is no significant linear relationship, a non-linear relationship could be established in this case.

Spearman's rank-order correlation (ρ or r_s) is used to examine if two variables are monotonically associated (both increase at the same time, or one increases and the other increases, not necessary linearly). Both variables must be ordinal or better. Normality of variables is not required.

Although the technique is 'rank-order' based, the data we provide does not have to be. SPSS will process ordinal/interval/ratio data into rank for the analysis.

Click on **Analyze, Correlate, Bivariate** … and check the box for **Spearman**.

A student conducted a survey to examine the difference in opinion between the size of the firm (1 = small, 2 = medium, 3 = large) in the use of computerised techniques. The question asks for the opinion on whether computer techniques enhance the effectiveness of project management (1 = Strongly agree, 2 = Agree, 3 = Neutral, 4 = Disagree, 5 = Strongly disagree).

RESULTS

Correlations				Firm	Opinion
Spearman's rho	Firm	Correlation Coefficient		1.000	−.529**
		Sig. (2-tailed)		.	.005
		N		26	26
	Opinion	Correlation Coefficient		−.529**	1.000
		Sig. (2-tailed)		0.005	.
		N		26	26

** Correlation is significant at the 0.01 level (2-tailed).

A Spearman's rho of −0.529 is computed with a very high significance of 0.005. Another method to test the strength of relationship between two ordinal (or better) variables is **Kendall's Tau** (τ). It is used to examine if two variables are monotonically associated. Normality of variables is not required.

Kendall's Tau b is suitable for square tables and **Kendall's Tau c** is more suited for rectangular tables.

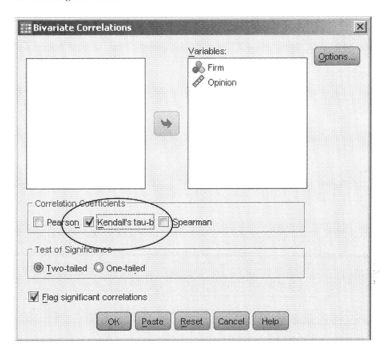

RESULTS

Correlations			H&S score	Percentage of profit
Kendall's tau_b	H&S score	Correlation coefficient	1.000	0.248
		Significance (two-tailed)	.	0.117
		N	22	22
	Percentage of profit	Correlation coefficient	0.248	1.000
		Significance (two-tailed)	0.117	.
		N	22	22

A Kendall's Tau b of 0.248 with a significance of 0.117 indicates no relationship between the variables.

REGRESSION

After correlation analysis, suppose a significant linear relation between the two interval/ratio variables is confirmed, we wish to find out **how** the variables are related.

Click on **Analyze, Regression, Linear** …

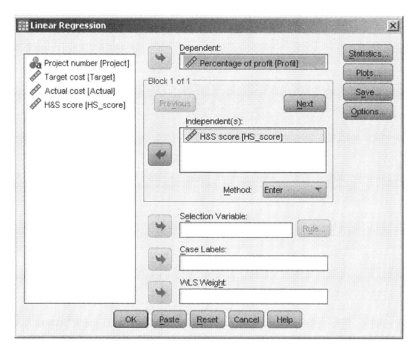

Question: Which is dependent and which is independent and why?

The following results are shown:

Coefficients[a]					
Model	Unstandardized Coefficients		Standardized Coefficients	t	Sig.
	B	Std. Error	Beta		
1 (Constant)	−46.328	30.306		−1.529	.0142
H&S score	.652	.328	.406	1.985	0.061

a Dependent variable: percentage of profit.

In this case, the 'best-fit' line that relates Profit (y) and H&S Score(x) has the equation:

$$y = 0.6546x - 46.328$$

When analysing nominal variables, chi-square (χ^2) test or Fisher's exact test is used to compare two groups of data to see if there is a difference between them, or to examine if the variables are related (test of independence).

H_0: No difference between variables

Condition to apply Chi-square test

2-by-2 table   All cells must have a frequency count of at least 5.
Larger tables   80% of the cells have a frequency count of at least 5, and no cell with 0 count.

When the condition is not met, Yates' correction is automatically applied by SPSS.

Condition to apply Fisher's exact test

Small sample, sparse or unbalanced data (<20). No blank cell.
Does not work well when the table is adequately filled.
SPSS automatically generates Fisher's exact test results under chi-square test when the condition is met.

Suppose we wish to establish if there is a relationship between the size of the firm and its location.

Click on **Analyze, Descriptive Statistics, Crosstabs** …

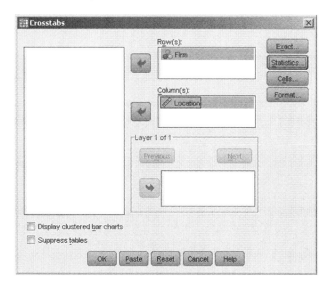

Click **Statistics**.

The following results are shown:

Chi-square tests			
	Value	df	Asymp.Sig. (2-sided)
Pearson chi-square	6.727[a]	8	0.566
Likelihood ratio	8.029	8	0.431
Linear-by-linear association	0.871	1	0.0351
No. of valid cases	26		

a 15 cells (100.0%) have expected count less than 5. The minimum expected count is 1.08.

This table shows a p of 0.566, which is not significant to reject H_0.

For ordinal variables, **Mann–Whitney U test (Wilcoxon rank sum W test)** is used to compare two groups of data to see if there is a difference between them. When more than two groups are considered, Kruskal–Wallis one-way analysis of variance (K–W one-way ANOVA or H test) will apply.

It is used when sample sizes are small and/or the variables are not normally distributed. The method can also be used for interval and ratio measurements.

H_0: No difference between variables

For the previous example on examining the difference in opinion between the size of the firm (1 = small, 2 = medium, 3 = large) and on whether computer techniques enhance the effectiveness of project management (1 = Strongly agree, 2 = Agree, 3 = Neutral, 4 = Disagree, 5 = Strongly disagree).

Click on **Analyze, Nonparametric Tests, Independent Samples** … and on the
following screen, click **Run:**

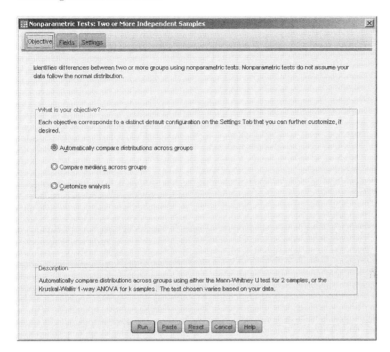

Move the variables into the corresponding boxes and click **Run**.

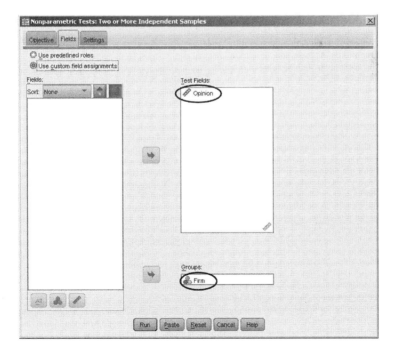

RESULTS

Hypothesis Test Summary

	Null Hypothesis	Test	Sig.	Decision
1	The distribution of Opinion is the same across categories of Firm.	Independent-Samples Kruskal-Wallis Test	.029	Reject the null hypothesis.

Asymptotic significances are displayed. The significance level is .05.

The output from SPSS not only indicates the test it has used but also the decision!

When the measurement is Interval or Ratio, parametric tests are often used. Requirements for parametric test:

• Variables must be normally distributed
• Variability of variables should be low (homogeneity of variance)

Parametric methods such as the *t*-test can be used to test the hypothesis H_0: **no difference between the means of two groups**. In other words, we are testing if there is any difference between the two groups of data.

Suppose we wish to compare our research results with those from a previous research.

Click **Analyze, Compare Means, Independent Samples T Test** … Move the variables into the appropriate boxes. You may wish to Define the Groups but it is optional.

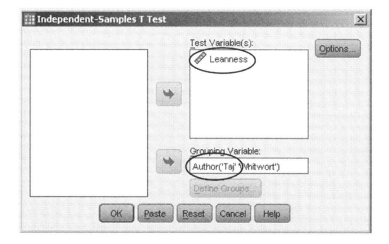

RESULTS

Group statistics

	Author	N	Mean	Std. Deviation	Std. Error Mean
Leanness	Taj	65	55.2654	12.29832	1.52542
	Whitwort	37	53.5054	19.81432	3.25745

Independent samples test

		Levene's test for equality of variances		t-test for Equality of Means					95% Confidence Interval of the Difference	
		F	Significance	t	df	Significance (two-tailed)	Mean difference	Standard error of the difference	Lower	Upper
Leanness	Equal variances assumed	16.621	0.000	0.554	100	.581	1.75998	3.17802	-4.54512	8.06508
	Equal variances not assumed			0.489	52.11	.627	1.75998	3.59693	-5.45742	8.97738

To interpret the results, we need to first look under the Levene's test of equality of variances column. $F = 16.6$ is significant ($p = 0.000$) means we have to use the results from the 'Equal variances not assumed' section.

For the results of our t-test, a t-value of 0.489 at $p = 0.627$ indicates there is no significant difference between the mean leanness score of construction projects surveyed in our research and that of the manufacturing projects in Taj's study.

If we wish to compare more than two means, **one-way ANOVA** is use for interval/ratio data. The conditions to run ANOVA are:

• The groups must be normally distributed.
• The variances of the groups must be equal.

One sample Kolmogorov–Smirnov test is used to check each group of data for normality. If normality does not hold, use the nonparametric **K–W one-way ANOVA** test.

Suppose we wish to examine if there is a difference in productivity between Germany, France and the UK.

Click **Analyze, Compare Means, One Way ANOVA** ... Bring the variables into the right boxes, e.g. Country is the independent factor in this case.

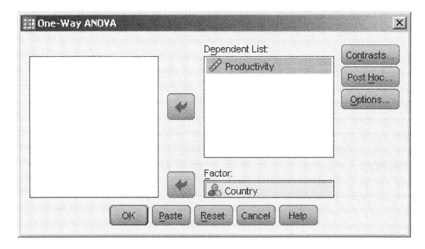

Click **Options** to specify some statistics and a test on equality of variances:

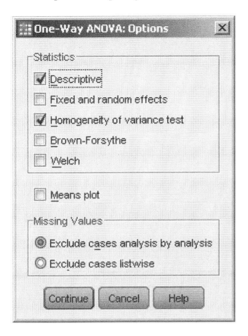

RESULTS

Descriptives								
Productivity								
	N	Mean	Std. Deviation	Std. Error	95% Confidence Interval for Mean		Min.	Max.
					Lower Bound	Upper Bound		
Germany	65	55.2654	12.29832	1.52542	52.2180	58.3128	30.61	77.42
France	37	53.5054	19.81432	3.25745	46.8990	60.1118	11.00	91.60
UK	22	52.7727	20.32810	4.33397	43.7598	61.7857	15.00	90.00
Total	124	54.2980	16.28678	1.46260	51.4029	57.1931	11.00	91.60

	df1	df2	Significance
	2	121	.000

ANOVA					
Productivity					
	Sumof squares	df	Meansquare	F	Significance
Betweengroups	135.255	2	67.627	0.252	0.778
Within groups	32491.631	121	268.526		
Total	32626.886	123			

In the Descriptives results table, the mean score for the three countries are shown.

As Levene's test of equality of variances shows significant (p = 0.000) difference between the variances of the three groups, the results of the subsequent ANOVA will not be relied upon in this case.

Appendix 6
Example of presenting interview results in a tabulated format

From an MSc dissertation by Zoë Elizabeth Mulholland (2010, pp. 59–63). The dissertation was supervised by Dr Shamil G. Naoum, MSc course in Construction Project Management, London South Bank University. For more of this research's findings see Naoum et al. (2011).

Question	Client A	Client B	Client C	Architect A	Architect B	Architect C	Cost Manager A	Cost Manager B	Contractor A	Contractor B
A) 1. What is your understanding of the term sustainable construction?	Acting responsibly, reducing impact of the company's operations on its surroundings, people and environment.	1. Briefing/design with renewable; low carbon and low energy. 2. Min. waste max prefab. Considerate contractors – no noise or pollution. 3. End product; build quality, longevity and running costs.	Carbon neutrality. The issue of carbon content seems to be driving the sustainable construction. However it is impossible to produce carbon neutral buildings economically.	Holistic view of buildings, thinking about energy, life cycle costs and durability. Not just technology but what you do with the building and how it is operated.	Triple bottom line: Environment; Economy; Society 90% focus on energy/ carbon. But not enough on social side. Get social and environmental aspects right then economics follows.	Totality of the building from the initial concept. Balance between capital cost and running cost. A traditional concept: avoiding waste.	What is developed today can still be developed in future. Minimising the impact on the environment and society. It's not just about being carbon neutral.	Use of renewable resources and materials.	1. Renewable 2. Long term 3. Minimum environmental impact.	1. Use of sustainable sources 2. Design & construction that reduces CO_2.
2. When were you first aware of sustainable construction?	2000 BREEAM was considered. Prior to that thinking about the way we operated e.g. source of timber, how much cement was being used.	2005 Campus consisted of 1960s building not built to last and hard to adapt. Look at Victorian buildings which scrub up really well.	2005/6	Late 1990s, early 2000	Early 1990s	Early 1990's. But more active in the last two years.	2000 Heard about BREEAM	2005/6	2005	2006

Question	Client A	Client B	Client C	Architect A	Architect B	Architect C	Cost Manager A	Cost Manager B	Contractor A	Contractor B
A) 1. When did you first implement sustainable construction practices?	2001 BREEAM 'Good' rating £65M.	2008 Academic building. New build £60M.	2009 High end residential. PV panels £10M.	2000 Sports centre, £7M BREEAM excellent.	1992 Commercial development with displacement vent; retractable shading.	1993 Office with sustainably sourced materials.	2003/4 School project. Rainwater harvesting; low voltage lights; facade performance; landscaping.	2007 Commercial office BREEAM 'Very Good' for operation and maintenance but not design. New build.	2006 Retail project in SE £9M BREEAM 'Very Good'.	2006 Office £7.5M new/part refurbish.
2. What sustainable construction practices do you have experience of?	Commercial office. BREEAM 'Excellent' 'Landmark' project in 2009. Waterless urinals; Green roof; Rain water harvesting; Bat boxes; Solar panels covered 30% roof; Bike spaces.	Teaching space Medical research Low velocity fume cupboards; Natural ventilation.	Private let new and refurb apartments. Code 4; Ecological & sustainability report; Green roofs; Green walls.	Housing association. CfSH L4–6. Office commended for low energy £3.5M using PVs obtain grant funding from DTI. FE College £1M Ground source heat pumps Guesthouse. £1M used biomass boilers.	Further education college 20M 2003 PVs sponsored by the government University admin 20M 2005 PVs 50% grant from the council; external shading BRE house Carbon zero house.	HE College new build BREEAM 'Excellent' HE College refurb BREEAM 'Good' Laboratory Bespoke BREEAM.	FE College used CHP £20M HEI project energy saving measures FE College BREEAM £20M looked at transport strategies HE College 2007 ground source heat pumps.	New build apartments £3.5M 2011 CfSH L4 Supermarket £2.5M 2009 Solar panels; Greywater.	Retail £9M 2006 BREEAM 'V.Good' Recycled bottles cladding; Sheep's wool insulation. Bank fit out PIRs; Long life lamps Bank HQ PV panels Retail Grey water; Ground source heat pumps; Green roofs.	Office 2006 Energy saving lights Natural ventilation Actuator windows Chimney 'false draught ventilation' Sustainable materials. No technologies used in any of projects.

Section 4 – Drivers for sustainable construction

	R1	R2	R3	R4	R5	R6	R7	R8	R9	R10
A) In your opinion what are the drivers for sustainable construction?	1. No choice. If you care about the environment, it has got to be done. Think of legacy left for our children. 2. Being 'seen' to be doing good. 3. It makes business sense, better ways of doing thing.	1. Funding source, in our case HEFCE, demands it. 2. Reputational issue – hot topic globally. 3. Personal conscience.	1. Planning permission. 2. Regulations. 3. Customer demand -20% premium on rent because of the sustainable development demand. 4. Belief that there is an issue that needs to be addressed.	1. Personal agenda of the client. 2. Cost of energy. 3. Legislation.	1. Funding in the public sector is dependent upon improved sustainability. 2. Social benefits. 3. Economic, there must be a business case. 4. Legislation.	1. Funding authority demands it. 2. Legislation. 3. Increase in energy cost. 4. Personal commitment to sustainable construction.	1. Public Relations, public perception. 2. Energy saving. 3. Access to funding.	1. Saleability. 2. Ethos of doing green things. 3. Regulations.	1. Image. Seen to be engaging. 2. Personal commitment.	1. Genuine desire to right the wrongs of the past. 2. 'Seen' to be sustainable. 3. Desire to save on running costs.
B) Rate the importance of these drivers on a scale of 1–10 (where 10 is most important and 1 is not at all).	B) Comment Comment was made and blended within the discussions of the results.	B) Comment	B)	B) Comment	B) Comment	B) Comment	B) Comment	B) Comment	B) Comment	B) Comment
CSR policy	10	7	4	5	3	8	8	6.5	8.5	9
Legislation	5	9	8	7	9	6.5	10	10	10	5
WLC benefits	7.5	7	6	3	5 Owners – 5 / 1 Rent – 1	8.5	5	5	7.5	9
Competitive advantage	10	7	1	5	8	5	3	3	6	1
Customer demand	9	6	6	7 Public – 7, 3 Private – 3	6	5	10 Public 10, 8 Private 8	2	9.5	8
Green incentives	7	6	3	9	8	7	6	6	2	6
Peer pressure	2	9	3	6	4	4.5	8	4	8	9
Better buildings	10	8	7	6	7	8.5	8	2	7	6
C) In light of the recession, do you think these drivers will increase (I), decrease (D) or not change (NC)?	C) Comment	C) Comment	C) Comment D More concerned about bottom line.	C) Comment	C) Comment	C) Comment	C) Comment	C) Comment	C) Comment	C) Comment
CSR policy	NC	D	NC	NC	NC	D	D	NC	1	D

(continued)

Question	Client A	Client B	Client C	Architect A	Architect B	Architect C	Cost Manager A	Cost Manager B	Contractor A	Contractor B
Legislation	NC	D	I Legislation is going to increase.	I	NC	I New Part L even more onerous.	I	NC	NC	NC
WLC benefits	NC	D Clients focus on the initial capital Costs.	I Oil more expensive plus increasing energy demand.	I	D Clients do not see beyond the initial outlay.	I	NC	I Benefit realised of lower running costs.	I Running costs will increase.	I Clients focus on running costs.
Competitive advantage	I Bigger incentive to differentiate your business.	I Need to distinguish themselves.	NC	NC	I Need to be more competitive in recession.	NC	I	I Do anything to distinguish yourself from competition.	I Desperate for anything to give an advantage.	I Do anything to increase advantage.
Customer demand	I	NC	I As awareness grows so will demand.	I Public – increase Private – decrease D	I	I Customers are gradually becoming more aware.	I Public – increase. Private – no change. NC	NC	I	NC Depends on the client and project.
Green incentives	NC	D Less money around, even from Gov.	I Green bank noted in Gov. 2010 budget.	NC	I	I Follow from legislation.	D	I	NC But note 9 for Education more grants.	NC
Peer pressure	NC	NC	D	D	NC	NC	NC	NC	NC	NC
Better buildings	I	D A nice to have nor essential.	NC	D	D Clients cannot afford these measures.	I	I	NC	I Best possible for least amount.	NC
Section 5 – Barriers to sustainable construction										
A) In your opinion what are the barriers to sustainable construction?	People do not like change.	1. Larger capital outlay. 2. Difficult to persuade academics of the importance. 3. End users are very intolerant of change.	1. Technology not as advanced as the politicians state. 2. Lack of transparency of the feed-in tariffs/ grants. 3. Building industry set in their ways.	1. Lack of knowledge of the benefits. 2. Reluctant to change way of working. 3. Limit of technology – no track record. 4. Perception of cost.	1. Not enough in-use and capital cost data. 2. Cost. 3. Changing legislation. 4. Risk of emerging technology.	1. Perception that it costs more money. 2. Split incentives.	1. Public perception: unaffordable and does not work. 2. "eco bling", BREEAM just a badge. 3. Difficult to refurb existing buildings.	1. Capital cost. 2. Nonstandard installations. 3. Perception that it is more expensive to run.	1. Clients do not know what is out there and are unfamiliar. 2. Resistance to change. 3. Perception of cost.	1. Increased capital outlay. 2. Lack true desire and interest 3. Too risky in a recession 4. Poor professional advice. 5. CDM – access and maintenance can be costly.
B) Rate the importance of these barriers on a scale of 1–10.	B) Comment	B) Comment	B) Comment	B) Comment	B) Comment	B) Comment	B) Comment	B) Comment	B) Comments	B) Comments
Increased capital outlay	5 If thought about early enough then no increase.	10	8	8	8	8	10	8	7	8

Lack of demand	2 Huge demand, customers need to be seen to be green.	5	8	8	8	8	6	7
Physical barriers	5	8	5	5	8	8	6	8
Poor knowledge by client	1 Developer has their own sustainability department.	3	8	6	7	9	3	8
Split incentive	7 Need to educate the client.	8	8	8	10	8	7	9
Unknowns of new tech	5 Need more new tech; old products and ideas.	9	8	7	7	5	5	5
SME	2	5	7	4	8	7	7	7
Lack of training	4	3	3	5	3	5	3	4
C) In light of the recession, do you think these drivers will increase (I), decrease (D) or not change (NC)?	C) Comment	C) Comment	C) Comment	C) Comment	C) Comment	C) Comment	C) Comment	C) Comments
Increased capital outlay	I Clients focus on every penny of expenditure.	D As tech and competition improves capital costs will go down.	I	I	D Clients see as an opportunity for saving money.	I	I	I
Lack of demand	NC	D Increasing awareness and growing demand.	NC	I	D There will be an increase in demand.	I	I People are just not spending.	NC
Physical barriers	D Increased awareness and changing attitudes.	D Industry find new ways of working and adapt.	NC	NC	D Greater application of sustainable construction in all areas.	I There will have to be more refurb.	D	NC
Poor knowledge by client	D Projects on hold there so more time to explore.	NC	NC	NC	NC	NC	NC Education and but not commercial.	NC

(continued)

Question	Client A	Client B	Client C	Architect A	Architect B	Architect C	Cost Manager A	Cost Manager B	Contractor A	Contractor B
Split incentive	D Tenants are trying to be more efficient with current financial pressures.	NC	NC	D	NC	D More holistic approach will be taken due to the economic situation.	NC	NC	I	I Pressure on capital budgets not FM.
Unknowns of new tech	NC	D	D We will become more familiar with the technology	NC	NC	D Increasing awareness and benefits of new technologies realised.	I	I	I	NC
SME	I	NC	I SMEs cannot access debt, let alone pay premium for sustainability.	NC	NC	D	NC No change to those with small portfolio.	I	I	NC
Lack of training	NC	D	D As with awareness it is improving.	NC	I Reduced training with budgets cuts.	D	I	NC	I Very diverse among sector.	NC

Section 6 – Impact of the recession

Question	Client A	Client B	Client C	Architect A	Architect B	Architect C	Cost Manager A	Cost Manager B	Contractor A	Contractor B
A) 1. In what ways has your organisation been affected by the recession?	All work on hold. Last development came to the market in 2009. The next development is likely to be in 2011.	Moderate effect. Cut in capital spend 10% voluntary redundancy. But science is well supported by the government.	Moderate effect. All building is focused on rent income. Rent reduced by 7–8%. There is a much higher risk of contractors going bust.	Moderate. Maybe in future. Large number of bids but projects are not being commissioned. Ones that are – smaller budgets. lower fees.		Moderate effect.	Moderate but boosted by public work. Fewer project with smaller budgets. Increased competition for work. Redundancies.	Moderate. Starting to notice downturn in projects as public sector slowing down. Staff redundancies.	Smaller value projects; more tendering opportunities but with bigger list; reduced margins and some negative bids. Projects awarded but on hold.	Reduce turnover and costs. Suffer competition. Larger contractors are dropping down to smaller works as there are less big projects.
2. Which industry or clients have been worst affected?	Commercial office,	Housing,	Residential,	Commercial office,			Commercial,	HE,	Commercial dried up.	Financial.
B) 1. Since the recession have you encountered a change in the amount of sustainable construction?	Yes, increase.	Increase. Only just started in past two years.	Increase.	No change.	Decrease,	Increase. Sustainability become higher profile.	Increase because of legislation.	No change.		It's being talked about less, finding it is less of a driver.

2. Since the recession has there been a change in the type of sustainable construction?	Yes, in future going to really challenge approach to building. Buildings will be dramatically different. Look at air flow, orientation, shading – focus on passive measures.	Considered using PVs but removed because of their poor WLC not because of the recession – even if the project budget was more flexible it would not have been implemented.	CfSH reduced from L6 to L4 to make a viable return. Future is domestic CHP cheap electricity and potential income from feed-in tariffs up to 40% reduction in running costs. Passive measure, i.e. insulation. Project completed in 2009 full of air conditioning – never again. Market will accept natural ventilation.	More emphasis on passive approach by using efficient materials and design. PVs are excluded from projects unless they are subsidised by some form of grant. Code 6 housing has increased.	More formal measures being used like BREEAM. About achieving targets rather than talking about it SWMP legislation is proof.	PVs and other renewable energy tech were used before. Now rationalising existing stock. BREEAM will continue to be used a "stamp" of sustainability. More refurbishment rather than new build.	Level to which they are implemented has sometimes been downgraded. E.g. pipeline development is going from Code 6 to A due to financial constraints. Hospital new build project still going for BREEAM excellent.	Awareness increased. More focus on natural ventilation. Increased number of suppliers providing renewable technologies and the competition is increasing among them. Lack of new ideas. Always natural ventilation; rainwater harvesting; green roof. Need more innovation.	Small/medium jobs do not address sustainable construction in a major way. Only minor details such as PIRs etc. not bigger investments like technologies.
3. In your opinion what is the cause for these changes?	Using two year gap to innovate. Tenants are being educated; they will accept wider temperature ranges.	As we are really looking to save money the focus is on air conditioning as it has potential to be a huge saving if removed. Need strong business case and energy efficiency. Convenient that this is being green!	Running costs and capital. Air conditioning very expensive. People are aware enough of the environmental issues to put up with warmer environments.	Running costs need to be reduced in future. Otherwise need Government grant in order to subsidise other renewable technologies.	Increased pressure on capital budgets, opportunity to invest decreases. Each project is subject to much great scrutiny. The 2%, 5%, 10% increase for sustainable buildings is not justifiable.	Organisations are concerned about energy efficiency, material and maintenance. The recession will not make people go backwards legislation will ensure that.	Lack of capital funding Running costs of building for owner/occupiers.	Clients better educated but also they are looking to save money. Clients are switched on about saving on maintenance costs. No longer blinkered.	Good intentions but companies just want to look good. Most initiatives government led – legislation or incentives. Contractors only have a minor role limited to construction phase.
4. Which sectors do you think have been the most willing to continue with sustainable construction?	All.	Higher Education.	Institutions education; hospitals; local government; prime residential. Green leases will push the commercial world longer term.	Social housing; Higher Education and any other sector where their funding source stipulates sustainable buildings.	All of the public related sectors.	Public as the sustainable construction agenda is driven by central government. Legally binding commitments to reduce CO_2.			

Note to students

The above table should be inserted at the start of the results chapter and each section should be analysed and discussed individually. For example, Zoë analysed and discussed the sections on the definition of sustainability and the barriers to sustainability (as seen by the interviewees) as follows:

Definition of sustainable construction

A broad range of responses were given for the definition of sustainable construction. Some respondents gave very specific responses such as 'being carbon neutral' while other detailed more in-depth definitions touching some of the complexities of the field. In particular, Client B gave a detailed outline of what it means from design, construction to occupation of a building. Nevertheless, there were common themes with many overlapping definitions. The most common statements were: to reduce the impact of construction on people and the environment; a holistic approach to building; and the use of renewable energy and materials. It is interesting to note that both the Contractors' responses focused on renewable energy and materials as this is the end of the supply chain with which they are involved. The more general concepts of holistic buildings and impact on society or surrounding environment are mentioned by architects and clients. Client B also mentioned under the broader definition of sustainability that the 'Considerate Contractors' Scheme' was key with its bid to reduce impact of noise and prevent pollution to the surrounding area during the construction of a building.

The next most common definitions were low- or zero-carbon status buildings and consideration of life cycle costing and running costs. Finally, minimising waste in design and construction and longevity of buildings were stated by two of the interviewees. It was noted by Architect C that these last two concepts were in fact very old-fashioned ideas and stated that 100 years ago, all construction professionals were interested in building to last and reducing costly waste.

Some respondents also stated what they considered not to be sustainable construction. Cost Manager A and Architect B made the point that it is not just about being carbon neutral but must be a more far-sighted view of the impact on the society and environment. Similarly, Architect A asserts that sustainable construction is not just about technology but how buildings are used and operated.

The wide-ranging answers showed that there was a good body of knowledge amongst the respondents, with many demonstrating a deep level of understanding.

An interesting trend can be seen in the timeline of when respondents became aware of sustainable construction (Figure A6.1). Two of the architects had heard of the concept of sustainable construction under different terminology in the early 1990s. These concepts have been dubbed 'proto sustainability' and include energy saving, ethically resourced materials and non-polluting construction. In the late 1990s a second group (a client, the other architect and a cost manager working at a dynamic practice) were introduced to the concept. These probably

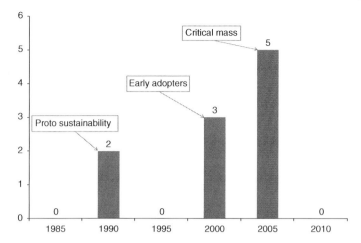

Figure A6.1   *Timeline showing frequency of when respondents first heard about sustainable construction.*

represent 'early adopters' of sustainable construction in its current format, working on landmark projects, first examples of BREEAM and with forward-thinking clients. Then there is the critical mass, where half of the other interviewees stated that they had first heard about it in 2005 or 2006. Both contractors state this as the time they became aware of sustainable construction.

Drivers for sustainable construction

The first part, investigating the drivers for sustainable construction, asked respondents to give their opinion on the top drivers without prompting from a list to exclude any bias from academic literature. This gives an overview of their perception from personal or company experience of the subject matter. There was a danger that interviewees could state what they felt they ought to but they were encouraged to be candid in their responses.

The open-ended responses were coded into eight categories, which were then grouped in three themes: social, financial and external drivers. Figure A6.2 shows the results according to the frequency with which each driver was mentioned. By a clear margin the most frequent answer was personal commitment of the client or developer with 80 per cent of respondents stating this was a key driver. The next highest at 50 per cent were reputation/image and funding/planning authority demands. These were closely followed by legislation and increased energy costs at 40 per cent. It is worthy of note that only two of the ten respondents stated business case or customer demand as a motivation for adopting sustainable construction, areas which traditionally would be considered a strong driving force behind company strategies.

When the results are weighted according to the order in which the respondents listed the drivers, a different trend appears (the first response was assumed to

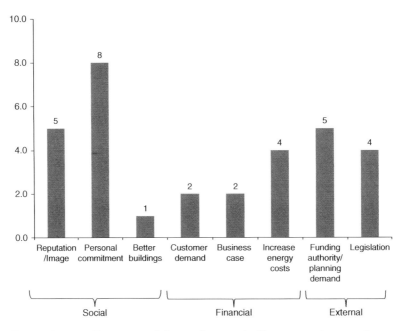

Figure A6.2 *Frequency of drivers for sustainable construction stated unprompted by respondents.*

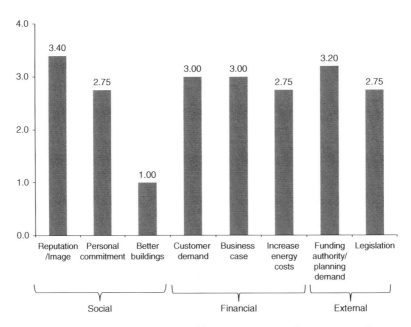

Figure A6.3 *Drivers for sustainable construction with priority ranking stated by respondents unprompted. The higher the bar, the more often the driver was stated first by respondents (the scale has arbitrary units).*

be the most important for the respondent, the second assumed to be the second most important, and so on). Figure A6.3 reveals that a company's concern for their reputation or image overtakes personal commitment to be the top priority, showing that the clients in the construction industry are primarily concerned with being 'seen to be green'. Closely behind reputational drivers is the external demand of the funding/planning authority. The two respondents that did state customer demand and business case as drivers for sustainable development ranked them very highly, raising their profile in the results. With such a small sample size, single or infrequently listed drivers can distort the results. However, it is worth noting that there is a group of respondents that not only consider customer demand and business case as a driver for sustainability but rate it as a top priority.

References

Mulholland, Z.E. (2010) *An examination of sustainable construction in the recession*, MSc dissertation, Department of the Built Environment, London South Bank University.
Naoum, S.G., Mulholland, Z., Fong, D. (2011) Sustainable Construction in the Recession, *11th World Sustainable Building Conference SB11*, October, Helsinki, Finland. Paper ID 1666853.

Appendix 7
Scoring matrix of project performance

Source: Naoum, S.G. (1989) 'An investigation into the performance of management contracts and the traditional methods of building procurement', PhD thesis, Brunel University, Middlesex.

Notes to students

1   This research was updated in 2016. (See Naoum and Egbu, 2016.)
2   This is an example of an achieved research aim. The aim of this research was to construct a scoring matrix showing the level of performance between management and traditional form of contracts (see Proposal 2 in Appendix 1).
3   This scoring matrix is related to the research road map shown in Figure 2.4 on page 22 and also to the research model shown in Figure 4.5 on page 63.
4   This type of an achieved aim (i.e. end of research product) is usually inserted in the conclusion chapter of your dissertation.
5   The content of this scoring matrix may not apply to today's clients' and projects' criteria as the characteristics of the construction industry have changed significantly over the last two decades or so. (See Naoum and Egbu, 2016.)

Project performance

Client and project characteristics	Management contracts											Traditional contracts										
	Design time	Build time	Total time	Speed (a/w)	Unit cost	% ±time	% +/–cost	Level S time	Level S cost	Level S quality	Total scores	Design time	Build time	Total time	Speed (a/w)	Unit cost	% +/–time	% +/–cost	Level S time	Level S cost	Level S quality	Total scores
Speculative <£5m N=4MC. 3TRC	2	1	2	1	2	1	2	2	2	2	17	1	2	1	3	3	2	2	3	3	3	23
Speculative >£5m N=14MC. 6TRC	3	2	3	3	1	2	3	2	2	1	22	2	2	2	3	3	2	2	3	3	3	24
Bespoke <£5m N=12MC. 11TRC	3	2	3	3	1	2	2	3	3	3	25	1	2	2	2	3	2	2	2	3	2	21
Bespoke >£5m N=7MC. 4TRC	3	2	3	3	3	2	2	3	3	2	26	2	1	1	3	2	2	3	2	2	2	20
Bid rate <50,000 N=10MC. 21TRC	3	2	2	2	1	3	3	3	3	2	24	2	2	1	2	3	2	2	2	2	3	21
Bid rate >50,000 N=29MC. 9TRC	3	2	3	3	1	3	2	2	3	2	24	1	2	1	3	2	1	1	1	3	2	17
Industrial <£5m N=8MC. 13TRC	3	2	3	3	2	3	2	2	3	3	26	2	2	2	1	3	3	1	2	3	3	22
Industrial >£5m N=8MC. 5TRC	3	2	3	3	3	3	2	23	3	3	27	1	2	1	2	3	1	2	2	2	3	20
Commercial <£5m N=8MC. 5TRC	3	1	3	2	1	3	2	3	2	2	22	2	2	2	3	3	2	3	3	2	3	25
Commercial >£5m N=18MC. 8TRC	3	2	3	2	1	3	2	3	3	2	24	1	1	1	3	2	2	1	1	2	3	17
Area <7000 sqm N=15MC. 18TRC	3	3	3	2	1	2	3	3	2	2	24	2	2	2	2	3	2	2	3	3	3	24
Area >7000 sqm N=24MC. 12TRC	3	2	3	3	3	3	2	3	3	2	28	1	1	1	3	2	2	2	2	2	3	20
Normal complexity N=20MC. 20TRC	3	2	3	2	2	3	3	3	2	2	26	1	2	1	2	3	2	1	2	2	3	19
Highly complex N=19MC. 8TRC	3	2	3	3	2	2	2	3	2	1	23	1	1	1	3	3	2	1	1	2	2	17
TOTALS	44	29	43	37	26	36	34	39	39	31	358	22	26	21	35	41	31	27	31	40	41	315

Measurements

Average performance for projects costing less than £5 million: design time = 34 weeks; building time = 52 weeks; total time = 96 weeks; speed (a/w) = 81 area/week; cost/sqm = 562 £/sqm; % ± time = 5%; % ± time = 5%.

Average performance for projects costing more than £5 million: design time = 55 weeks; building time = 88 weeks; total time = 140 weeks; speed (a/w) = 125 area/week; cost/sqm = 775 £/sqm; % +/– time = 8%; % ± time = 7%.

Score 1 = low performance; score 2 = average performance; score 3 = high performance.

Reference

Naoum, S.G. and Egbu, C. (2016) Modern selection criteria for procurement methods in construction: A state-of-the-art literature review and a survey. *International Journal of Managing Projects in Business*, 9(2), pp. 309–336.

Index

Printed in Great Britain
by Amazon

85508057R00181